RHINOCEROS BOUND:
Cluny in the Tenth Century

"The rhinoceros, that is, any powerful man,
is bound with a thong so that he may crush
the clods of the valleys, that is,
the oppressors of the humble."

Odo of Cluny, Vita Geraldi i.8

THE MIDDLE AGES a series edited by
EDWARD PETERS *Henry Charles Lea Professor
of Medieval History, University of Pennsylvania*

RHINOCEROS BOUND: *Cluny in the Tenth Century*

BARBARA H. ROSENWEIN

 UNIVERSITY OF PENNSYLVANIA PRESS
1982 · *Philadelphia*

Copyright © 1982 by the University of Pennsylvania Press
All rights reserved

Designed by Adrianne Onderdonk Dudden

Library of Congress Cataloging in Publication Data

Rosenwein, Barbara H.
  Rhinoceros bound.

  (The Middle Ages)
  Bibliography: p.
  Includes index.
  1. Cluny (Benedictine abbey) 2. Cluniacs.
I. Title. II. Series.
BX2615.C63R67   271'.14   81-43525
ISBN 0-8122-7830-5   AACR2

Printed in the United States of America

To Tom

CONTENTS

Acknowledgments

This book would not have come into being were it not for my teacher and colleague, Lester K. Little. His undergraduate survey course in medieval history first awakened my interest in that field. His graduate colloquium on monasticism introduced me to Cluny. He has continued to be my most important critic and collaborator. I owe him an immeasurable debt of gratitude.

Professor Karl F. Morrison has read all of my work, including a draft of this book, and he has unfailingly offered me acute criticisms and perceptive comments. Dr. Constance B. Bouchard read the entire manuscript and played an indispensable role in its final revision. She was for me a model of scholarly generosity, giving freely both information and ideas. I also want to thank Professor Bernard McGinn, Dr. Joyce Galpern, and my colleagues Drs. Allen Frantzen and Michael Masi for their help.

The funded leave of absence awarded to me by Loyola University of Chicago for Fall, 1978, gave me the opportunity I needed to complete a first draft of the manuscript. In addition, the support of Loyola's Research Services, offered generously and without question by its director, Dr. Thomas J. Bennett, made possible the technical preparation of the final manuscript. The staff of Cudahy Library at Loyola, especially Sr. Bonaventure Price, did everything possible to satisfy my voracious appetite for books on interlibrary loan. I am grateful to my research assistants, including Ms. Kari B. McBride, Mr. Stephen Ryan, who checked the notes, and Ms. Anie Sergis, who prepared the maps for this book. I would also like to thank my editor, Mrs. Ingalill Hjelm, and members of Karon, Morrison, and Savikas, Ltd., for their help.

Finally, I want to thank my family. My parents set an example of love and respect for ideas and creativity that continues to inspire and nourish me. My children, Jessica and Franklin, have patiently borne "Mommy's work" as a normal part of their young lives. My husband, Tom, has supported me in more ways than I can say; this book is dedicated to him.

Chicago, 18 May 1981   BARBARA H. ROSENWEIN

Abbreviations

C	*Recueil des chartes de l'Abbaye de Cluny,* A. Bernard and A. Bruel, eds.
CCCM	*Corpus Christianorum. Continuatio Mediaevalis.* Turnhout, 1966 on.
CCM	*Corpus consuetudinum monasticarum,* K. Hallinger, ed. Vol. 1: *Initia consuetudinis Benedictinae*
CCSL	*Corpus Christianorum. Series Latina.* Turnhout, 1954 on.
CM	*Consuetudines monasticae,* B. Albers, ed. Vol. 2: *Consuetudines cluniacenses antiquiores*
CSEL	*Corpus Scriptorum Ecclesiasticorum Latinorum.* Vienna, 1866 on.
LCL	Loeb Classical Library
MGH	*Monumenta Germaniae Historica*
MGH, Leg. 2: Capit. reg. Fr.	*MGH, Legum* sectio 2: *Capitularia regum Francorum.* Hanover, 1883–1897.
MGH, Script. rer. Mer.	*MGH, Scriptores rerum Merovingicarum.* Hanover, 1884–1920.
MGH, SS	*MGH, Scriptorum Tomus.* Hanover, 1826–1934.
PL	*Patrologiae cursus completus. Series latina,* J. P. Migne, ed. Paris, 1844–88.

RB	*Benedicti Regula,* in *La Règle de Saint Benoît,* A. de Vogüé, ed. and trans.
SC	*Sources Chrétiennes.* Paris, 1941 on.
SSA	"Social Structure and Anomie," R. K. Merton

Note on the Maps

Compared to the usual maps depicting the expansion of Cluniac houses, these maps look uncrowded. In part, this is because the maps here are limited to the tenth century. But it is also the result of the strict definition of a "Cluniac house" used throughout this study. A monastery is considered to come under this rubric only if there is evidence that a Cluniac abbot was called upon to effect its reform. Some monasteries were held as property by Cluny, but they cannot be simply assumed to have come under Cluniac reform. For example, the houses of St.-Jean and St.-Martin in Mâcon were part of Cluny's possessions; this is all we know about them. (Agapit II, *Epistola* 9 [an. 949], *PL*, 133: col. 901.) The map also does not necessarily include houses which later became part of the formal Order of Cluny, because the question of dependence on Cluny is quite distinct from that of reformation by a Cluniac abbot. Further, the maps were prepared in the light of Hallinger's warning against considering reforms by Cluniac "disciples" to be "Cluniac" reforms (see below, pp. 17–18.) In borderline instances, where a Cluniac abbot was called upon to effect a reform but was unable to complete it, I have exercised discretionary judgment. For example, Chanteuge is not on the map because Odo of Cluny was too busy to reform it, and its founders immediately turned it over to Arnulf, abbot of Aurillac and Odo's disciple. (E. Sackur, *Die Cluniacenser in ihrer kirchlichen und allgemeingeschichtlichen Wirksamkeit bis zur Mitte des elften Jahrhunderts,* 2 vols. (Halle a. S, 1892–94), 1:85, citing É. Baluze, *Histoire généalogique de la maison d'Auvergne, justifiée par chartes, titres, histoires anciennes, et autres preuves authentiques,* 2 vols. [Paris, 1708], which I have been unable to consult.) On the other hand, St.-Denis is on the map because Hugh Capet asked Majolus to reform it, and Majolus agreed to do so, but died before he was able. Finally, the map does not include doubtful cases. All that is known about Lézat, for example, is that after its foundation its abbot was Adacius, Odo of Cluny's co-abbot at Tulle. (C. Devic and J. Vaissette, *Histoire générale de Languedoc,* 15 vols. [Toulouse, 1872–92], 4:586.)

MAP OF FRANCE

Cluny and monasteries which Cluniac Abbots, Berno (B), Odo (O),
Aymard (A) and Majolus (M) were called upon to reform.

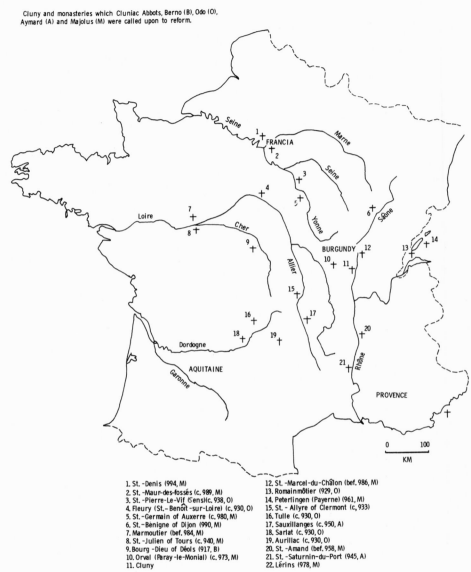

1. St. -Denis (994, M)
2. St. -Maur-des-fossés (c. 989, M)
3. St. -Pierre-Le-Vif (Sens)(c. 938, O)
4. Fleury (St. - Benoît -sur-Loire) (c. 930, O)
5. St. -Germain of Auxerre (c. 980, M)
6. St. -Bénigne of Dijon (990, M)
7. Marmoutier (bef. 984, M)
8. St. -Julien of Tours (c. 940, M)
9. Bourg -Dieu of Déols (917, B)
10. Orval (Paray -le-Monial) (c. 973, M)
11. Cluny
12. St. -Marcel-du-Châlon (bef. 986, M)
13. Romainmôtier (929, O)
14. Peterlingen (Payerne) (961, M)
15. St. - Allyre of Clermont (c, 933)
16. Tulle (c. 930, O)
17. Sauxillanges (c. 950, A)
18. Sarlat (c. 930, O)
19. Aurillac (c. 930, O)
20. St. -Amand (bef. 958, M)
21. St. -Saturnin-du-Port (945, A)
22. Lérins (978, M)

✝ Monastery

In parentheses are dates of foundation or reform, Abbots called upon
to effect foundation or reform

MAP OF ITALY

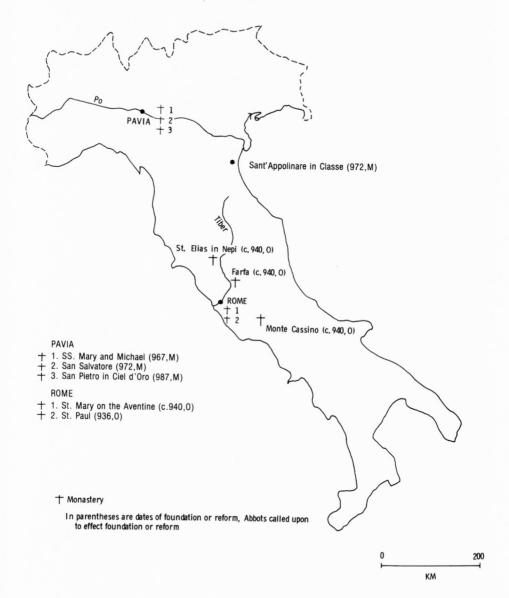

Cluny and monasteries which Cluniac Abbots, Berno (B), Odo (O),
Aymard (A) and Majolus (M) were called upon to reform.

Po

† 1
PAVIA   † 2
† 3

Sant'Appolinare in Classe (972,M)

Tiber

St. Elias in Nepi (c.940,O)
†

Farfa (c.940,O)
†

ROME
† 1
† 2   †
Monte Cassino (c.940,O)

PAVIA

† 1. SS. Mary and Michael (967,M)
† 2. San Salvatore (972,M)
† 3. San Pietro in Ciel d'Oro (987,M)

ROME

† 1. St. Mary on the Aventine (c.940,O)
† 2. St. Paul (936,O)

† Monastery

In parentheses are dates of foundation or reform, Abbots called upon
to effect foundation or reform

0   200
KM

Introduction

The monastery of Cluny was founded in 909 near Mâcon. Its founder, a rich layman named William, was duke of Aquitaine (886–918) and also count of Mâcon. In his foundation charter, William stipulated that Cluny follow the *Rule* of St. Benedict.[1] Whatever precise meaning this may have had for William and the Cluniac monks (see Chapter 4), it clearly was meant to give the monks a predominantly spiritual role. Indeed, William wanted the Cluniacs to spend their time in prayer for the redemption of his soul and the souls of his family and other faithful. This vocation resulted in a very long liturgy, a fact noted by contemporaries with pride and admiration in the tenth and eleventh centuries, but generally greeted with scorn thereafter.

William also provided for Cluny to have local immunity (i.e., freedom from the taxation and jurisdiction of any outsider) and to be dependent upon the papacy (i.e., to be the property of and under the protection of SS. Peter and Paul). The significance and importance of these clauses have been much discussed and debated by historians. Two points are most often mentioned. First, freedom from local lay control allowed Cluny to maintain its religious commitment at a time when most monasteries were dominated not only by the laity but by lay mores as well. Second, Cluny's special position with the papacy blossomed, in the eleventh century, into a working partnership for church reform. This movement, often called the Gregorian reform after Pope Gregory VII, one of its chief exponents, was directed primarily against simony (buying church offices) and lay investiture (broadly speaking, lay prerogatives in the choice and ordination of churchmen). Most textbooks continue to make these two points about Cluny, although, as will be seen, they are now criticized as misleading and simplistic by many historians.

What is incontrovertible is that Cluny's abbots—Berno (909–26), Odo (926–44), Aymard (944–64), Majolus (964–94), Odilo (994–1049), and Hugh (1049–1109)—were active in monastic reform.[2] Presumably, William chose Berno to be the first abbot of Cluny at least in part because of Berno's reputation as abbot of Baume. When Berno became abbot of Cluny, he did not give up his position at Baume but held both monasteries—along with a few others—under his direct jurisdiction. When he died, some of these monasteries were handed over to his nephew, while Cluny and Déols were placed under the direction of Odo. Odo continued to reform monasteries, as did his successors. Some of the monasteries reformed by these abbots became integral members of the eleventh-century Order of Cluny, that is, their abbot was the abbot of Cluny, and they were directed in day-to-day affairs by a prior. Other monasteries reformed by Cluny maintained an independent position with (and sometimes without) ties of friendship to Cluny. Although, as we shall see, the ideal was to effect a reform in Cluny's image, reformed houses followed Cluny's *ordo* (its regular way of life) only to varying degrees, depending on individual cases. Some of the monasteries reformed by Cluny went on to become reform centers in their own right. Other houses spontaneously adopted Cluniac practices. Given all this, it is extremely difficult to say what was or was not a "Cluniac" monastery. However, for all its complexity, one thing is certain: by the end of the eleventh century, Cluny was seen as the preeminent monastery, "the light of the world," as Pope Urban II put it.[3] Its prestige diminished soon thereafter, as new religious ideals gained prominence. However, it continued as an institution and retained a symbolic significance until the time of the French Revolution, when the community was disbanded and the buildings pillaged. This tale of rise and fall has drawn historians irresistibly to study Cluny.

Historical studies of the past reflect their own times: the aphorism embraces this book as well. I first became interested in Cluny when the United States was waging a war in Vietnam. Cluny, I knew, had been founded in a period plagued with wars. Its ritual, discipline, order, and calm seemed to me an antidote to violence, both in fact and in purpose.

Later, the issues of Watergate revealed wider problems to me; the war was only one side of a multifaceted abuse of power. Other facets, now familiar, became clear: the contempt for law, the advancement of self-made, self-serving definitions of virtue; the manipulation of symbols to create an image rather than to express the substance of government; the diversion of public institutions to private ends. I did not try to find these subjects in Cluniac texts; but their existence in the present influenced the sorts of questions I asked about the past. I realized that Cluny was involved in nothing less than understanding, exercising, and altering the use of power. In a world which saw the breakdown of royal political authority, Cluny's emphasis on divinely enjoined behavior—its ritualism—substituted the rule of God's law for fragmented power. Faced with crucial issues of morality, such as exploitation of the poor and self-serving uses of violence, Cluniac writings affirmed an old morality adjusted to new needs and circumstances. Cluny's fame and institutional success were due, I came to see, to its unsurpassed mastery of highly charged symbols and iconic acts in an age which put a premium on gesture.

This manipulation of image had a substantive meaning. Its very essence was to link Cluny's monasticism, and the donors and patrons who supported that monasticism, to old and hallowed customs, rules, laws, and responsibilities. Cluniac formalism implicitly showed how clergy and laity could be reformed on the basis of old laws. The modern search for "roots" has allowed historians and sociologists to understand a motive force behind this. The anxieties of social dislocation make people look to traditional forms for a niche in life.

The ideas and practices at Cluny were responses to its world. This is no doubt partly because Cluny, like other institutions, was dependent upon a public. Simply for its survival Cluny needed donors. It was founded not by a monk but by a layman, who stipulated what style of life Cluny was to have from the beginning. It was dependent on its benefactors, too, for the opportunity to spread its brand of monasticism to other houses. Finally, it was dependent on the world for the very forms and modes of its behavior even as it sought to change those forms. Hence, although there are no lessons from Cluny for Watergate, Cluny does provide a model for comparison with our own day: it shows the ways in which a moral institution responded to issues involving the use and abuse of power by conforming to, clashing against, and trying to alter social norms.

In the eleventh century, when Cluny was rich and famous, this interaction with the outside world was obvious. Historians have been drawn especially to the turbulent years of church reform, beginning in the mid-eleventh century, and to the question of Cluny's role in it. This has been the great issue for Cluniac studies from the beginning of its modern historiography. However, historians have taken only a perfunctory look at the manner in which Cluny fit into the world of its naissance and growth before that later age.

Such an approach is understandable but perilous, for, in point of fact, Cluny's participation in the movements of the eleventh century was dependent upon its survival and its development in the tenth century. Cluny did not spring forth fully blown at the time of the Gregorian reform. It was founded in the early tenth century under St. Berno. Its second abbot, St. Odo, provided the structures that served the physical needs of the brethren for the next half-century, set the tone for much of its spiritual program, and spread its brand of monasticism to other houses. SS. Aymard and Majolus, Cluny's third and fourth abbots, respectively, wrote no works that survive. But we know that, during their tenure, the abbey continued to receive donations; to found or reform other houses; to demand its privileges from popes, kings, and princes; and—so far as we can tell—continued to hold to and practice the monastic round that, by Cluniac standards at least, was one which followed the *Rule* of St. Benedict, as stipulated in Cluny's foundation charter.

Majolus's abbacy takes us to the end of the tenth century. There is no question that Cluny was flourishing by then; indeed, during the last two decades of the century, its wealth—a barometer of its reputation—grew enormously. With the solid foundation of its early years behind it, Cluny was launched onto its enormously successful eleventh-century career by Abbots St. Odilo and St. Hugh.

The forces which brought Cluny into being and shaped its development, then, were rooted in the tenth century. The general issues concerning the interaction between religious and political norms, between morality and the use of power, between ideal and normative life-styles, must first be explored in that century. The present study proposes to do this. Its purpose is to understand the significance of Cluny in its original, formative context. Historiographical contributions have made clear, as we shall see, that Cluny was not the center of all monasticism in its day. On the contrary, it was one of a number of popular monastic reform nuclei. Nor was it unique or radically different from its predecessors or contemporaries in idea and style. Rather, Cluny was quite typical of many monasteries. Yet, precisely because the myths of Cluny's originality and centrality have been demolished, Cluny remains instructive for an inquiry into tenth-century forms, values, and ideas. Its documents are unusually rich. It excited (and we still have, in the form of charters) the devotional outpourings of generations of every class of men and women. We can often trace who and where they were. Moreover, even in its own day, Cluny was considered by many to be a model monastery.

The present book is, in the strictest sense of the term, a case study. There is need for many more studies of other monasteries and institutions during the tenth century if we are to have a rich and subtle view of even one aspect of this period. But the result should be worth the effort: that century was of crucial importance, particularly for the political development of Europe. Above all, people in the tenth century confronted problems of changing political institutions, of violence, of the use and abuse of power, and of the values that justified all of these. Understanding Cluny's involvement in these issues should lead to a deepened appreciation of the tenth century, to the contribution its solutions have made to our own civilization, and to some mechanisms of social adjustment not readily apparent today.

Why there is a tenth-century gap in Cluniac studies heretofore, and on the other hand, what enormous territory has already been explored, is the topic of Chapter 1. It will become clear that the present work rests from first to last on the accumulated gains of a large and important body of research and approach. Chapter 2 will begin to answer the question of Cluny's significance in the tenth century by looking at its benefactors. The work of previous historians will be assessed and used here again, for this chapter, like Chapter 1, is directly about historians' perceptions. What historians have not heretofore noticed, or at any rate, considered significant, will be argued in detail in this chapter: the people who fostered Cluny had in common an experience of social dislocation, that is, of social mobility up or down. (In Chapter 5 this observation will be assimilated into modern anomie theory.) Chapters 3 and 4 will shift to Cluniac perceptions, first of society at large (Chapter 3), then of their monastery (Chapter 4). The point here will be to explore Cluniac ideals, which, it will become clear, presented an affirmation of stability, of lawfulness, and of discipline; in short, they were the antithesis of anomie. Chapter 5 will demonstrate how modern anomie theory can help to relate the spiritual ideal at Cluny to the political disintegration and social mobility of the tenth century. In turn, tenth-century Cluny will expand our understanding of possible responses to anomie.

This study presents no previously undiscovered facts or new primary source materials. It is intended instead as a synthesis and interpretation of materials already long known, worked with, and explained. The use which has been made of these elements in the past determines what needs to be said in the present book.

RHINOCEROS BOUND:
Cluny in the Tenth Century

1 | THE LINEAGE OF CLUNIAC STUDIES

The historiography of Cluny needs to be undertaken here for three reasons. First, since this book attempts to review the ways that historians look at Cluny, it needs to be preceded by an assessment of how Cluny has been seen in the past. Second, since its new view of Cluny uses modern anomie theory to explain both spiritual and social phenomena, it is important to see that the application of the social sciences is called for by the very direction of Cluniac historiography. Third, since the questions asked and the approaches used here are partly born out of modern concerns, a proper perspective must begin with an understanding of the ways in which past studies of Cluny have similarly been products of the times in which they were written.

The first modern historians of Cluny were ungrateful heirs of seventeenth-century erudition, in particular of the work of the Maurist monks, who had edited some Cluniac manuscripts.[1] The first historians simply ignored the bequest. They were interested in Cluny because they thought of themselves as French patriots; immediate concerns, not critical scholarship, determined their approach.[2] Writing in the wake of the upheavals of the nineteenth century (Lorain first wrote about Cluny in 1839, Cucherat in 1850, Pignot in 1868), painfully aware that familiar institutions were crumbling, foreseeing the barbarization of all aspects of life and the rule of the masses (Lorain spoke of their "vulgar prejudices"), these men looked to the institutions and ideals of the Catholic church of their own day to preserve their own civilization: "Catholicism is still the soul of France, the soul of its nationality, the ameliorator of its morality."[3] And they looked to history to prove that the church had been the bearer of organized society in the past: "Cluny was a bright beacon in the midst of darkness, a sacred leaven of virtue in the midst of vices and corruption."[4] All the great events of the tenth and eleventh centuries were creations of the church. The crusades, the truce of God, and the Gregorian reform were merely the most glorious products of the church's leadership in bringing about social progress.[5]

If the Napoleonic era had needed a Napoleon to run it, so did the brave deeds of the past need a hero at the helm.[6] For nineteenth-century historians, the pope took this role. But it required an upheaval—the investiture controversy (1077–1122)—for him to achieve this supreme position. That the pope emerged the winner from this crisis was the contribution of Cluny, which served as the support, the model, indeed the source of papal power: "If there were error or excess in the claims of the Roman pontiff, Cluny should assume the glorious responsibility."[7]

Such a view of Cluny's function on behalf of the papacy was rooted in an interpretation of Cluny's position *vis-à-vis* the lay world. The crucial document for the nineteenth-century French historian was Cluny's foundation charter with its clauses of local immunity and papal dependency.[8] Liberated from the encroachments of local laymen, reasoned the nineteenth-century historians, Cluny was able, under the leadership of its heroic and farseeing abbots, to forge a chain of monasteries similarly independent of worldly ties. From its centralized and powerful position, Cluny could then help the papacy itself achieve its freedom.

Since it was leadership in the church that determined Cluny's significance for the nineteenth-century French historians, once the church was under the firm reins of the papacy, Cluny became of secondary importance. If the tenth century had been for Cluny the age of organization and the eleventh century the age of power, the twelfth century was to be the age of decline. Cluny's work was over.[9]

The purposes of the French historians were served with only passing reference to the sources edited by the Benedictine Maurists in the seventeenth century. German historians, however, were beginning to conceive of the historical task as one rooted first and foremost in the primary texts.[10] Influenced by Leopold Ranke's emphasis on *Quellenkritik,* convinced that the historical purpose was to describe the past "wie es eigentlich gewesen," and armed with the critical textual editions in the great historical collections such as the *Monumenta Germaniae Historica,* these historians attempted to assess the past on its own terms.[11] In the early 1890s Ernst Sackur, himself an editor of the *Monumenta,* undertook to write about the "real significance" of Cluny.[12] With a passing nod to his French predecessors, Sackur gave grateful acknowledgment both to the Maurists and to the recently completed critical edition of Cluniac charters.[13] He expressed the conviction that his French predecessors had been handicapped without these charters, and he charitably overlooked their disinclination to use sources in general.

Sackur traced Cluny's history from its origins to the death of Abbot Odilo. Although he devoted many pages to the life of the monastery—its art, liturgy, economy, and scholarship—his main focus was on Cluny's role in reforming other monasteries to the discipline of the Benedictine *Rule.* For Sackur, this was no cosmetic procedure; it was nothing less than a moral awakening. In this way, Sackur's book, which was otherwise so different from the books of his French predecessors, had an odd resonance with them. If Cluny had been responsible for leading the Middle Ages out of barbarism for the French writers, it was responsible for a "general renaissance" for Sackur.[14] Cluny acted as midwife to bring forth, out of the womb of a France devastated both materially and spiritually by the Viking invasions, the new and unique culture of the Romanesque.

Sackur ended his study with the accession of Abbot Hugh (1049–1109). At that time, he argued, Cluny's focus changed.[15] It no longer was primarily interested in monastic reform: it was interested in supporting the papacy in its reform of the ecclesiastical hierarchy. As part of its new program of leadership, the papacy became embroiled in a series of quarrels with temporal authorities (including the famous investiture controversy between Henry IV and Gregory VII and their successors [1077–1122]). This latter point was the crucial one for Sackur: he considered the Gregorian reform to have been a political movement. Its essence was the redistribution of power from the hands of bishops and kings into the hands of the popes. Of course, there were some spiritual issues as well: the papal reformers stressed clerical celibacy and opposed simony. Sackur argued that, until the time of Hugh, the Cluniacs supported the papacy only regarding these spiritual matters, and at the same time, they supported pious emperors, such as Henry III, on precisely the same issues. There was no need to take sides.

As for the "political" aspect of the papal reform, the Cluniacs took very little interest until the time of St. Hugh: "Cluny had an idealistic goal, fluid and abstract." The papal goals had been the opposite: political, clearly defined, concrete. When, under Hugh, the Cluniacs opted for the papal position, its independent history ended; its story became inseparable from that of the church as a whole.[16]

There was another reason for Sackur's ending with Hugh's election. Sackur's deliberate use of the word *renaissance* inevitably evoked Burckhardt's 1860 vision of the Italian city-state civilization of the fifteenth century.[17] That had been, above all, a created civilization, a "work of art." For Sackur, Cluny too had been a creative force. But under St. Hugh, it underwent a notable stiffening of forms: its statutes were codified, its internal administrative apparatus was formalized, its relations with its dependencies were systematized, its position as a political force was institutionalized. In short, its creative days were over.

Whence came Cluny's creativity? For Sackur, as for Burckhardt, the nature of historical circumstances sometimes forced men to reassess themselves, impelling them to re-create their moral and material conditions in time of stress. The Viking invasions had destroyed the old order; the Carolingian world had disintegrated. The feudal nobility, newly powerful, independent, and undisciplined, was the first to recognize the need for its own moral regeneration as well as for a newly regenerated society:

> It is, in fact, the noble [*Adel*], himself so utterly sinful, who first gathers himself up against the disrupted elements of the time; and the more sensitive souls, disgusted with the horrors that in part still were taking place around them, in part remaining in the memory of all, flee the circles out of whose center calamity was spread or maintained over the world [i.e., they became monks at reformed monasteries]; or, seized by remorse and sympathy for the thin and hungry masses, they place at least their means at the disposal of the church, the only surviving institution that was in a position to effect a reform in social conditions. It is a delightful picture to see men like Hugh of Autun, Berno, William of Aquitaine, Fulk of Anjou, and Odo, all of whom had come from the nobility, work towards the resuscitation of monastic spirituality.[18]

The political leaders of society, prodded by the more sensitive of their peers, thus brought about their own regeneration. Unlike his French predecessors, Sackur looked to the king and the duke—the secular rulers

—to recognize the need for reform and to utilize the proper institutions to effect it:

> The need to support the church was first revived in the highest circles [e.g., at the court of Hugh Capet]. If these led the way, the vassals and people would follow.[19]

The movement begun by these forces became self-generating, and penetrated much of Europe. With his scrupulous adherence to the sources, Sackur could not but acknowledge that Cluny's influence in the Empire had been greatly exaggerated by previous historians; that English monastic history had followed a line of development independent from Cluny; that opposition to Cluniac reform by the French bishops north of the Loire modified its program and diminished its influence there.[20] Nevertheless, Sackur's work left the impression—supported both by a few explicit statements and by the general tone of his exposition—that there had been an essential unity to the monastic reform movements of the tenth and eleventh centuries, a unity that was based on the Cluniac model.[21] In this conception of the nature of the monastic reform movement, Sackur revealed his debt to Ranke's notion of the unity of European history.

Perhaps Sackur was also influenced by the successful fulfillment of German cultural and material goals under the political leadership of Prussian statesmen. During Sackur's lifetime, Germany had achieved national unification and had expanded westward, inflicting a humiliating defeat on the French in the 1870 war. Perhaps the same fact also explains why Sackur's work found few sympathetic echoes in a France newly defeated by his countrymen. Scholars of the Third Republic continued to study Cluny, but they tended to avoid Sackur's contribution. Many retreated from the question of Cluny's significance, which Sackur had addressed, to the less polemical concerns of the archivist, the cataloguer, the editor of Cluniac documents. Always they saw Cluny as a French national institution. The contribution they made toward a coherent picture or assessment of Cluny was minimal. None of them attempted to write a history of Cluny thorough enough to supercede Sackur's nor comprehensive enough to serve as the foundation for smaller, more specialized studies. The articles and brief histories that were produced in late nineteenth-century France were isolated and uncoordinated. They were divorced from any general conception of Cluny except, perhaps, the one set forth by French studies of a half-century or more before. When, in 1911, Chaumont published the second edition of a short history of Cluny "from beginning to end," he avoided even passing reference to Sackur, preferring to describe Cluny in the old terms of pre-Sackur historians.[22] But even for Chaumont the old vision was outmoded: Fustel de Coulanges had long ago called for a separation between patriotism and history.[23] Besides, the desire for heroic leaders was no longer so keenly felt. Chaumont's Cluniacs were civilizers not because they supported the papacy, but because they fostered the study of letters.[24] Chaumont's work could not serve to integrate the more specialized studies of his peers. A congress organized by the Académie de Mâcon to commemorate the thousandth year anniversary of the foundation of Cluny found French historians (only one "foreigner" was represented—a Swiss) engaged in studies that, if not antiquarian on the one hand or archaeological on the other, were decidedly independent of any chronological or geographical limits.[25] M. Leonce Lex wrote about Cluny's organization in the eighteenth century while Mgr. Dom Guépin asked "why Cluny had not survived the twelfth century." Egger described Cluniac houses in Switzerland; Guilloreau spoke about the Cluniac priories in England. Bauchond found a short sermon which he edited, translated, and ascribed to the eleventh-century Abbot Odilo; Virey commented on a fourteenth-century Cluniac manuscript.[26] A roster of topics so wide-ranging would doubtless have been fruitful had it been explored within a larger conceptual framework of Cluniac history. But, in fact, it flew in the face of the only comprehensive picture that did exist. Sackur's Cluny had been carefully defined both geographically and chronologically; the contours of his picture could certainly be expanded—this is precisely what German, American, and English students of Cluny undertook to do—but only in a way organic to the whole.

If Sackur's study had little impact upon French historians,[27] it tended, conversely, to determine the studies produced in Germany, England, and America. These historians claimed, at least, to be working within the rubrics defined by Sackur; if their interests lay outside of those rubrics, they usually came to conclusions that took into account and did not contradict those of the larger study.

Yet the very historians who deliberately worked within Sackur's framework imperceptibly changed its character. When Lucy Smith, for example, explored Cluny's relationship to the Gregorian reform, she reiterated Sackur's conclusions about the period before St. Hugh and then proceeded to extend those conclusions to the abbacy of St. Hugh himself: "In the struggle between pope and emperor, [Hugh] may be regarded as neutral."[28] But that contradicted Sackur's notions about the nature of Cluny's monasticism under St. Hugh. In her subsequent book on Cluny's early history, Smith emphasized the internal development of the monastery rather than the reforming activities of its abbots; the Romanesque "renaissance" of Sackur became the isolated efflorescence of one monastery for Smith.[29] Later, in 1930, she was to publish a book intended simply to extend the chronological limits of Sackur's study.[30] But by that very attempt, she implicitly challenged the reasons behind Sackur's periodization.

Similarly Ernst Tomek, while claiming to work within Sackur's thesis, radically altered it by claiming the monasteries of the empire for Cluniac studies.[31] While Sackur had left the general impression that Cluny was the prime mover of all the monastic reform movements of the tenth and eleventh centuries, he never made quite so sweeping a claim explicit. Indeed, precisely in regard to the reform of imperial monasteries, Sackur acknowledged that Cluny had had a minimal role. Bertha, mother of Empress Adelaide had, it is true, given Peterlingen to Abbot Majolus, thus establishing "close relations" with Cluny, but the real impetus for reform in Germany came from the imperial court itself, and the new monasteries were integrated into the military and economic system of the empire, not of Cluny.[32] Tomek argued that through its Lotharingian houses, particularly Gorze, Cluny was the indirect center of German monastic reform. But Sackur himself had not included Gorze in the constellation of strictly Cluniac houses.[33]

The turn of the century brought with it new historical approaches and interests that were also to affect Cluniac studies. The development of sociology under Durkheim and Weber and the maturation of economics into an academic discipline in the nineteenth century led to the study of social and economic history in the twentieth. Thus, Georg Schreiber examined Cluny as a social group—a community—with a form and function determined by the needs both of its own members and of society at large.[34] He studied monastic constitutions to determine the interaction between the activities of the monks and the activities of the lay world. None of Schreiber's work overtly challenged Sackur's picture, but it did mark a shift in focus. Sackur had sought above all to explain the origin and nature of Cluny itself. Schreiber sought first to explain the nature of social phenomena; Cluny became, secondarily, a part of this explanation. Thus, when Schreiber noted that the laity of the eleventh and twelfth centuries were donating proprietary churches to reformed monasteries—an observation that grew out of his desire to understand the impulse and impact of the Gregorian reform—his primary concern was to determine lay motives. These, he discovered, were inseparable from people's expectations about the nature and function of the monastic life itself, a life spent, above all, in the choir. The donor contributed his church to the monastery "in order to obtain" (as Schreiber put it) a burial spot in monastic ground and a place in monastic prayer.[35] The lay community thus participated in the monastic community. By means of the liturgy, both groups were linked to the community of saints, apostles, and martyrs.[36]

In the course of his exploration of medieval social groups, Schreiber was to return to Cluny again;[37] in the *interim* his student, P. W. Jorden, had expanded his findings on the donation of proprietary churches into a comprehensive study of the connections between monastic liturgy, lay needs, and land ownership.[38] For Jorden, as for Schreiber, lay needs came first: the desire for salvation motivated the laity to give economic support to monasteries which would devote themselves to intercessory prayer. The liturgy was a "repayment" *(Gegengabe)* for the donation.[39] Seeing Cluny above all as a social group with a particular form and function meant that in order to appreciate its significance properly, careful studies would have to be made of its internal constitution. In 1911, Schreiber had made the appeal for such studies, but they were not to be undertaken until the 1930s and then for different reasons and under different circumstances.

Thus, in the first quarter of the twentieth century, students of Cluny shared one characteristic in common: they deliberately chose an intellectual tradition in which to work. Until 1910, French studies remained in the pre-Sackur tradition. Then, perhaps because of the inadequacy of that tradition for serious historical work, there was, in France, a virtual hiatus in Cluniac studies until the 1930s. On the other hand, German, American, and English studies grew directly out of Sackur's thesis and/or out of the concerns of ancillary sciences such as sociology, economics, and the study of art and architectural history. Art history became an academic discipline in Europe in the nineteenth century. In the United States, it "began" in the early twentieth century; the year 1913 saw the first publication of the *Art Bulletin.* In the 'twenties, under the auspices of the Mediaeval Academy of America, Kenneth John

Conant began excavations at Cluny, thus harnessing the methodologies of both the art historian and the archaeologist. At the same time, Conant worked within the assumptions contained in Sackur's tradition: he began his work with the conviction that Cluny had been the "centre of Western monasticism." After his initial dig, he became convinced that Cluny had begun a new and advanced sculptural and architectural style in the eleventh century that set the pattern for the twelfth-century Romanesque. (His assessment in 1968, after almost a half-century of work on the project, supported his earlier conclusions.)[40]

By adhering to one or more academic tradition, the Cluniac historians of the early twentieth century avoided overt challenges to their predecessors or to one another. This polite disengagement seems to have been part of a broader distaste for political matters. Schreiber, writing in 1915, simply expanded on the implications of his work of 1911 without a hint that he now wrote in a Germany at war. L. M. Smith in 1911 stressed Cluny's lack of involvement in the political arena of Gregory VII; in 1920 she revised her position only in the sense that she decisively repudiated politics as a topic fit for study in her internal history of Cluny. It is, then, perhaps significant that the first overt challenge to Sackur—that of Brackmann in 1928—grew out of a political question, a question which may have grown, indeed, out of the aftermath of the Great War in Germany.

The German question, as historians saw it, was to explain why Germany had failed to follow the "natural" course of development into a nation-state. Their answer generally pointed to imperial Italian policy as the culprit; the emperors allowed themselves to become embroiled in Italy and left domestic affairs to the princes, who naturally proceeded to set up political institutions antithetical to the formation of a centralized state. In 1928, in a Germany faced with the still-burning humiliation of defeat and war reparations, Albert Brackmann argued against the notion of the inevitability of historical phenomena.[41] Failures were not to be assessed on the basis of *a priori* notions of a "proper" evolution. On the contrary, failure was simply a descriptive term to indicate that an institution had been unable to survive. Nor was the source of this inability to be sought in the wrong policy of those in control but rather in the very nature of the institution and the stresses upon it from other institutions. The medieval German empire had failed because it had not survived; the responsibility for this failure was not misguided imperial policy but the dependency of the universal empire on a universal papacy. Imperial power was based on a theory of mutual leadership by emperor and pope: the papacy was to preside over spiritual matters such as prayer and sacraments; the emperor was to protect the church and serve as a political leader. But (Brackmann argued) the pope did not share these notions: he had theocratic aspirations of his own. The weakness of the popes in the ninth through the eleventh centuries disguised this fact; when they gained power under Gregory VII, the universal ideal was shattered and the empire fell.

The crucial issue for Brackmann, then, was not the history of the empire but rather the history of the papacy. Had the papacy remained weak, the empire would have survived. Brackmann lay the responsibility for the growing power of the pope at the feet of the Cluniacs. They were the ones who had provided the papacy with its model of centralization and political organization. Moreover, they had given the papacy the secrets of their power quite deliberately. When Brackmann saw Cluniac abbots hobnobbing with popes and princes he could not believe that questions of politics were avoided: "None of these [abbots] was so unworldly that he did not know what was going on in front of him on the political arena of his day."[42] From the beginning, indeed, the Cluniacs had had a "political core": they were never interested in just their monastery. By the eleventh century, Cluny was even involved in setting up and leading a church-state *(Kirchenstaat)* in Spain and was attempting to do the same thing in Germany through its center at Hirsau.[43] Not only were such activities necessarily anti-imperial, argued Brackmann, but they also provided ready-made power for the popes: Urban II recognized this when he put the German monasteries organized by Cluny under Roman rather than Cluniac protection. Thus, Cluny was indirectly responsible for destroying the balance of power between papacy and empire.

Although Brackmann's assessment of the contribution of the Cluniacs to the Gregorian reform adhered to the letter if not the spirit of the pre-Sackur French tradition, Brackmann had no desire to avoid Sackur under the protective umbrella of the French. Rather he chose, quite in line with his general view that men and institutions interacted on the basis of power, to attack Sackur directly. Sackur had claimed that the Cluniacs were nonpolitical; Brackmann rejected the very possibility, then marshalled his evidence.

The fact that most of the proof for Brackmann's assertion came from the period of St. Hugh did not prevent his views from receiving wide attention as a refutation of Sackur. With the publication of Brack-mann's article, Cluniac studies became revivified. Between 1930 and 1950 a plethora of books and articles on Cluny were published that were, in one way or another, reactions to the Brackmann-Sackur debate.

Implicit in the initial responses lay the uncritical acceptance of Brackmann's position that political activity was equivalent to worldly activity and that both were the opposite of religious. Thus, if Cluny had been a political institution, it was to be studied primarily as it operated in the world. On the other hand, if Cluny had not been political, then it was to be studied as an ascetic retreat. The lines were drawn, and students of Cluny tended to opt for one side or the other. While one camp looked at Cluny's role in the world, the other looked at Cluny's internal monastic life. Historians of the pre-Brackmann era had been able to look at Cluny's impact as a center of monastic reform on the world at large because they saw no necessary contradiction between piety and action. But in the 1920s and early 1930s, there was a tendency to see dichotomies where harmonies had been discerned before. The futurists were an example of this: they set "bold deeds" against "weak thoughts." The fascists translated the conflict into a political program. The mental climate of the time was pervaded by this new version of the old conceptual dualism between the *vita activa* and the *vita contemplativa*.

This distinction appeared in more than just Brackmann's work on Cluny. Boissonnade argued that Cluny had actively participated in the Spanish reconquest. For Boissonnade this was an essentially political fact; it proved that the Cluniacs were worldly.[44] The same opposition between religious and political was evident in Berthelier's 1938 study of the expansion of the Cluniac order. She concluded that Cluny before St. Hugh had been nonpolitical: it set about the task of monastic reform in a haphazard manner, depending on disciples to spread its essentially religious program. This changed under Hugh: monastic reform became systematic and took deliberate advantage of contemporary circum-stances: Cluny became involved in the ". . . great political movements of the age."[45]

Other historians of this postwar period were convinced that Cluny had always been a purely religious institution. They began to explore the organization and character of Cluny's internal life without speaking of its activities, even its reforming activities, in the world. In 1931, Evans, maintaining that she had "neither thesis to maintain nor theory to develop," created a detailed composite picture of Cluniac monastic life in its first two and one-half centuries.[46] Guy de Valous did the same in 1935 with evidence culled from sources extending to the fifteenth century.[47] These studies suggested, implicitly, that Cluny was so completely cut off from the rest of the world that it was uninfluenced and unchanged by it; the spiritual program set up originally in the tenth century remained intact in the twelfth or even, for Valous, in the fifteenth century.[48] Such an assumption made it possible for Evans and Valous to discuss the formation of a Cluniac order without discussing politics. The order was simply the institutionalization of Cluny's spiritual program; it was to be discussed descriptively as an organization, not historically as an organism evolving with time and circumstance. When this ceased to be true—when Cluny's internal life became dependent upon its abbot's external activities (for Evans, the change began under St. Hugh; for Valous, it came with Abbot Jean III de Bourbon in the fifteenth century)—Cluny began to decline.

The notion that Cluny was to be seen primarily as an ascetic retreat also set the tone for a number of studies that did not deal directly with Cluny's interior life. Cluny's art and architecture were described, its written work explored, even its economy analyzed, not as expressions of Cluny's impact on nonmonastic areas, but in order to grasp the material and spiritual foundations of the Cluniac life-style.[49]

These studies rarely mentioned the Gregorian reform, but that topic lurked in the wings nonetheless. Due partly to the assumption that power and piety were incompatible, partly to the terms in which Brackmann had framed the problem, Cluniac historians of the 'thirties and 'forties tended to see the Gregorian reform as essentially political. The implications for Cluny followed almost inexorably: if Cluny had been worldly, then it must have participated in papal politics; if it had been ascetic, then the reverse was true. Evans never mentioned the Gregorian reform.[50] Hayden White, on the other hand, associated the "political" Abbot Pons with the "worldly" Gregorians.[51] But by the time White wrote, in 1958, the assumptions upon which he rested his dichotomy between worldly and ascetic had long since been challenged.

In fact, it had been challenged almost simultaneously in the mid-thirties by at least three historians. Carl Erdmann was the first. He argued that Cluny's very religiosity impelled it to become worldly precisely in order to reform the world spiritually. The point, however revolutionary for its time, was almost an aside in Erdmann's larger inquiry. He presented it in a book only peripherally about Cluny, and he modestly ascribed it to the nineteenth-century theologian Harnack.[52] The next year, however, the same idea was argued at length by Gerhart Ladner and Gerd Tellenbach in independent publications.[53] Both asserted that the distinction between politics and religion was a modern notion anachronistically imposed on the early Middle Ages. Both argued that for the Cluniacs politics and religion were inextricably mingled. However, in Ladner's view, this synthesis was first made in the time of the German emperor Henry III. With this *proviso,* Ladner was able to maintain the old dichotomy between action and asceticism, while at the same time introducing the notion that the two poles came together for a moment in the mid-eleventh century. Ladner argued that the Cluniacs had been an essentially religious movement; their only political activities involved attempts to preserve their liberty, that is, their immunity from lay control. When Henry III guaranteed imperial Cluniac houses this very privilege, they began to support him in other endeavors as well, just as older Cluniac houses had supported the popes who protected them. But in neither case did this backing mean that the Cluniacs were political, since in the eleventh century, imperial and papal power were both seen as a fusion of the spiritual and the worldly.[54] With this argument, Ladner took a position midway between those historians who, following Brackmann, claimed that contact with popes and emperors was evidence of political—*ergo* nonspiritual—activity, and historians like Erdmann and Tellenbach, who claimed that Cluniac asceticism had always been both spiritual and political without contradiction.

Tellenbach's argument for Cluny was a vigorous exposition of the Harnack-Erdmann thesis. Tellenbach maintained that Benedictine monasteries had always had the dual character of a retreat for ascetics and a base for proselytizers. Cluny was no exception. Its spiritual program not only determined the forms of piety to be practiced by the monks themselves but also imposed the ascetic life on society at large. The Cluniacs were worldly and unabashedly political precisely because they were driven by religious ideals:

> The ascetics set out to be the front-line troops of the church in the battle for Christ and against evil; and by their merits they hoped to save not only themselves but also their fellow men from damnation. This purpose determined the nature of their relations with the great ones of the world. They became their spiritual advisers, and kings and emperors, bishops and popes, princes and nobles listened to their words.[55]

A few years later Erdmann drew out the implications of this reconciliation between politics and religion when he asserted that the Cluniacs had been leaders in furthering the idea of the *imperium Romanum.* [56] The argument in effect attacked Brackmann on three fronts: the Cluniacs had not supported the papacy; they had actively promoted the imperial cause; they had at the same time remained strictly true to their religious ideals. For the Cluniacs the *imperium Romanum* was the equivalent of the *imperium Christianum.* There was nothing worldly in their support of the Salian kings.

Thus liberated from an anachronistic dichotomy, historians began to resume their study of Cluny's relationship with lay society without denying Cluny's essentially religious nature. Schreiber, who had been silent on the subject for years, now produced, as part of a project to explore Cluny's "place in the history of piety," a study of Cluny's active role in emancipating the parish church from lay ownership.[57] What was needed, wrote Schreiber at the beginning of his own, admittedly preliminary investigation into one facet of the problem, was a study of the impact of Cluny on the institutions of feudal society and the impact of these in turn upon Cluny. Schreiber envisioned research that would encompass institutions such as the proprietary church; movements such as the Crusades, the Peace of God, and pilgrimages; and modes of thought and expression, such as the cult of the saints. Yet, even though he clearly considered piety consonant with action, Schreiber was still haunted by the ghost of the old dichotomy: at the end of his study, he found it necessary to point out that the Cluniacs had not violated their spirituality by being at the same time worldly.[58]

Both Erdmann and Schreiber wrote in a world at war. Their studies reflected nothing of the chaos raging around them; on the contrary, they picked up the thread of topics left from their prewar days. In the face of cataclysm, they affirmed a continuity with the past. But when the war ended, and a new social and political order was established, the changed circumstances contributed to the formulation of new approaches. In particular, the creation of a divided Germany seems to have been crucial in the writings of Ernst Werner and, to a lesser extent, Kassius Hallinger, whose work was to change the course of subsequent Cluniac studies.[59]

Ernst Werner, an East German scholar, used the methodology of Marx and Lenin to show that the significance of Cluny's reformed monasticism had been misinterpreted. The key to Werner's reformulation was the Marxist analysis of society: the economic mode determined a dominant and an oppressed class; the interests of the dominant class determined political forms and the cultural superstructure. In the tenth and eleventh centuries, the economy was agrarian; the dominant class was that of the feudal landowner; the political structure of greatest benefit to it was the principality.[60] Cluny was an important component of the cultural superstructure of feudal society because its particular form of monasticism was created to benefit the magnates' position materially, politically, and ideologically.[61] Cluny's economic contribution was, through its system of priories, to consolidate heretofore scattered lands into compact territories.[62] Its political contribution was, first, to allow the great feudal magnates to function as advocates for these enormous and well-administered economic units and, second, to oppose central, monarchical power, both theoretically (because of its own desire for liberty) and institutionally (through such substitutes for royal power as the Peace and Truce of God). Cluny contributed to an ideology that justified the control of feudal landowners over the masses in two ways: it kept the powerless content with their lot by mitigating the worst aspects of their condition with guarantees of peace and protection, and by dazzling the laity with piety and ceremony, it prevented both peasants and merchants from looking to heretical movements for ideological alternatives.[63] In short, Cluny was an extremely specialized weapon in the arsenal with which the feudal classes maintained their dominant position.

Like Werner, Hallinger too wrote from a distinctly German perspective, but his was the Germany of the *Bundesrepublik.* Although he expressly denied writing out of chauvinist partisanship, the terms in which Hallinger couched his argument seemed to have nationalist undertones.[64] His thesis was that Cluny, which he characterized as Western and (equivalently) French, had no influence on Eastern, that is, German, monasticism. Rather, German monasteries had been reformed under the aegis of Gorze, a Benedictine house in Lotharingia which historians, following Tomek and (less correctly) Sackur, had long considered Cluniac.[65] Hallinger argued that Cluny and Gorze belonged to two different, indeed hostile, traditions. Gorze stood for simplicity in life-style, Cluny for elaboration; Gorze was a center of intellectual and literary culture, Cluny of cult; Gorze had been a proprietary church, Cluny had been "antifeudal"; Gorze had supported the emperor, Cluny the Gregorians. Nor did these differences describe antagonisms confined to the isolated world of the cloister. Gorze served the empire not only as a model of monasticism but also as a cultural center. Thus, the lines were drawn: Gorze *versus* Cluny, Germany *versus* France, East *versus* West:

> Already in the tenth century, indeed even long before the tenth century, a deep spiritual line of demarcation developed between Lotharingia [whence Gorze] and the Burgundian West [whence Cluny]. The cultural ferment of Lotharingian monasticism was without question directed toward the German East and not toward the Burgundian or French West.[66]

Hallinger's promotion of Gorze to a position rivaling Cluny was crucial in determining the course of subsequent Cluniac studies. His was not the first assertion of multiple reform centers, but it was the one worked out in the most compelling detail. Yet it was precisely this concentration on minute differences that constituted the greatest weakness in Hallinger's argument. It tended to slight the monastic forest for the trees: the notion of a monastic reform movement was in danger of fragmenting into two hostile species. Issue was taken with Hallinger almost immediately on two levels: the first was to assess the importance of Cluny and Gorze as reform centers; the second was to interpret the significance of their differences.[67]

In an early review of *Gorze-Kluny*, Theodor Schieffer tempered a generally favorable response with the *caveat* that the evidence was not all in and that Hallinger's verdict was premature.[68] Further research would reveal, Schieffer asserted, that many monasteries originally reformed by Gorze in the tenth century had gravitated to the Cluniac orbit a hundred years later. The abbacy of St. Hugh saw a veritable "Clunicization" of houses not only in the West but also in Lotharingia.[69] Schieffer's restrained enthusiasm was supplemented the same year by Dauphin's response to Hallinger in the *Downside Review.*[70] Dauphin did not dispute Gorze's newly recognized role as an important and enduring reform center, but he did question whether the hostility between Gorze and Cluny had been as extreme as Hallinger claimed. A case in point was St. Vanne, a monastery in Lotharingia which had practiced a mixed observance more unabashedly Cluniac than Hallinger had allowed.

The implications of Dauphin's argument were drawn out by Leclercq in a series of publications over the next two decades.[71] Each of his studies focused on separate issues, but the thesis common to them all was that the differences between Cluny and Gorze were more properly to be seen as nuances within a common tradition than as antagonisms between two disparate spiritualities. Further, the cleft between East and West, the Empire and France, which Hallinger had stressed, seemed to Leclercq to be an artificial contrivance.[72] His arguments were paralleled by European political events: the 1950s and '60s witnessed attempts to integrate Western Europe politically and economically. Distinctions between nations were not denied, but they were seen as variations within the European community. In Leclercq's vision of a pan-European tenth- and eleventh-century monastic tradition, too, variety was a necessary corollary. There had been many kinds of Benedictine forms, he argued. Some houses, despite a location in Lotharingia or in the Rhineland, had followed "a practice and a doctrine similar to that of Cluny."[73] Other houses reformed directly by Gorze nevertheless used necrologies commemorating Cluniac abbots.[74] On the other hand, there were monasteries situated even in Burgundy which were centers of reform independent from their famous neighbor. Cluny itself, then, had been one—albeit important—monastery among many. It was not an archetype. The Cluny of Hallinger was a myth, a strawman.[75]

Thus resurrected on the new foundations of Hallinger's thesis as modified and tempered by its critics, Cluny lost its position as the sole monastic reform center of the tenth and eleventh centuries, but gained new status as the home of a particular and sophisticated form of Benedictinism. When, in the 1960s, a number of studies of Cluny's internal life were published, their purpose was not so much to illustrate the nature of "Cluniac" monasticism as to appreciate the life-style unique to Cluny.[76] At the same time, studies of Cluny's interaction with the world, which had, since Brackmann, often been seen as a question of Cluny's political activities, once again turned to Cluny's social role. These new studies, informed by the techniques and approaches of the social sciences, were now to merge with the research that had been confined to Cluny's internal monastic culture. The result was to be a much richer synthesis than Schreiber had been able to make, since when Schreiber was writing both sides of the amalgamation had been insufficiently explored. Schreiber had pointed out connections between Cluniac piety and its social context in general terms: the liturgy provided the motive for donations. But in 1967, when Wollasch and Schmid made a similar connection, they did so by studying the relationship between a specific necrology used at Cluny and the particular social groups it served.[77]

The conceptual framework upon which such a study rested had

been provided by earlier works of synthesis. The methodologies of the social sciences were welcomed into historical research with the advent of *Les Annales d'histoire économique et sociale,* founded by Lucien Febvre and Marc Bloch in 1929.[78] The journal became associated with a school, the school with a tradition. It was fed by streams from many disciplines: anthropology, sociology, linguistics, economics, geography. It viewed civilization as the product of interconnected human activities, themselves the creative responses to the possibilities and limitations presented by material conditions. It emancipated itself from the constraints of national histories and based itself squarely on whatever structures—whether regional or supranational—were fundamental. Thus, in the early 1950s, when Georges Duby turned to study medieval society in the region surrounding Cluny, all his conclusions were literally rooted in the soil: the social structure and the political regime of the Mâconnais were ultimately determined by the land and the people's relations to it.[79] Duby chose the Mâconnais not because he was especially interested in Cluny, but because the Cluniacs had been party to, and therefore had kept excellent records of, most regional land transactions. Yet this very fact revealed at once the clear connection between monastic piety and lay society. Donations to Cluny fluctuated with political conditions and economic realities; the anxieties and the peace of mind which arose from these outside causes were translated into religious acts.[80] In the 1960s, Duby published a number of studies exploring the nature of Benedictine piety and its connections with feudal society.[81]

It was, however, on the nature of the conjunction of social order and monastic *ordo* that historians from the two disciplines—the sociological on the one hand, the traditional historical on the other— were to clash. Ever since Tellenbach's work in the thirties, few historians of Cluny denied the importance of exploring the role of the Abbey within its external environment. But now the definition of that context came into dispute.

Implicit in the traditional historian's work, and reinforced in Cluniac studies by the influence of Brackmann's terms, was the assumption that the important facts about men and institutions were at bottom a function of political position. Ideology, behavior, and interests had all been seen as a function of power. Hence, Lemarignier's approach in 1937 to the question of monastic exemption. The exempt monastery was freed from the spiritual jurisdiction of the local bishop in favor of papal jurisdiction. When Lemarignier found that this exemption increased the power of both the papacy and the central monarchies, he concluded that exempt monasteries could not have been part of the feudal (nonmonarchical) world.[82] In 1956, at a conference in Spoleto, Lemarignier linked his argument to Hallinger's: Cluny, by setting up a hierarchy of power independent from any other authority, placed itself in direct opposition to feudal control. It was, in a word borrowed from Hallinger, "antifeudal."[83]

But in this communication, Lemarignier was not content with reiterating the older view; he supplemented it with a new definition of the nature of feudal society. Along with his argument of political opposition, he introduced a new and quite different thesis. The Cluniac hierarchy, because it had been orderly and regulated by laws, was by its very structure antagonistic to the disorderly, arbitrary hierarchy of feudal society.[84] The sociologists had made their impact.

For the sociologically informed historian, the basic unit of human organization was the social class, defined by wealth or occupation. Society was the arrangement of these classes in relation to one another. In the discussion following Lemarignier's presentation, Masai, using the political definition of feudalism, challenged Lemarignier on the grounds that real political control over Cluny had not been in the hands of the pope, who was too weak, but rather in the hands of lay advocates.[85] But Courtois, using the sociological definition of feudalism, countered Lemarignier on the ground that Cluny's organization of a mother house and dependent priories mirrored the feudal system of a lord and dependent vassals.[86] In 1959, Violante was to reconcile Lemarignier and Courtois by arguing that feudal society had constantly alternated between a tendency to disintegrate and, in compensatory efforts, a tendency to centralize.[87] The Cluniac order developed in a parallel manner. Extending control over formerly independent abbeys was as much a symptom of anarchy as a hypothetical castellan's attempt to control as many castles as he could; but at the same time both the abbey and the lord were revealing the wish and the possibility of creating a united organism.

If Violante was convinced of Cluny's feudal nature because of the structure of its order, other historians found it equally feudal because of its personnel.[88] The warlike character of the Cluniacs had been a charge leveled against the monks even in their own day.[89] Modern historians had occasionally spoken of the aristocratic origins of many

Clunic monks, noting that many came from families of titled rank.[90] But a systematic study of the social origins of the monks at Cluny was not attempted until the postwar synthesis of social science methodology and historical studies described above. In 1959, under the triumphant title of *New Research on Cluny and the Cluniacs,* Tellenbach assembled a number of detailed reports whose collective import was that the Cluniacs came from and shared the values of the great feudal lords of the tenth and eleventh centuries.[91] Mager revealed that the Cluniacs had been quite content to leave proprietary churches in the hands of the laity. Wollasch, using new prosopographical methods, argued that the monastic policies of Abbot Odo of Cluny were tied to the politics of the *seigneurie* of Berry and the king of France.[92] Similarly, in 1959, Schieffer concluded that:

> Without any doubt the aristocratic elements predominated [at Cluny] entirely. All the abbots, who frequented the courts of kings and princes, were products of the high nobility; St. Hugh himself was related to the Capetian dynasty. It is frequently counts and princes who become monks at Cluny. On this point even the charters are eloquent: we read there that some of the monks who entered the order gave the monastery part of their property, allowing us to suppose that most of them belonged to the landed nobility.[93]

The "eloquent charters" were made to yield up further riches. Already Duby, in his several studies of the Mâconnais, had made extensive use of them in analyzing the social structure of the region. Then, seven years after Schieffer wrote, Johannes Fechter subjected them to a systematic analysis designed in particular to reveal the social origins of the monks at Cluny.[94] He concluded that Cluny began with a balance between the upper and lower classes—between *Adel* and *Volk,* to use his terminology—and then, in the course of the eleventh century, it became a house of nobles.

Had the monks been isolated from the world, the question of their social origins would have had little importance. The significance of Fechter's analysis lay in the insight it could give about the function and motives of monastic activities as they connected with the lay world. This, in turn, led Fechter to look at the Peace Movement and the Spanish *reconquista.* Although Fechter did not mention it, these two movements developed in tandem with the movement for church reform. Along with those many other studies that posed the issue of Cluny's feudal character, Fechter's work called for a complementary, sociologically informed study of the relations between the classes in the monastery and the papacy. The need was partly met in 1970 by Cowdrey,[95] who had earlier looked at the question of Cluniac alliances with laymen and bishops.[96] Ironically, his conclusions concerning Cluny and the Gregorians largely flew in the face of the expectations of those whose work had set up the new terms of his problem in the first place. Schieffer and Tellenbach's students, by showing that the Cluniacs shared the interests of their feudal neighbors, were led to conclude that Cluny had not promoted the Gregorians. But Cowdrey argued that, although their research was correct, their conclusions did not necessarily follow.

Cowdrey agreed that Cluniac interests did not coincide with the interests of the Gregorians on the question of cooperating with powerful laymen, but on other matters monastery and papacy found common ground. The Cluniac need for liberty and the papal need for supremacy in the church, for example, were not only compatible objectives, but complementary as well. Although coming from different directions, the Cluniacs and the popes had mutual interests and embarked on a path of mutual advancement. Indeed, Cowdrey challenged the very basis of previous assumptions. He argued that the feudal world itself was not utterly opposed to the papacy or to the Gregorian reform. Everyone in eleventh-century society shared at least one interest in common: the remission of sins. In connection with this need, the Gregorians could and did look to the laity for support:

> Because St. Peter had such power over the affairs of men even in this life and because his vicar was so straitly charged with the proclamation and fulfillment of righteousness here upon earth, the pope necessarily looked to all men, and especially to those with any kind of ecclesiastical, social, or political preeminence, for active service in this world in the cause of St. Peter. . . . The warfare of Christ was the warfare of knights upon an earthly battlefield. . . . Gregory sought, with varying degrees of success, to commit kings and magnates; but above all it was to the lower feudal classes that he appealed.[97]

Thus, Cowdrey dealt with the issue of the Cluniacs and the Gregorian reform in terms of class interest; but he also neatly shifted it from a question of sociology to one of spiritual needs. In doing so, he was drawing upon yet another discipline, the study of spirituality.

This field had a long history in its own right, responding to many of the same intellectual currents as the study of Cluny itself. The word *spiritualitas* had been used in the Middle Ages, but not with a specifically religious meaning. Rather it signified the nonmaterial in a general sense. In the nineteenth century this association remained, but theologians began to use the term to describe, in particular, programmatic ascetical exercises, such as those of St. Ignatius. Such a view lent itself to the new historical sensibilities taking root in the nineteenth century and made possible a survey of the development of ascetic and mystical thought. Following the predilection of the time, spirituality was rooted in the *vita contemplativa;* it was found in texts, not in acts. When Pourrat was writing his books on *Christian Spirituality* in the 1920s, he defined his topic as a specific aspect of theology and mysticism.[98]

By 1960, this definition was no longer satisfying. When Bernard Bligny wanted to write about the religious life in the kingdom of Burgundy, he explicitly avoided discussing *"spiritualité proprement dite."* He preferred to concentrate, as he put it, "less on doctrines than on men."[99] Influenced by the *Annales* school, Bligny saw the importance of fitting religious life into the larger context of mental attitudes, themselves products of more basic contextual configurations such as geography, social structure, and political life.

The concern to show the interdependence of thought and deed was the root of the dissatisfaction with the old definition of spirituality. Already in 1956 at the conference at Spoleto referred to above, historians such as Lemarignier had been waging a battle for this interdependence as part of their response to Hallinger's thesis.[100] Like Bligny, the participants at that conference did not actually change the definition of the word *spirituality* (when it was used, it was to differentiate the "spiritual world" at Cluny from the "feudal world" outside). But the heated debate at Spoleto over the monastery's relationship with other social and political structures set the stage for a broader definition.

That definition came at the 1958 conference at Todi. To be sure, some scholars at that conference, such as Jean Leclercq, continued to be guided by the old definition. Leclercq argued that Cluny had a rich intellectual—indeed scholarly—tradition; that Cluny was, in effect (and possibly in fact), a "school of spirituality."[101] However, at the same conference in which Leclercq was defining spirituality primarily as doctrine, the results of other, more radical definitions of spirituality were being aired. The title of this conference, *Cluniac Spirituality,* implied no more than a nineteenth-century notion of programmatic asceticism, now newly associated with Cluny. But the organizers of the conference envisioned a problem of far greater scope: to explore the nature and influence of Cluny "on the political, social, and religious world of the high middle ages."[102]

One year after the Todi conference, a seminar at La Mendola was showing a willingness to push the boundaries yet further. Todi, for all its pathbreaking, still held to the view that spirituality was a topic appropriate only to people and institutions primarily devoted to religion. However, at La Mendola, historians like Delaruelle spoke of "spiritualité populaire."[103] And a few years later, in 1965, the third conference at the La Mendola center was entirely dedicated to the "laity in 'Christian society.'"[104]

So forceful was the new wave that in 1960 Leclercq, and a few other influential scholars, gave their blessing to at least a part of it. The multivolume *History of Christian Spirituality* which they wrote began with a nod at the field of psychology. Psychology (the authors said) had to be included in any discussion of "religious consciousness." On the other hand, psychology was not to overwhelm religious truths with an anthropological outlook that saw spirituality as a universal human sensibility divorced from specific dogma. The solution Leclercq and his colleagues arrived at was a compromise: spirituality was to be seen as the response of the worshiper and, at the same time, the object or idea that was worshiped. The history of spirituality was to be a survey of changes in the perception of—and in the modes of responding to—religious things that were eternally fixed.[105]

This break with pure theology freed the *History of Spirituality*, especially Leclercq's contribution to it, from the contemplative text. Indeed, Leclercq is now treating spirituality as an aspect of mankind's psychological makeup.[106] Meanwhile, R. W. Southern brought to the study of the Western church his unique sensitivity to the nuances of medieval culture. Like the scholars at Todi, Southern sought to show how religious forms meshed with social and political needs. Southern did not use the word *spirituality*, but his work implicitly reinforced the Todi definition.[107] The integration of social and religious forms has become the watchword of the most recent and up-to-date studies of medieval spirituality.[108]

Nevertheless, the latest books on Cluny have not reaped the full harvest of these historiographical changes. Cowdrey's work may serve to sum up the collective gains and gaps which have accrued over time in the study of Cluny. In the wake of Hallinger's challenge to the Cluniac universe of Sackur, Cowdrey recognized that historians could no longer speak of Cluny as central to all pre–twelfth-century monasticism. On the other hand, if Cluny was no longer impressario, it was still a key figure in the drama: it was a supremely characteristic, a model post-Carolingian monastery. "Far from being unique," wrote Hunt in 1967, referring to Cluny's liturgy, "her timetable was typical of the black monk's horarium in the tenth and eleventh centuries. If anything, Cluny followed rather than led."[109] Cowdrey accepted this point of view for Cluny's original position—*vis-à-vis* its founder, its lay supporters, its papal sponsors—then traced the process by which Cluny became, in fact, unique in the eleventh century.

Cowdrey did not wholeheartedly embrace the use of the social sciences to illuminate Cluniac studies. The impact of sociology, psychology, and anthropology on the ideas, questions, and assumptions made by modern historians had been unavoidable, even if the latter eschewed using new-fangled methodologies and terms. Cowdrey was somewhat sensitive to the issues of class raised by sociologists and, in a vague way, to the issues of systems of belief raised by anthropologists. But he did not elaborate on these themes.

Also left to Cowdrey was the decisive repudiation of the conceptual dichotomy between political and religious. Although bridged as early as the 'thirties, this view had continued to haunt Cluniac studies in disguise. Hunt, for example, had argued that Cluny's spiritual, interior life deteriorated as a result of Abbot Hugh's activities beyond the cloister walls. It was a new argument, but it led to the old conclusions. However, at the same time Hunt was writing, even historians of spirituality were insisting on the political ramifications of spiritual ideals. By 1970, then, Cowdrey was able—indeed found it necessary—to speak in the same breath of the Cluniacs' mission to save souls and their work as "agents of the reformed Papacy."[110]

Within this last point, however, is the one large gap in Cluny's historiography: the tendency to bypass the tenth century in favor of the eleventh. Cowdrey's work is only one of the latest to fall into this pattern.[111] A short review of those studies which have looked even fleetingly at Cluny in its early days makes clear that the foray into the tenth century has generally been directed at discovering the sources of Cluny's subsequent development. At first concerned with Cluny as the prime mover of heroic deeds, historians, as we have seen, tied Cluny to eleventh- and twelfth-century chivalry, morality, and papacy. When, toward the beginning of the twentieth century, students of history began to shift their focus from the theater of great events to the backrooms of politicians, so too did Cluny become variously described as the scene of Gregorian political machinations or, on the contrary, the retreat from questions of church power altogether. In every case, rarely has more than a passing glance been bestowed upon Cluny's initial monasticism; by and large, this has been in order to contrast it with its eleventh-century character.

A case in point is Sackur's pioneering study, which admittedly rooted Cluny in the chaotic conditions of the ninth and tenth centuries. But Sackur was less interested in the roots than in the harvest: out of chaos the Cluniacs had created a renaissance, the civilization of the Romanesque. In the 1920s, Hessel, a lesser figure in Cluniac historiography, contributed an article on tenth-century Cluny. But the gist of his argument was that the Cluniac "reformation" was in part responsible for the formation of eleventh- and twelfth-century French culture.[112]

A similar perspective pervaded the proceedings of a scientific congress held at Cluny in 1949. This conference proposed to look at Cluny in the time of St. Odo and St. Odilo, in its very purpose mixing tenth- and eleventh-century abbots. In point of fact, the ultimate focus of the conference was on the future Cluny of St. Hugh. Lemarignier, for example, researched the question of monastic exemption at Cluny in order to connect it with the Gregorian reform. Hourlier sought in the tenth century the origins of Cluny's eleventh-century congregation. Dom Cousin looked at Cluny's Mariolatry from Odo to Hugh to demonstrate spiritual continuity. Leclercq discussed the monasticism of Odo in order to show the spiritual foundations of Cluny's later social role. The congress had as many feasts in honor of the abbots as papers; indeed, many of the writings had a devotional, sometime apologist, purpose in addition to a scholarly one. When Dom Laporte studied St. Odo as a disciple of St. Gregory the Great, it was to demonstrate that Cluny fit into the larger monastic tradition established by the fathers.[113]

Nothing is more telling with regard to the magnetic effect of the Gregorian reform than a 1951 dissertation on Odo's ideas that concentrated on numerous comparisons between Odo and Gregory VII.[114] The author concluded that Odo did not have Gregorian ideas. That ought to have been expected, since Odo died in 944, and Gregory was not born until c. 1015. Yet, apparently it was unthinkable to the author to study Odo without Gregory.

Again, in 1954, when Hallinger surveyed the problem of Cluny and pronounced it still unsolved, he began to fill the gaps by studying Cluny's original monastic ideal.[115] Taking up where Leclercq and Laporte had left off in 1949, Hallinger placed tenth-century Cluny squarely within the monastic tradition rooted in the Fathers and harvested in St. Francis, in mysticism, and in later religious forms. Hallinger's exposition recognized the richness of the tenth century ("the ideas [expressed by Odo at Cluny] are anything but elementary platitudes") but its goal was the future. Hallinger's last pages were devoted to St. Hugh and the papacy.

The conference on Cluny held at Todi in 1958, so pathbreaking with regard to its definition of spirituality, was in the mainstream when it dedicated itself to the "Cluniac movement in fullest bloom."[116] All papers, even those touching on the tenth century, were focused on this point in time. Thus, when Raffaello Morghen spoke about Odo's spirituality, he fixed on the elements within it which were connected with or opposed to later impulses toward Church reform.[117] A short paper at the same conference by Capitani addressed itself to Odo's teaching on the eucharist in part for its intrinsic interest, but also because it prefigured an aspect of Gregorian spirituality.[118] The eleventh-century perspective was, of course, even more pronounced in most of the other studies. Dom Schmitz's description of Cluniac prayer, for example, was largely based on late eleventh-century customaries.[119]

In summary, Cluniac studies have almost always treated tenth-century Cluny as an introduction to eleventh-century Cluny. Only J. Wollasch's rather specialized article began and ended with Cluny in its tenth-century milieu.[120] Wollasch propounded a very speculative hypothesis. He maintained that Abbot Odo's father was Ebbo I (d. 936), lord of Déols, and he argued that Odo's reforming activities were in the political interest of Odo's immediate family. Here a different gap—or better, disconnectedness—in Cluny's historiography is once again pointed up. Wollasch was not at all concerned with Cluny as a religious, moral, or spiritual institution. He was interested in personalities and politics. Once more we see a separation between those interested in Cluny's spirituality and those interested in its policies in the world. In this case, the implicit choice of sides is especially curious, because Wollasch was Tellenbach's pupil!

The legacy of Cluniac historiography is now clear, and the work that needs to be done is manifest. Cluny must be seen as both a worldly and a spiritual institution. It must be studied with the sensitivities of the sociologist, the psychologist, and the anthropologist as well as the historian and theologian. Above all, it must be viewed in its original, formative context.

That context was, in a general sense, the entire tenth century. However, within that broad framework Cluny may well have been peripheral; one cannot simply assume that it held meaning for the broad spectrum of tenth-century society. To understand what Cluny meant in its time, it is necessary to look specifically at those with whom Cluny was involved and to whom it was compelling. These are the people who found Cluny important enough to donate property to it or to found other monastic houses along the Cluniac model.

Modern historians have understood this supportive context in a variety of ways. They have looked at the distribution of land donated to the monastery. They have mapped the new monastic foundations or monastic reforms sponsored by Cluniac supporters. They have looked at the benefactors themselves to find clues to Cluny's significance. A survey of these historical perceptions is the necessary prelude to the particular interpretation advanced in this study. In the next chapter, then, we shall look at the gift-givers and the pattern of gift-giving at tenth-century Cluny.

2 | LOOKING AT THE TENTH CENTURY: *The Historians' Perception of Cluny's Benefactors*

Cluny's benefactors are known through charters of donation and foundation. Collected, edited, and published, these charters have been readily accessible since the turn of this century. However, the six huge volumes in question have never been indexed, and many of the charters have not been dated, or they have been misdated or dated so broadly as to be of little use. Historians have exploited the charters as best they can, but it is not surprising that they have emerged from the sources with very different conclusions.[1]

The earliest study of donations to Cluny was undertaken by Guy de Valous in 1920. He surveyed the growth of the order and the domain of Cluny from its inception until the reign of Abbot Hugh (1049–1109). Cluniac houses spread, he argued, gradually but unremittingly across the whole of Western Europe. Beginning in Burgundy, Cluny's reforms had, by the end of Abbot Odilo's time (994–1049), found their way to Italy, Germany, all of France, Spain, England, Hungary, and Poland.[2] Here, Valous followed the work of Sackur and Tomek. Valous then turned to Cluny's domain. He found that Cluny's landholding followed a development parallel to the organization of its order: beginning with fragmentary landholdings, especially those near to the mother monastery, Cluny embarked on a campaign of consolidation that left it, by the end of St. Hugh's abbacy, a great landowner with vast, united dominions. In the realm of landholding, as in the work of monastic reform, Cluny proved to be a great organizer.

There were a number of questions which Valous did not answer in his article. He thought that his discovery of the originally fragmentary nature of the land donations to Cluny was crucial. But he did not question why the donors should give such gifts, nor did he question why there was a distinction between the gifts given to Cluny in its immediate neighborhood (gifts that were especially fragmentary), and those given to Cluny in other areas (which tended to be larger and more consolidated). Moreover, in spite of his careful sorting of charters by geographical region, Valous did not see any significant pattern emerge from his material corresponding to regional differences. His point was, rather, to demonstrate the Cluniac genius in wielding together so disparate a group of lands.

Two decades after Valous wrote, M. Chaume attempted to answer some of the remaining questions. Chaume argued that Cluny's expansion depended on personal and political ties.[3] The figure of William, duke of Aquitaine and founder of Cluny, was pivotal. His name figured in many of the early donations to Cluny and in the foundation charters of monasteries handed over to Cluny for reform. He probably chose Berno to become abbot because—and here Chaume took a speculative leap into the realm of prosopography—Berno might have been the count of Escuens and, thus, attached to the kingdom of Vienne, which William supported. Berno, in turn, had a personal following. Again, Chaume argued that it was personal and family relations which explained Odo's accession to the abbacy as well as the areas in which Odo received donations or monasteries to reform.

A problem in Chaume's thesis was the leap of faith by which he titled Berno a count and gave Odo a birthplace in Maine. Indeed, the recent study of Wollasch removes Odo entirely from Maine and places him instead in Berry.[4] But Wollasch's reconstruction, though destroying the particulars of Chaume's argument, at least preserves its terms: both conclude that Cluny grew because of personal and political ties among great men.

The survey in Chapter 1 has shown that this sort of formulation of the issue became less compelling to historians in the 1950s. When, in 1957, Lemarignier tackled the question of Cluny's monastic growth, it was in terms of structures rather than in terms of personal ties.[5] For Lemarignier, politics played a key role in Cluny's growth, but for reasons having to do with sociology rather than friendships. In brief, Lemarignier argued that a general phenomenon of political fragmentation—with power falling into the hands of castellans—occurred at the end of the tenth and the first third of the eleventh century. The Order of Cluny was significant as a counter-structure to this political anarchy. This thesis, intriguing as it was, may be questioned on a variety of grounds. First, it (in effect) refounded Cluny at the end of the tenth century. Instead of looking at Cluny's growth, which began as early as Berno's abbacy, it discounted everything until 1016, when Benedict VIII first proposed the idea of a formal Order of Cluny.[6] Second, Lemarignier spoke of the phenomenon of fragmentation as if it occurred at the same time everywhere. Yet historians have increasingly become aware of the extreme variety of experiences in French political life. Third, by speaking in terms of parallel but opposing structures, Lemarignier rightly avoided relying on personal ties as the explanation for the growth of Cluny. Such ties might suggest why certain individuals were involved, but they would not explain the nature of the institution that was created, and this latter problem is what Lemarignier sought to solve. On the other hand, one cannot ignore the fact that personal ties were involved; Cluny's survival and growth, after all, were fostered by men and women from the outside world. At least some of these were the "anarchical" castellans against whose very existence Cluny was said by Lemarignier to be organized.

Thus, historians still needed to look at the people who supported Cluny, their social position, and the connection of both of these to Cluny's institutional character. J. Fechter's 1966 study of Cluny's donors in the Mâconnais did just that.[7] Fechter looked at donation charters, speculated as to the class of people behind them, and connected the very style of Cluniac monasticism to the life-styles of these donors. Briefly, his argument went as follows. During the tenth century, Cluny was supported by both rich *(Adel)* and poor *(Volk)* in the Mâconnais. Imitating the social experience of many of its supporters, Cluny glorified the notion of poverty in its writings; it set up an *ordo* that reiterated the simplicity of poverty; it understood its mission to be the protection and defense of the poor. In the eleventh century, a transformation of both donors and style occurred. Now the *Adel* became the principal donor, and Cluny abandoned its identification with the poor to take on the concerns of the rich. The monks transformed their simple liturgy, adding lavish prayers for the souls of their noble benefactors. They began to use chivalric imagery in their writings. They refrained from supporting the Peace of God against unruly warriors while, on the other hand, they joined in promoting the "Christian knight" in his mission of Spanish reconquest.

In Fechter's analysis, the key elements in Cluny's spirituality changed to meet the needs of its local donors, mirroring the very style of life of its benefactors. Were Fechter correct, the only major problem remaining for a synthesis of Cluny's spirituality and its social context would be to understand why an institution which, for over one hundred years, had been associated largely with the plight of the poor should suddenly reflect the aspirations of the rich.

However, Fechter's analysis cannot be correct as it stands. It most certainly overlooks a number of key facts, and it may possibly misinterpret some others. Let us look at Fechter's problem anew. Georges Duby's study of the Mâconnais—which Fechter used extensively—provides several correctives to his analysis.[8] Rather than dividing the society of the Mâconnais into *Adel* and *Volk,* Duby discussed a tripartite social order that remained fairly stable until the 980s, a crucial turning point that will be discussed below. First were the major land-owning families, one of which dominated the lands around the city of Mâcon and held the comital office. Other rich families in effect divided between them the northern, central, and southern portions of the region. A few of their members, whom Duby calls castellans, manned the defensive structures originally set up by the Carolingians, and they acted as the count's functionaries in military and judicial matters. But prior to the 980s the social and economic status of these castellans was not significantly different from that of their rich neighbors.

Duby also described a "middle" class of allodists (i.e., people who owned their own land), unrelated to the great families. Their lands were situated in the interstices, as it were, of the major properties. Yet, the members of these families were not economically subject to the wealthy, nor were they dominated judicially or militarily by their rich neighbors. They were, indeed, free men, and prior to the 980s, they kept their small properties intact for their heirs through a judicious use of charters of division *(cartae divisionis)* and modest almsgiving.

Finally, there were peasants in the Mâconnais. This was the group that Fechter termed the *Volk.* He identified them with the poor, so that when he read the word *pauper* in a Cluniac text, he assumed it referred to them.[9] He equated the *Volk,* too, with a certain kind of donor at Cluny, one who gave land *post obitum,* reserving the usufruct until death.

Since more than half the total number of donation charters to Cluny before the 980s were couched in these terms, Fechter concluded that peasants formed more than half of Cluny's patronage.[10]

However, according to Duby, the peasants of the Mâconnais were not poor. They were humble men, to be sure; by definition, they were those who worked their land themselves. But most of them owned outright at least some of the land that they tilled—how else could they have deeded anything to Cluny?—and some of them extended their allodial holdings in the course of the tenth century. Even serfs in the region often claimed a small patrimony of their own. But, prior to the crucial decade of the 980s, most peasants in the Mâconnais were not serfs; they were free men. Nor were they known as *pauperes;* indeed the charters distinguish between the *laboratores,* peasant laborers, and the *pauperiores,* the manual workers, who had no plough and were forced to eke out a living with their hoes.[11]

Who among these groups patronized Cluny? The charters are not very revealing about social levels, and this is why Fechter relied on post-obit gifts to make his point. But the *post obitum* donation was a formula of choice for all levels of men. Guy de Valous's early study of Cluny's domain had already observed this fact, and recent work on the post-obit gift elsewhere confirms its popularity among all classes.[12] Thus, it is not surprising that in 936 Count Gauzfred and his wife had no more compunction about giving Cluny a gift which reserved the usufruct until their death than did one possibly impoverished man who, in 949, donated land to Cluny, provided that "if I need it, you will aid me out of your own property."[13] Middling allodists of the Mâconnais, too, were represented in these charters. What is striking in almost every instance is not the poverty of the donors but rather the pettiness of the gifts. On the whole, these post-obit concessions netted Cluny only negligible amounts of land: a manse here, a vineyard there. The same was true of outright gifts.[14] As a result, aside from its original bequest from Duke William, Cluny held only fragments of land in the Mâconnais until the 980s. These bits and pieces of property certainly do not suggest that Cluny was extraordinarily important either to the population of the Mâconnais as a whole, or to any particular social group within it.

This is further borne out by the evidence from the one group of donors that can be identified most positively: the very rich. These local magnates did not avoid Cluny. The counts of Mâcon donated land there and acted as advocate on its behalf.[15] Others, as we have seen, made contributions and often received reciprocal gifts of land in precarial tenure. That is, they enjoyed the usufruct and, ostensibly, protected land for Cluny. Duby has pointed out that this mutual generosity benefited the aristocracy more than it did the monastery.[16] The relationship between the monastery and the great local families stretched over generations. A piece of property at Verzé may serve to illustrate the point. In 924 or so, just after his first wife died, Letbald, whose family later became the lords of Brancion, gave some land at Verzé to Cluny. For fifty years no more is heard about this property; then, in 978, Abbot Majolus gave this same land to Letbald's nephew *in precaria*.[17] The mutuality of such arrangements does not show, however, that there was a peculiarly close relationship between Cluny and the rich. The great families contributed to Cluny, to be sure, but they also associated themselves in the same way with the two other major religious centers in the vicinity. Documents for the monastery of St.-Philibert in Tournus are sparse, but we know, for example, that the count of Mâcon contributed land to it in 971, while, ten years later, a man named Henry, who was wealthy enough to donate a church to St.-Philibert, received in return a chapel and some land.[18] Similarly, the church of St.-Vincent in Mâcon had numerous donors and precarists, including rich families, all through the tenth century.[19] In short, the evidence suggests that prior to the 980s, Cluny was not exceptionally compelling to any social group in the Mâconnais, whether rich, middling, or peasant.

The 980s witnessed a change from this lukewarm support to avid patronage. Cluny's new status was connected, Duby has shown, to a local political transformation. Before the 980s, the counts of Mâcon had presided over a society that retained the forms, the institutions, and the social and political roles handed down by the Carolingian state. Some of these have already been mentioned. The economic backbone of this society was the "middle class" allodist. The peasants were held to account not by the seigneurial power of the ban but by the public power of the count. Those public powers included calling men up for military service and hearing disputes and crimes—even those involving the aristocracy of the region—in court. Indeed, the count was able to compel the *fideles*—the wealthier, more important men of the region—to sit on his court. In addition, the count delegated functionaries to hear legal disputes locally, a service for those who could not afford to come to the court at Mâcon. Finally, the count controlled the mint and collected the market tolls.[20]

However, the situation was potentially unstable. The counts were independent agents, whose legitimacy came from custom rather than from delegated power. Already, before the middle of the century, the viscomital family simply had taken outright the title and functions of the count. But these new counts continued to exercise their office in the spirit, if no longer at the behest, of the Carolingian kings.

The 980s witnessed a more radical transformation when a new man, an outsider, became count of Mâcon. Otto-William, who held the position 982–1026, was son of the deposed king of Lombardy, Adalbert.[21] He married Ermentrude, widow of the late count of Mâcon, thus claiming the county by marriage. Through his wife, he also got four counties across the Saône, in the kingdom of Burgundy. When Henry, duke of Burgundy and Otto-William's stepfather, died in 1002, Otto-William vied for the inheritance of his stepfather with Robert the Pious, who was Henry's nephew and, more importantly, king of France. The wars between them, ending in about 1015, helped work a social and political transformation in the Mâconnais. The count was no longer the main guarantor of law and order in the region. The sources that witness to this decline begin, on the whole, from the time of the wars, but even before then, it seems that Otto-William was not providing the sort of government people expected. As early as 994 a group of churchmen assembled at Anse in an effort to keep the peace, which, in their opinion at least, was not being kept. Anse was in the kingdom of Burgundy, and the council drew local bishops, but it was attended also by bishops from the duchy of Burgundy, including, significantly, those of Mâcon, Chalon, and Autun, as well as Abbot Odilo of Cluny. The council declared, among other things, that no count or other public official could exercise judicial or military authority at Cluny, and that no layman, whether powerful warrior or simple neighbor, could despoil Cluny of its property. The penalty was the pain of anathema.[22] Shortly thereafter, the documents concerned with court proceedings in the Mâconnais show that a similar evolution was taking place for other groups in the region. The comital court was no longer functioning as a public institution, commanding all free persons. It was a personal court, consisting of the count, his relatives, and his own entourage. It no longer had an important role in the lives of the rich, particularly the castellans; it neither compelled them to sit on court nor did it judge them.[23]

Thus, around the turn of the century, effective authority in certain areas of the *pagus* of Mâcon was no longer held by the count of Mâcon, but rather was taken by a number of different groups. These included local ecclesiastical institutions, such as Cluny, for whom, as we have seen, the Council of Anse functioned as a virtual Declaration of Independence. Another group was the counts from nearby *pagi*, such as the count of Chalon, who extended his influence into some areas of the Mâconnais.[24] Finally, there were the castellans of the region, who took advantage of the new conditions and of their own relatively impregnable position to consolidate their lands and to extend their power over their neighbors. Formerly independent middling allodists and even members of the richest families who lacked their own fortresses were compelled—by need and by force—to turn to the castellans. Some became vassals; some were reduced to humbler dependency. By 1050, the Mâconnais was a "feudal society."[25]

In addition to establishing ties of dependency in the period 980–1050, the people of the region turned to older and more familiar sources of bodily and spiritual protection. They parcelled out their holdings to all their heirs in return for the safety of the family group.[26] They fragmentized their lands in charitable contributions to ecclesiastical institutions in order to insure a refuge for their souls after death.[27]

During this transitional period, Cluny's fortunes in the Mâconnais witnessed a dramatic turn for the better. In its immediate neighborhood the effects were striking: endowments, sales, and exchanges made Cluny a major landowner in the area. At the commune of Igé (about 7 km from Cluny), for example, Cluny had held only six pieces of property during the period 909–980; between 981–1025 it gained seventeen more pieces of land. At Saint-Vincent-des-Prés, about the same distance to the northwest, Cluny held three pieces of land during 909–980 but obtained thirty-six more pieces during 981–1025.[28] The last years of the tenth and the first third of the eleventh century saw gifts pour in from every part of the county. Rich families depleted their wealth in pious donations; middling allodists impoverished succeeding generations of heirs.[29] All the ecclesiastical institutions in the Mâconnais experienced some of this new generosity, but not on a scale comparable to that of Cluny.[30]

Who were these generous donors? Paradoxically, some of them

KEY CLUNIAC DONORS AND CAROLINGIAN KINGS

Counts of Anjou	Counts of Chalon	Counts of Mâcon	Capetians	Dukes of Burgundy

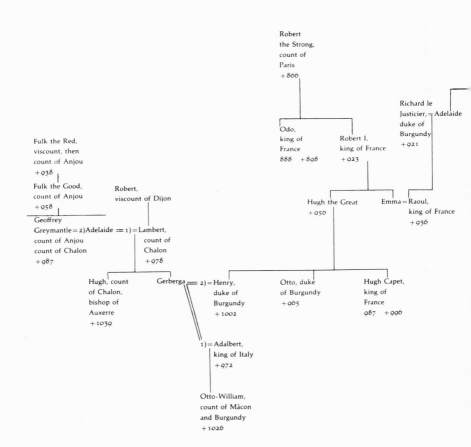

Robert
the Strong,
count of
Paris
+866

Richard le
Justicier, = Adelaide
duke of
Burgundy
+921

Fulk the Red,
viscount, then
count of Anjou
+938

Odo,
king of
France
888   +808

Robert I,
king of France
+023

Fulk the Good,
count of Anjou
+958

Robert,
viscount of Dijon

Hugh the Great
+050

Emma = Raoul,
king of France
+936

Geoffrey
Greymantle = 2)Adelaide == 1) = Lambert,
count of Anjou   count of
count of Chalon   Chalon
+987   +978

Hugh, count
of Chalon,
bishop of
Auxerre
+1039

Gerberga == 2) = Henry,
duke of
Burgundy
+1002

Otto, duke
of Burgundy
+065

Hugh Capet,
king of
France
987   +996

1) = Adalbert,
king of Italy
+972

Otto-William,
count of Mâcon
and Burgundy
+1026

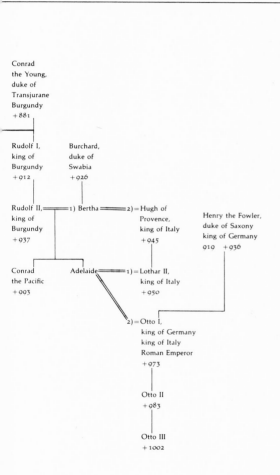
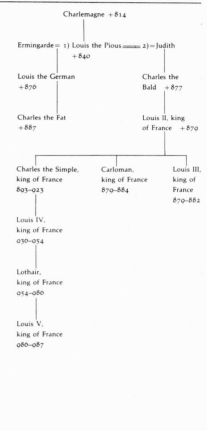

Kings of (Transjurane) Burgundy	Kings of Germany	Carolingians

Charlemagne +814

Ermingarde = 1) Louis the Pious ===== 2) = Judith
+840

Louis the German +876   Charles the Bald +877

Charles the Fat +887   Louis II, king of France +879

Charles the Simple, king of France 893–923   Carloman, king of France 879–884   Louis III, king of France 879–882

Louis IV, king of France 030–054

Lothair, king of France 054–080

Louis V, king of France 086–087

Conrad the Young, duke of Transjurane Burgundy +881

Rudolf I, king of Burgundy +912   Burchard, duke of Swabia +926

Rudolf II, king of Burgundy +937 ===== 1) Bertha ===== 2) = Hugh of Provence, king of Italy +945   Henry the Fowler, duke of Saxony king of Germany 010 +936

Conrad the Pacific +003   Adelaide ===== 1) = Lothar II, king of Italy +950

2) = Otto I, king of Germany king of Italy Roman Emperor +973

Otto II +083

Otto III +1002

were Cluny's persecutors. When the Council of Ansè spoke of men who were attacking and robbing the monastery, it no doubt referred, at least in part, to the castellans of the region, all of whom gave alms to the monastery after 980.[31] The Cluniacs continued to attach this group to themselves with the material ties of *precaria* in addition to the spiritual ties of prayer, friendship, and community with the saints, which were set up more or less explicitly by a donation. The rich castellan families, alone among the families in the Mâconnais, were able to hold on to and, indeed, increase their landholdings, while, at the same time, gaining effective, private command (banal and feudal) over the people in their vicinity.[32] Other generous donors, however, were not men on the rise. On the contrary, they experienced the loss of the security of established public institutions, and they did not have a private castle to turn to as the center of alternative power. These were the free allodists—middling and peasant—of the region. That all these groups should become attached to Cluny at the same time suggests a conjunction between their changed circumstances and their perception of Cluny's signifi

What is important about Cluny's donors in the Mâconnais is not that they came from one particular social class, whether *Adel* or *Volk,* but that, whatever their class, they had experienced a sudden shift in their status and fortune. Recently, Alexander Murray has suggested using stasis and mobility instead of wealth and poverty as ways to classify medieval social groups.[33] What we witness in the Mâconnais is not the sort of movement Murray had in mind (he was talking about mobility in an urban setting), but it is amenable to the same sort of analysis. Indeed, we may carry Murray's point further by asking what people experience during swings of fortune, especially if there are no clear normative patterns for people to follow as they rise or fall. Murray did not ask this question because he took much of his evidence from a period in which paths for ambitious men were already well worn. But in the tenth century, men on the rise (or descent) could not have known that they were forging a "feudal society." As we shall see from the writings of Odo, the profound social and institutional transformations in the tenth century produced a disjunction between men's expectations about how society ought to work and the way it worked in fact.

Sociologists have a term that implies both the experience of upward and downward swings of fortune and the disjunction just described: anomie. The term anomie fits both the rise of the castellans of the Mâconnais and the fall of other allodists in the region. The various theories of anomie and the conclusions that flow from them will be discussed in Chapter 5. There I hope to show that anomie theory is useful in analyzing the relationship between the monastic spirituality at Cluny (Chapters 3 and 4) and the world of its supporters (the present chapter). The most important purpose of the remainder of this chapter is to show that social mobility, up or down, is a common phenomenon among Cluny's benefactors.

A few cautions are in order here. One must not expect that all of Cluny's donors experienced vicissitudes of status or fortune, nor should it be necessary to prove that all people who experienced ups and downs supported Cluny. In the eighth century, the Carolingians were an upwardly mobile family. But the Carolingians supported a monasticism of quite a different temper from that of the Cluniacs (see Chapter 4). In the ninth century, devastation by Carolingian dynastic wars and Viking invasions produced social dislocation, but the ninth century is the age *par excellence* of monastic decay. Social mobility does not necessarily lead to Cluny. However, in Chapter 5, I shall argue that Cluny was a particularly constructive response to Fortune's wheel. In that sense, its popularity reinforces the view that the tenth century witnessed a creative reorganization of society out of the chaos of the ninth century. The makers of this reorganization were, as we shall see, some of Cluny's most avid supporters. Some, however, were not. And, to shift the argument slightly, we should not expect that even supporters of Cluny adhered to that one monastery alone. There were other religious houses that drew their support, perhaps because they were local favorites or were of special importance to certain families.[34] Allowance, too, must be made for personal choice or idiosyncracy.

These are the limitations inherent in the hypothesis of social mobility. Other limitations grow out of the sources themselves. It is very difficult in most cases to know anything at all about the background of a donor to Cluny. However, some of Cluny's supporters are more amenable to such an analysis simply because they were rich, often noble, and left evidence about themselves. These are the men and women who sponsored the reform or the foundation of a monastery in accordance with the Cluniac norm. Even before 980, when people in the Mâconnais gave Cluny only half-hearted support, people elsewhere were such devotees of Cluny that they asked (and payed for) its abbot to set up a replica of Cluny at other monasteries. It is to these people we shall now turn.

First, however, we must establish what it is we will be looking for. Recently, Constance B. Bouchard has convincingly argued for a tripartite phenomenon of social mobility extending from the end of the ninth century to the beginning of the eleventh century.[35] At the end of the ninth century, independent kings and dukes established themselves; these were men who came from families with high positions—e.g., count or duke—in the Carolingian state. In the course of the tenth century, these nobles were joined by men whose origins derived from a viscomital status, which was a relatively low position, since viscounts were originally dependent functionaries of the counts. But in the tenth century, many of these viscounts rose to become counts. Finally, at the beginning of the eleventh century, castellans began to consolidate their power and join the swelling noble ranks. Bouchard's formulation has the great merit, among others, of reconciling two opposing views. Historians like Lemarignier speak of a general fragmentation of power at the end of the tenth century.[36] Historians like Evergates remind us that "the collapse of the Carolingian *pagus* and the rise of independent castellans now appears to have been the exception, not the norm, in much of northern France," where strong counts prevented disintegration.[37] Bouchard shows that both phenomena were happening side-by-side. The rise of the castellans did not mean the fall of the count; both increased their power at the same time over humbler men. The elasticity of the noble class and the enormous amount of power available to enterprising men are the striking features of tenth-century society. While Bouchard's timetable may differ in different regions (she was thinking mainly of Burgundy), the pattern is clear and the criteria objective. They may be used to examine the sponsors of Cluny's reforms.

Let us precede the evidence with the conclusions. Of the twenty-eight tenth-century initiators of Cluniac reforms, one was a Cluniac abbot, twenty were examples of social mobility and seven were not, or not clearly so.[38] Because sources are poor and social and regional studies are still pending, these conclusions and the survey that follows are provisional.

The case of William the Pious, the founder of Cluny, is the obvious preface to our discussion. Unfortunately, the ancestry of William is a much-debated issue, and its resolution one way or the other is decisive for any certain pronouncement. If William's ancestry could be traced to St. William of Gellone, count and duke of Toulouse, then William himself would not be considered an example of social mobility, for in that case, he would have belonged to an aristocratic family well established in Aquitaine for generations.[39] On the other hand, if William was the grandson of Bernard of Poitiers, he would be of far more obscure origins.[40] In that case, William's power in Gothia, the Lyonnais, the Mâconnais, the Auvergne, the Limousin, and Berry, as well as his taking the title *dux* would indicate a decided enhancement in status and fortune.[41]

Whatever his background, the monastery that William set up at Cluny came to represent the proper, normative monastery for many men of unstable position. The founding itself was a traditional, even old-fashioned act. It had long been an unofficial part of the position, function, and privilege of families of power to found and support houses of prayer. The practice went back to the Merovingian court in the time of St. Columban.[42] Although Charlemagne and Louis the Pious had put the monasteries of the kingdom under royal supervision, wealthy families continued to be involved in their support and protection.

Nor was William's foundation charter, in which he set forth the conditions and expectations under which the monastery was to operate, extraordinary.[43] It specified that Cluny follow the Benedictine *Rule,* but, as will be made clear in Chapter 4, this was no more and no less than the expectation ever since Charlemagne's day. It provided that Cluny be under no power save that of SS. Peter and Paul, but this famous clause of local immunity and dependency on the papacy was, as Cowdrey has shown, an arrangement characteristic of a number of monasteries founded before Cluny.[44] It asked that the monks at Cluny busy themselves with prayers on behalf of the souls of William, his family, his friends, and other faithful Christians, but this had been a standard request ever since the Merovingian period, producing numerous monasteries dedicated to an elaborate liturgical round.[45] Thus, Cluny was founded in the best noble, conservative tradition. As we shall see, the promoters of Cluniac reform sought it out precisely because they considered it a model monastery. Although newly founded, it had firm roots.

The first sponsor of a Cluniac reform was a *fidelis* of William, Ebbo, who founded the monastery of Bourg-Dieu at Déols in 917.[46] (For Bourg-Dieu and other monasteries, see maps.) Ebbo was the ancestor of the lords of Déols. His grandfather had had allodial land in Berry, but Duke William enriched Ebbo further by placing him at the head of two *vicariae* (subdivisions of the *pagus*) of Bourges.[47] Geronce (911–948), probably Ebbo's relative and possibly his uncle, was archbishop of Bourges. Ebbo's son, Laune, followed Geronce into archiepiscopal office (948–955). The evidence points to a man of substance who gained, in the course of his lifetime, considerable local power. Indeed, with Ebbo in mind, Devailly dates the emergence of the independent castellan in Berry at the very early date of c. 920.[48]

But if Ebbo's status defies Bouchard's timetable for the rise of the castellans, his foundation charter for Bourg-Dieu breathes not a word of innovation. Wollasch has shown how both the vocabulary and form of the document imitate William's foundation charter for Cluny, written nearly a decade earlier.[49] In effect, Bourg-Dieu was to be a miniature Cluny. Both in the foundation charter and in a subsequent codicil, Ebbo spelled out the sort of *ordo* he wanted Bourg-Dieu to have. It was to be a strikingly fixed and unabashedly derivative monastic regime, following Berno's monastery (i.e., the monastery that William founded) in all particulars:

> We ask [he wrote] that the monks live according to the purpose of the monastic profession and, if not better, at least up to the example of those whom the venerable and reverend Abbot Berno first put there; and that the successors who remain have the same quantity of psalmody, the same humane hospitality, the same perpetual abstinence from all meat in favor of fish.[50]

Ebbo's example leads to a new hypothesis. If mobility describes the experience of Cluny's supporters, then stability describes their expectations and wishes for the monasteries they handed over to Cluny. They wanted strict adherence to the clear and well-charted norms already followed by Cluny. Once again this cannot be demonstrated in every case, for the desires of Cluny's supporters were not always set down. Nevertheless, it is made explicit a number of times in the charters, and as we shall see, the Cluniac abbots certainly understood the strict imposition of the Cluniac *ordo* to be their task as reformers.

Abbot Berno was succeeded by St. Odo (926–44), under whom Cluny's reforming activities began in earnest. Odo himself was directly responsible for no less than eleven reforms. The first was Romainmôtier, handed over to Odo in 929. The donor was Adelaide, sister of Rudolf I (king of Jurane Burgundy), widow of Richard le Justicier (duke of Burgundy) and mother of Raoul I (king of France). (See genealogical tables for these and other Cluniac benefactors.) Each of the men in her life requires comment. All are examples of the social mobility available to members of the Carolingian nobility at the end of the ninth century. Adelaide's brother, Rudolf, inherited c. 866 the duchy of Transjurane Burgundy from his father, who had held it from Louis II, Carolingian emperor of Italy. The deposition of Charles the Fat in 887 marked a turning point in Rudolf's career, as it did in the careers of many other men. The political repercussions are evident in the rash of new kings declared in 888, among them Odo in France, Arnulf in Germany, Berengar in Italy, and Rudolf in Burgundy. Rudolf held the new title and position to the end of his life (912) and passed it on to his heirs.[51]

The origins of Adelaide's husband, Richard, are obscure, but we know that by 880 he was count of Autun; we have a charter from Carloman referring to him as *comes Augustodunensis*.[52] The year 888 brought new opportunities to Richard as well, particularly since Burgundy was then the object of devastating Viking attacks. Richard led the battle against the Vikings, becoming the undisputed military leader in the region. His military preeminence was no doubt the source of his growing political ascendancy. After 888 we find that Richard's acts were no longer simply of local interest, but compelled the presence of the counts and great ecclesiastics in Burgundy.[53] We find him intervening in church elections.[54] We find him replacing the count of Sens with a viscount.[55] The documents make belated recognition of his position; 918 is the first date in which extant sources refer to him as *dux*.[56]

Richard died in 921 and was succeeded by his and Adelaide's son, Raoul. By marrying Emma, the granddaughter of Robert the Strong, Raoul became part of a family which, since 888, had already twice occupied the Frankish throne. Odo, son of Robert the Strong and great uncle of Hugh Capet, had been elected by a faction of the Frankish aristocracy as king in 888, an act that overlooked the young Carolingian claimant, Charles the Simple. Charles did succeed Odo ten years later, but he was not allowed to hold the crown for life. Robert, Odo's brother, took the throne in 923. When Robert was killed, within the year, his son-in-law, Raoul, was elected in his stead and crowned at Soissons.

Raoul's reign allows us to glimpse some of the painfulness attending at least this example of upward mobility.[57] His election once again bypassed Charles the Simple and also the son of Robert I, Hugh the Great, who, however, supported Raoul. The election was supported by a small faction of the aristocracy, and much of Raoul's time was spent waging wars to neutralize enemies and gain recognition as king. But Raoul himself may have had some doubts about what he was doing. Perhaps it is not very telling that, in 924, when he fell ill, he went to Reims to ask God's mercy and to donate his possessions to churches and monasteries; this was a well-worn model of contrition.[58] More extraordinary was Raoul's act of humiliation, in December 928, before Charles the Simple, who was then in prison and powerless. "When king Raoul came to Reims, where Charles was being held, he made peace with him, humiliating himself in his presence and returning to him the fisc of Attigny."[59]

Adelaide asked Odo to reform Romainmôtier only six months after this event. Clearly hers was not a static society. She was part of a group of people who were on the rise, sometimes painfully so, as opportunities made advancement possible. She married Richard in 889, just at the beginning of his ascent, and just after the coronation of her brother. She donated Romainmôtier at a moment of crisis for her son. Yet Adelaide's charge to Cluny—as we have come to expect—did not breathe even a hint of change. It called explicitly for the perpetuation of old norms and for a revered tradition:

> Let the monks living there so preserve the way of life which was transmitted by Cluny to educate future monks, that they in no way change the norm in food and clothing, in abstinence, in psalmody, in silence, in hospitality, in mutual love and submissiveness, and in the goodness of obedience.[60]

So full an account of the circumstances and goals of a monastic reform is rare. Shortly after the reform of Romainmôtier, in the early 930s, the Cluniacs were involved in four reforms in southern France: two in Limoges (Aurillac and Tulle), one in Sarlat, one in Clermont. In these instances the information is less bountiful. The first of these reforms, at Aurillac, was sponsored by Aimo, then abbot of Tulle, and his brother, Turpio, bishop of Limoges (after 897–944). Aimo was also responsible for turning the direction of Tulle over to Odo.[61] These men were friends of Odo's. Turpio had ordained Odo priest when Odo was still a monk at Baume.[62] At Turpio's request, Odo wrote the *Collationes,* and at the request of both Turpio and Aimo, he wrote the *Vita* of St. Gerald of Aurillac (see Chapter 3). Turpio was the founder and reformer of a number of monasteries in his diocese, while Aimo served as abbot of St.-Martial de Limoges from 936 to 942.[63] We may view the sponsorship of Odo at Aurillac and Tulle to be a matter of friendship and shared interest. However, it seems likely that even here political and social changes in the Limousin played a role. Aimo and Turpio were also brothers of Rainald, viscount of Aubusson.[64] We do not know much about Rainald and his viscomital office except that it was relatively recent in origin. The first viscount in the region, the viscount of Limoges appeared only at the end of the ninth century. Other viscounts in the Limousin—at Aubusson and Turenne, for example—are mentioned only in tenth-century documents. These viscomital titles were associated with fortresses, not with any preexisting offices. A document drawn up by Turpio c. 934 mentions as *nostris consanguineis seu obtimatibus* (our relatives or [and] important men) the viscounts of Limoges and of Aubusson. One commentator has concluded that the viscomital families of the region were all related, with the main trunk of the family tree at Limoges.[65] Whether related or not, all benefited from the death of William of Aquitaine's ducal heirs (927); the Limousin became a locally controlled frontier between the south, politically centered at Toulouse, and the north, controlled from Poitiers.[66] The viscounts of the region in effect divided control over the area. Odo's reform of Tulle and Aurillac in the early 930s may be associated with the new status of the family of Turpio and Aimo.

Shortly after his reform of Tulle, Odo was asked to reform Sarlat by Bernard, count of Perigord, and his wife Garsin. Bernard does not appear to be an example of social mobility; his grandfather was made count of Angoulême and Perigord under Charles the Bald, and his father, William, inherited the position of count of Perigord (Bernard's uncle, Alduin, became the count of Angoulême). William left Perigord to Bernard, who also shared the county of Angoulême with his cousin (i.e., Alduin's son).[67] In his donation charter, Bernard says that the monks at Sarlat were leading an irregular life, and he decided to restore the monastery to its proper dignity by handing it over to Odo.[68]

The restoration of St.-Allyre and its reform under Odo (c. 933) is, on the other hand, associated with social and political changes. Bernard I, who appears as count of Auvergne in 930, was brother of Acfred and William II, hence a *nepos* of William the Pious, duke of Aquitaine.[69] William had used the title duke, as had Acfred, but Bernard did not (it was soon—by the mid-930s—taken by Raymond III Pontius, count of Toulouse).[70] At the same time, local viscomital families in the region were beginning to rise in status and power (by the 980s one of these, of the viscomital family of Robert I, had taken the title of count).[71] The reform of St.-Allyre of Clermont was a joint venture of Bernard, the bishop of Auvergne, the local barons *(baronum Arverniae)*, and Raymond Pontius.[72]

Still in the 930s, Odo was called upon to reform a house in the Loire valley: Fleury (St.-Benoît-sur-Loire). Evidence about the sponsor of this reform is very scanty. St. Odo's biographer gives the fullest account:

> At that time [the early 930s, when Odo was reforming Auril-lac],[73] Elisiardus, who was then an illustrious count but who has now taken the monastic habit, hearing of the infamy of those monks [at Fleury], begged and received the abbey from Raoul, the king of the Franks, and when he had received it, he gave it to our father [Odo].[74]

The cartulary of Fleury includes a donation by a man named Eli-siernus in 941. He expresses the desire to become a monk; the richness of the donation (much land and two churches) shows that he was a man of substance. We are justified in identifying him as the count who sponsored the reform of Fleury. Nevertheless, we know nothing certain about him.[75] Another source, a letter from Pope Leo VII dated 938, attributes the reform of Fleury to Hugh the Great, Raoul's brother-in-law, but does not mention Elisiardus.[76] The evidence is too fragmentary to do more than note that the impetus for reform seems to have come from men associated with King Raoul.

Another northerly monastery, St.-Julien of Tours, was reformed by Odo a few years later. This monastery had been destroyed by the Normans. The sponsor of its reform was Archbishop Teotolo, who made Odo its abbot c. 940. Teotolo had been a canon at St.-Martin of Tours at the same time Odo had been there, and when Odo became abbot of Cluny, Teotolo became a monk there under him. A few years later (931), he became archbishop of Tours. Teotolo's solicitude for St.-Julien and his desire for Odo to effect its reform may be attributed simply to personal ties. However, it would be helpful to know Teotolo's family origins, for it is clear that he was a powerful and wealthy man in the region of Tours, and he and his sister, Garsin, endowed St.-Julien largely out of their own patrimony.[77]

The last northerly monastery to be reformed by Odo was St.-Pierre-le-Vif, in Sens. St.-Pierre had been burned by the Magyars in

937. Its abbot, Samson, died shortly thereafter. "St. Odo succeeded him" is the way the chronicler of St.-Pierre puts the matter, continuing, "Odo, summoning Archbishop William, with the consent of the monks of St.-Pierre, made Arigaud, monk of St.-Benoît [-sur-Loire] . . . abbot at this monastery."[78] It is impossible to tell from this brief account at whose initiative came the reform of St.-Pierre.

St.-Pierre concluded Odo's Cisalpine reforms. For many of these French and Burgundian monasteries, the evidence is so scanty that little can be said about the sponsors of reform. More is known about the sponsor of Odo's Italian reforms. Alberic, prince of Rome 932–54, initiated the reform of no less than five monasteries, making him the most avid single supporter of Cluniac reform in the tenth century. To understand Alberic's position, a brief discussion of the region around Rome which he came to rule is in order.[79]

The Carolingians had placed the region immediately contiguous to Rome under the aegis of the papacy, fixing this as the *terra sancti Petri*. The papacy was to carry out the rights of royal sovereignty: minting, justice, levying of the army, and so on. However, papal power was never effective at all except, perhaps, in Rome proper. Local aristocrats living in the cities south of Rome dominated the neighboring countryside. In the north, the monastery of Farfa, through an accumulation of immunities, controlled almost the entire region. Thus, even in the Carolingian period, the area around Rome was ruled not by public counts but by private magnates. The Saracen invasions disrupted—as they (and the Vikings) had in France—the routine of daily living and the sway of traditional customs. Peasants-turned-brigands and Moslems alike terrorized the population. But, unlike France, the painful reconstruction of law and order in this region was not modelled upon still-remembered Carolingian forms, for these had never been implanted in the area.

Theophylact (c. 900–925), who in his capacity as papal *vestiarius* and *magister militum* was authorized to carry out some of the papacy's sovereign rights, began the reordering of the region. He mobilized and united the aristocracy to oust the Saracens and put down the peasant marauders. His grandson, Alberic, went beyond this and, in fact, forged a new Roman regime.[80] His rule was innovative; it has even been called revolutionary by historians who have seen in his work the formation of a centralized principality.[81] However, Toubert's recent study demonstrates that Alberic's innovation lay not so much in concentrating power as in organizing its use by local aristocrats to their own advantage. Save for a hazy allegiance to the "prince" of Rome (Alberic), these magnates were largely independent in their own spheres. This was true both in the south, where Alberic allied himself with the old, powerful families, and in the north, where Alberic broke up Farfa's dominion, to the advantage of local men of wealth. In each case, Alberic was instrumental in getting the aristocracy to act, albeit as private, local men, in administrative capacities. In other words, institutions of local peace were set up and in effect conceded to the aristocrats.

Alberic was a man on the rise; his self-endowed title of *princeps omnium Romanorum* shows his consciousness of the fact. Moreover, he made possible the rise of an organized local aristocracy. His regime put the *incastellamento* movement, the reorganization of the agricultural life of the countryside around a castle stronghold dominated by a local aristocrat, on its feet. Thus, Alberic spearheaded a radical change in the social, political, and economic structures in the region as he made his way to the top.

To achieve his position, Alberic had to struggle against Hugh of Provence, crowned king of Italy in 926. St. Odo was involved in making peace between the two men. In 936, with the wars over, Odo began to reform monasteries at Alberic's request: St. Paul (Major) in 936, St. Mary on the Aventine, Monte Cassino, Farfa, and St. Elias in Nepi, all c. 940.[82] (See map.) These reforms have been interpreted by Antonelli simply as an act of power politics, and it is true that the reform of Farfa was accompanied by the forcible destruction of Farfa's territorial autonomy. But Hamilton has pointed out that there was a genuine spiritual component involved as well. Alberic was not interested merely in controlling his monasteries but in controlling monasteries that followed the Benedictine customs of Cluny. There is no doubt that real reforms were attempted in each case. At St. Elias there was great difficulty getting the monks to stop eating meat. At Monte Cassino the monastery was "led back to the norm of the regular order." At Farfa the opposition against the reform contingent Odo brought was too great for the reform to work in Odo's lifetime; Alberic had to eject forcibly the recalcitrant monks in 947.[83] In Alberic's case, social mobility and monastic reform once again coincide.

Odo's Italian reforms were to be his last. He was succeeded in the abbatial position by Aymard (944–64), whose major project of monastic reform was Sauxillanges, in the Auvergne. The impetus came from the viscomital house of Robert I, which, as we have seen (p. 48), steadily advanced in social and political position after the mid-920s. Robert's son, Stephen, was bishop of Clermont by 945. Around 950 Stephen, together with his father and mother, handed Sauxillanges, which had been a house of regular canons, to Aymard, to be set up as a proper monastery.[84]

Abbot Majolus (964–94) was a far more active reformer than his immediate predecessor. Indeed, between 954 and 964, while Aymard still lived but was sick and weak, Majolus acted (as coadjutor) as abbot of Cluny. The first house that he was asked to order according to Cluny's norms was Saint-Amand. The donor was Boso, count of Arles. Arles had been one of several counties in Provence, but, with the Saracen invasions of the early tenth century, the other counties seem to have disappeared. It is likely that the comital office at Arles suffered a similar fate for a time, for Boso seems to be a new man. His father was one Roubaud.[85] Boso was called count in a document dated 948.[86] A source from 963 delimits the title more explicitly as *Arelatensis comes* (count of Arles).[87] Seven years later his son, William, was using the title *comes Provincię,* a position that he shared with his brother, Roubaud.[88] Some time before 958, when King Conrad the Pacific of Burgundy confirmed it, Boso handed Saint-Amand over to Cluny. Later (960) he obtained the confirmation of Lothair, the French king (954–986).[89] Clearly Boso was an important man, with influence at two royal courts and a local power base he could hand on to his sons.[90]

We infer that Boso was a self-made man from the fact that his father was obscure and untitled. We are on firmer ground when we look at other sponsors of Majolus's reforms. Undisputed documentation exists for the rise of the Ottonian kings of Germany, one of the most striking examples of social mobility in the tenth century.[91] The father of Otto I, Henry the Fowler, had been the first Saxon king of Germany (919–936). (His own father had been duke of Saxony.) Otto took his father's place on the German throne in 936, had himself crowned king of Italy in 961, and, a year later, was proclaimed Roman Emperor. It is not surprising that Otto and some of those in the circle around him supported and founded Cluniac monasteries.

The first reform sponsored by this group was that of Peterlingen (Payerne) in 961 or 962. Its foundation was probably the work of Bertha, mother of Otto's wife, Adelaide (not to be confused with Richard le Justicier's wife).[92] The time of foundation is significant, coinciding as it does with Otto's imperial ambitions. But Bertha was an example of social mobility, both up and down, in her own right. She was the daughter of Burchard, duke of Swabia. She married Rudolf II, king of Burgundy and son of Rudolf I, in 923, after he abandoned his attempt to conquer Swabia and turned, instead, to the conquest of Italy. Recognized as king of Italy that same year, Rudolf was forced to retreat in 926; it was Hugh of Provence (the same who fought Alberic for Rome) who was crowned king of Italy at Pavia in 926. In 937 Rudolf died and Bertha married Hugh (now of Italy). He soon repudiated her, and she returned to Burgundy.[93] Peterlingen was founded near the end of her life. Conrad, Bertha's son and now king of Burgundy, added to the endowment; Adelaide, Bertha's daughter and now empress, provided for the completion of the monastery.[94] Indeed, it is not impossible that Adelaide herself was the founder of Peterlingen.[95]

Adelaide was a benefactress of special importance to Cluny. Abbot Odilo wrote her epitaph to memorialize her many virtues, above all her patronage of monasteries.[96] Daughter of Bertha and Rudolf II, Adelaide married Lothar II, son of Hugh of Provence, at the same time that her mother married Hugh. When Lothar died, she married Otto, who now began to fulfill his ambitions in Italy.[97] In 972, ten years after her husband had been crowned emperor and coinciding with the marriage of her son, Otto II, to Theophano, Adelaide founded S. Salvatore, near Pavia, and "handed it over to Majolus to be ordered by the *Rule.*"[98] The same year Majolus "instituted the way of St. Benedict and made himself abbot" at Sant' Apollinare in Classe.[99] It is possible that this reform was sponsored by Otto I himself.[100]

The reform of SS. Mary and Michael of Pavia was not directly connected to the imperial family but was probably the act of a member of Otto's court. St. Mary's had been originally a simple chapel, belonging to Gaidulf, a judge at the imperial court *(judex domini imperatoris).* Gaidulf sold the chapel and some land to a priest named Adalgis on July 16, 967. That very day Adalgis donated the purchase, along with some other land, to Cluny. Two days later a judgment was handed down by the court at Pavia in favor of Cluny and against the claims of Gaidulf's heirs to the property. This, and the fact that the donation charter stipulates that daily prayers be offered up for Gaidulf's soul, suggests Gaidulf's sponsorship of the reform itself. Gaidulf—insofar as one can tell —does not, however, seem to be an illustration of social mobility. He was the son of a *judex* and grandson of another on his mother's side.[101]

A later Italian reform by Majolus was, it seems, unrelated to imperial initiative. S. Pietro in Ciel d'Oro at Pavia was reformed at the request of Pope John XV in 987.[102] John had been a parish priest and was elevated to the papal position by the powerful Crescentius family at Rome. A modern historian of the period, Bernard Hamilton, notes that John had little real power but claimed sovereignty all the same and, at least before 990, was referred to as apostolic lord *(domnum apostolicum)*. [103]

Beginning in the 970s, Majolus was called in to reform monasteries in Burgundy. The first of these was Orval (later known as Paray-le-Monial), founded around 973. The sponsor was Lambert, the first hereditary count of Chalon-sur-Saône. Lambert's father, Robert, had been viscount of Dijon, acting as a functionary for Dukes Richard le Justicier and his son, Hugh the Black. The process by which Lambert became a count is not known, but we find him first given the title in a document dated 960.[104] An account of the foundation of Orval, probably redacted after Lambert's death (c. 978), says that he began building the monastery to give thanks for his becoming count.[105] The house was consecrated in 977.

Lambert's widow, another Adelaide, also was a sponsor of reform. Soon after Lambert's death she married Geoffrey Greymantle, count of Anjou and now acting count of Chalon. Geoffrey himself is an example of social mobility; his grandfather had begun life as a viscount and in a process now familiar, took the title count. Geoffrey claimed the county of Anjou "by the grace of God and of Duke Hugh [Capet]."[106] He and Adelaide jointly handed St.-Marcel of Chalon over to Majolus some time after their marriage (i.e., after 978 and before 986, when Geoffrey died).[107]

Neither of these reforms was considered satisfactory. In 999, or shortly thereafter, Lambert and Adelaide's son, Hugh, formally gave the monasteries to Cluny as dependencies.[108] Hugh, it may be noted, continued the tradition of upward mobility begun by his father; he became not only count of Chalon but the bishop of Auxerre in 999 as well.[109] It is significant that his concern for Paray-le-Monial and St.-Marcel coincided exactly with his episcopal appointment. Even in Hugh's day and age, when church and state were remarkably intermeshed, a dual status like Hugh's was quite unusual.

Hugh's reforms bring us to the very end of the tenth century, and we need to backtrack a bit to pick up the thread of Majolus's Burgundian reforms. Hugh should be kept in mind, however, for the sponsors of those earlier reforms were linked, by blood or marriage, to his sister, Gerberga.[110]

The first of these reforms was the joint venture of Heribert, bishop of Auxerre (971–995) and his half-brother, Duke Henry of Burgundy, the husband of Gerberga. Henry had been the lay abbot of St.-Germain of Auxerre; he and Heribert asked Majolus to reform the monastery around 980.[111] Henry, the brother of Hugh Capet, had succeeded another brother, Otto, to the ducal position in Burgundy. His solicitude for St.-Germain cannot be attributed to vicissitudes of fortune, since he was from a well-established family accustomed to the ducal title.

Quite different is the case of Otto-William, Duke Henry's adopted son and the natural son of Gerberga and her first husband, Adalbert.[112] Born into a royal house c. 960 (Adalbert had been king of Lombardy), Otto-William was subject as a child to imprisonment and enforced hiding while his father fought against Otto I. Adalbert died when Otto-William was about twelve years old, and Gerberga soon married Duke Henry. Around 976, Otto-William married the widow of the count of Mâcon; we have already met him during this period. His rule marks the beginning of the social and political transformation in the Mâconnais associated with the growth of donations to Cluny. Otto-William himself gave some property to Cluny.[113] He also sponsored a Cluniac reform. He and his wife's brother, Bruno, bishop of Langres, asked Majolus to reform St.-Bénigne of Dijon in 990. Majolus sent monks from Cluny who were "instructed in the discipline of holy religion" to institute Cluny's way of life at the house.[114]

Majolus was also active in the north of France, beginning in the mid-980s. Here he was asked to reform Marmoutier by Odo I, count of Blois, Tours, and Chartres. Odo's grandfather, Thibaud, had been a viscount of Tours, but around 940 he took the title of count. His hold was solid, and he passed the comital office down to one son, Thibaud le Tricheur (the Trickster), who proceeded to extend his power to Blois and Chartres, while another son became the archbishop of Bourges, thus extending the family's influence into Berry.[115] Odo I, the son of Thibaud le Tricheur, succeeded his father c. 977 and in the early 980s succeeded as well to some of the land belonging to Herbert the Old of Vermandois. Odo continued his father's work of territorial expansion to the point that, by 995, he was plotting to get the title *dux Francorum* for himself by ousting Hugh Capet and bringing in Otto III to be king of France.[116] Early in Odo's career—Sackur puts it at the latest in 984 —he, his mother, and his brother (Hugh, who succeeded his uncle as archbishop of Bourges) asked Majolus to reform Marmoutier, at Tours.[117]

Odo was a vassal of Hugh Capet, but his rise was independent of this tie. Indeed, it often got in his way. When, for example, he determined to take the city of Melun, which belonged to Hugh, Odo had to put forward the legalism that Melun was not really King Hugh's city, as it was held by a vassal of the king.[118] That vassal was Burchard, who, unlike Odo, owed much of his power to the favor of the Capetians. Burchard's father was probably the count of Vendôme, and very likely Burchard succeeded his father in this position c. 950. His fortunes rose when Hugh Capet gave him the widow and the county of Corbeil and the county of Melun as well c. 960. After Hugh became king, he raised Burchard to the position of *comes regalis* of Paris.[119] A few years later, Burchard petitioned Hugh to reform St.-Maur-des-Fossés, an old monastery near Paris that had fallen into decay both spiritually and materially. Burchard called in Majolus, who effected a spiritual reform, but asked Hugh Capet to add to the material endowment.[120] Hugh gave an entire villa in return for prayers for himself and his family.[121]

Hugh Capet was, in fact, the last sponsor of a reform by Majolus, asking the aged abbot to reform St.-Denis in 994. Majolus died *en route*.[122] Hugh, whose family, since 888, had intermittently held the position of king of the Franks, was able to hand the position down to his son and, indeed, down to a long line of kings. He is a good example of the consolidation of power by new families at the end of the tenth century.

In the eleventh century, under Abbots Odilo and Hugh, Cluny's popularity rose so dramatically that historians' eyes have been fixed on this period ever since. In this later century, however, a combination of factors may well have been at work. It is clear that Cluny's expansion continued to coincide with the now widespread phenomenon of social mobility, both up and down. Castellans everywhere began to rise to prominence alongside counts, and less well-defended free men became subject to private powers. But it must be noted that by the eleventh century, Cluny's success was already so generally recognized that that fact alone may have generated the great bulk of its support for approximately the next fifty years. In the tenth century, the data are not complicated by this universal reverence. Cluny's support in that century was sporadic, regional, and dependent upon the initiative of a relatively small number of people. The one thing common among many of these disparate individuals was a social fact. They had been subject to vicissitudes of status. They had taken on new positions, or they had become subject to those who had.

That, at least, is the way in which a modern historian may perceive the context of Cluny's benefactors, i.e., those in the world who were closest to Cluny. But modern lenses were not the ones used by the Cluniacs when they viewed that same world. They used as tools, not regional or family histories, but rather the Bible and the writings of the church fathers. In the next chapter, then, we shall need to assess these tools and see how they were applied by the Cluniacs to describe the world around them.

3 | LOOKING OUT: *The Cluniac Perception of the World*

The Cluniacs had more than a passing interest in the world. They were nurtured by its charitable members, protected by lay advocates (e.g., the counts of Mâcon), and victimized by lay oppressors (e.g., those powerful men referred to at the Council of Anse). For the Cluniacs such temporal necessities had a spiritual counterpart. They were interested in the moral reformation of the world even as they were interested in the reform of monasteries. The Cluniacs understood that monks partook of the same human condition as the members of worldly society. They too were fallen yet redeemed. The monastery was not out of the world, but rather was set apart from it precisely to right the wrong in human society. The same morality—because the same humanity—applied within and without. Although the monk had withdrawn from the world and rejected its organization, its mores, and its institutions, the nature of the world was his initial concern.

The major extant sources that reveal the way in which the tenth-century Cluniacs understood the world are two texts by St. Odo. The *Collationes* were probably written around 925 (just before Odo became abbot of Cluny); the *Vita Sancti Geraldi* (Life of St. Gerald of Aurillac) is placed by the best guess at 930–31.[1] These works, the first an anthology, the second belonging to the well-worn genre of Saints' Lives, were deliberately derivative. They were based on the assumption that the truth revealed by Christ had been illuminated by many subsequent authorities. The most important of these authorities for Odo were St. Augustine (354–430) and Pope Gregory the Great (c. 540–604), himself heavily indebted to Augustine. These provided the "lenses," in effect, that shaped and colored the way in which Odo viewed the concrete details of his own society. On the other hand, Odo used his own eyes; he saw some things differently from his predecessors. To be precise, Odo saw the consequences of the new conditions—social dislocation, the rise of new men, the enforced dependency of others—described in Chapter 2. He modified the ideas he found in traditional authorities to make sense in the context of a new reality.

A few things need to be said about some of these ideas in order to understand the significance of Odo's work.[2] Fundamental here are ideas about human virtue and vice, about human society, and about the significance of the saints.

IDEAS ABOUT VIRTUE AND VICE

Two points need to be made here. First, the classical Latin world bequeathed to the Latin church fathers much of the vocabulary and some of the schemes they used to systematize the virtues and vices. For example, Cicero's list of virtues in the *De Officiis,* itself based on Plato, was a model for St. Ambrose's discussion of the cardinal virtues. Both spoke of *prudentia* or *sapientia* (prudence), *justitia* (justice), *fortitudo* (fortitude), and *temperantia* (temperance).[3] For the realm of evil, again lists were available: Horace's list of seven crimes (written c. 20 B.C.), for example, corresponded in part to later church doctrine on the seven chief sins: *avaritia* or *cupido* (avarice), *laudis amor* (vanity, pride), *invidia* (envy), *ira* (anger), *inertia* (sloth), *vinolentia* (drunkenness), *amatio* (sensuality).[4]

However, and this is the second point, although the words and schemes were borrowed, their significance was changed. Many of the Latin writers who left the legacy of such lists had invoked them in connection with serving the state or with a program of self-betterment. Cicero's *fortitudo,* for example, referred to courage on behalf of the common good.[5] Horace's vices referred to the distasteful aspects of human nature which could be purified through the discipline of philosophy. In the hands of the Latin church fathers, the virtues and vices were reoriented to the future life and to the realm of the supernatural. Ambrose rewrote Cicero because Cicero had misunderstood certain things. *For-*

titudo, in Ambrose's reworking, became the courage to despise the world for God.[6] Horace's notion that philosophy was the way to flee vice was dramatically disproved by St. Augustine, who tried philosophy and came to see that he needed God's grace instead.[7] But the notion that virtue had its source in God was much older than Augustine. It was part of the Jewish tradition. Here is what the psalmist says regarding patience, for example: "But be subject to God, my soul, since my patience is from him" (Ps. 61:6).[8] In the writings of St. Paul (Gal. 5:22–23) a long list of virtues is called the gift of the Holy Spirit.

The demons and the Devil who figure prominently in the New Testament show that vice, too, was linked to the supernatural. Morton Bloomfield has shown the deep roots of the association of sin with demons in pre-Christian, Hellenistic thought. The Latin church fathers often reiterated that link. Prudentius' *Psychomachia* (early fifth century) is a variant on the theme. It externalizes the moral struggle within men's souls, setting the virtues (led by Christ) and vices against one another in pitched and bloody battle.[9]

Thus, by the time of Gregory the Great, virtues and vices had been named, schematized, and integrated into a Christian world view. Gregory took the theme of seven chief sins and strengthened it with new imagery: pride was enthroned as a warrior queen, while seven other vices acted as her generals.[10] From 1 John 2:16, Gregory also adopted a scheme of vices, the Three Temptations: lust of the flesh, lust of the eyes, and pride of life. Gregory identified these as gluttony, avarice, and pride.[11] In his *Moralia,* he used a different three-pronged scheme. Here the sins of lust, malice, and pride were linked to the form of the Devil:

> In those, certainly, whom [the Devil] excites to the foolishness of lust, he is a beast; in those whom he inflames to the malice of harming, he is a dragon; in those, however, whom he elevates to the state of pride as if they were judges on high, he is a bird.[12]

Gregory's lists persisted, embedded within a tradition that was hardly challenged until the twelfth century. For example, in an abridgment of the *Moralia* traditionally attributed to Odo of Cluny, the two schemes of vices—with pride as queen and with the forms of the Leviathan—were retained.[13]

THE POLITICAL SOCIETY MEN MAKE

With the locus of virtue in God, not in man or the state, the importance of the social order was undermined. The Gospel set the Christian apart from the community and its mores: "Let the dead bury their own dead" (Matt. 8:22). Of what use was society when "my kingdom is not of this world" (John 18:36)?[14] Of course, by their ostentatious isolation from the rest of mankind, and by their own strong group identification, made manifest in communion, the early Christians formed subsocieties of their own. The question that confronted them was how to contend with the world outside.

Jesus was known to have paid his tithes and to "render to Caesar the things that are Caesar's" (Matt. 22:20–21). St. Paul argued that the powers that be were meant to be:

> Let every soul be subject to higher powers. For there is no power except from God. Those that are, are ordained by God. And therefore he who resists authority resists the ordinance of God (Rom. 13:1–2).[15]

Small wonder, then, that the Christian community was ready for Constantine when Constantine was ready for the Church. Under that "crowned Christian Apologist" (d. A.D. 337), the interests of bishops and princes were merged as never before. Constantine believed that the state could not exist without the Christian God. He took it upon himself to foster the saving religion. St. Paul's vision of the connection between church and state was fulfilled by these developments. The political order was considered a divinely ordained part of the Christian community itself.

Yet the Christian liason with the state was ambivalent. The martyrs had expressed a fundamental aspect of Christianity when they refused to obey civil authorities.[16] Rejection of the world was part and parcel of the Christian message. If nothing else awakened men to the fact, the sack of Rome (A.D. 410) confronted them with the stark difference between the fragility of the state and the safety of the eternal order of God.

St. Augustine, that great reconciler of traditions, most fully articulated the ambivalence. He worked out a justification for the political order that grew out of his abhorrence of it. The state was one of the tragic, but necessary, results of original sin. Two purposes were fulfilled by it: it was both a penalty for sin and an opportunity for salvation. Man, created to be equal and free, had fallen by his own act into inequality and servitude. Constantly striving for his own dominion, he was in turn dominated by others. This oppression, the origin of the oppression of the state, was part of the misery man had to suffer. At the same time, this inequality of power could be the means by which a form of peace, albeit imperfect and fleeting, might be established. At the very least, the peace imposed by the state would make a life of piety possible if only because it made survival possible. But there was more. Peace meant internal peace: the state forced men to adhere to laws. These laws could never perfectly represent the laws of God; by their very existence they betrayed corruption from the original design, where men obeyed God naturally and directly. But Christ's coming gave men the grace and the knowledge to reorder the laws of human society to harmonize with the laws of God. If the peace held, and the state were prosperous, such conditions would serve to test faith, as well as afford the leisure, money, power—in short the means—to perfect that faith. But even if the laws of the state did not attempt to approximate divine justice, and even if the ruler charged with carrying out the laws abused his power and replaced law by arbitrary will, men were obliged to obey those set above them. Tyranny, like all adversity, had its purpose and its justification in the divine scheme. It too could test faith, and at the same time, purge sins and recall the mind from the transitory things of the world to the permanent things of God.[17]

Pessimistic as such notions were, they were conducive to the practical task of setting up a state appropriate to the needs of Christian believers. To the increasingly self-confident and self-reliant Western clergy, the idea that states and their rulers were, willy-nilly, instruments of God came to mean that rulers should be under the direction of churchmen. From the clerical point of view it was in the interest of the ruler to be so. Already St. Ambrose (c. 339–97), bishop of Milan and Augustine's teacher, had monitored the emperor's behavior. In his eyes, Theodosius I (379–95) was a "son of the church" who should do penance for his misdeeds and who should use his temporal power to enforce the doctrinal decrees of orthodox bishops.[18]

Such ideas persisted in clerical circles in the Germanic successor states. Gregory of Tours (c. 539–94), who dreaded the Arians as much as he fiercely loved his local city, the resting place of St. Martin, pictured the barbarian king Clovis as an upright prince who conquered the heretics and spared the holy places.[19] Like Constantine, Gregory's Clovis learned how helpful the Christian God could be in battle. Piety and success were indissolubly linked for Gregory. When he accused Clovis's successors of being wicked, he threatened them not so much with eternal judgment as with military failure:

> What can be expected [he asked them, after recounting their sins] except that, since your army will fall, you will be left without consolation and you will be ruined instantly, overcome by enemy peoples.[20]

The Carolingian kings inherited the Frankish clergy along with the throne. Charles Martel and his grandson, Charlemagne, notorious for having used the church as a tool of statecraft, were used by the church in turn. Charles Martel confiscated land from the church, but at the same time, he opened up the eastern part of his empire to ecclesiastical ministry and domination. Charlemagne used churchmen as administrators, to consolidate his power, but he also took seriously the model of Old Testament kingship which the clergy expounded: his *Admonitio Generalis* was inspired by Josias.[21] Under these early Carolingians, the church was largely confounded with the state.

The later Carolingian kings were more clearly dominated by the clergy. Louis the Pious's bishops pointed out to him that "[the king] ought above all to be defender of churches and of the servants of God, of widows, orphans, and other poor people, and all the needy as well."[22] This was mainly an episcopal view, but Louis's heirs gradually adopted it as their own.[23] By the mid-tenth century, the king received the sword in the coronation ceremony only after God had been importuned to grant that it be used "to help and defend widows and orphans."[24] But in fact the most important duty of the king in these *ordines* was the defense of ecclesiastical rights and privileges. The institutionalization of originally *ad hoc* guarantees to the clerical order within the coronation ceremony itself, symptomatic of monarchical weakness and ecclesiastical strength, implied a contractual relationship: royal power defended, clerical power sanctioned.[25] King Odo (888–898) took a coronation oath that was filled with numerous duties toward the church:

> I promise and grant to each of you and the churches committed to you that I will preserve canonical privilege, due law, and justice. And, in accordance with my office, to the extent that

God gives me the ability, I will provide defense against the
predators and oppressors of your churches and of church property. And I will thus also preserve ecclesiastical law and canon
law for you and I will grant the property of your churches—
whether brought together by kings or emperors or by the other
faithful of God—to remain [together] in integrity and immunity without any dishonor, which property your churches re-
tain in a just and legal manner. And I will strive, just like my
predecessors, to augment and to exalt [your churches] in accordance with the service owed by each, just as God will grant
to me reasonably to know and be able and as the time will
require.[26]

King Odo, who was not of the Carolingian line, needed legitimation.
But kings did not turn to the clergy just because they needed them; they
had internalized clerical standards and outlooks. Thus, Carloman, who
was the son of Louis the Stammerer, was a *bona fide* Carolingian; he did
not owe his position to the church. But sometimes he viewed his world
like a clergyman. Gregory of Tours, a bishop, had already interpreted
military failure as an act of God. When Carloman's kingdom was in-
vaded by Viking marauders, he proved he had learned Gregory's lesson
well:

Truly, we plunder our brothers and therefore the heathens
justly rob us and our property. Therefore, how shall we be able
to march confidently against our [enemies] and the enemies of
the holy church of God, when the plunder of the poor lies in
our house?[27]

Hence, by St. Odo's day, St. Augustine's skeletal justification of the
ruler of the Christian community had been filled out by the successive
churchmen and kings of the Frankish empire with specific duties, obli-
gations, promises, and rewards. These specifics constituted more than
ideas, more than political theory; they expressed political expectations.
Worldly power was inextricably bound up with God's power. The fact
was shown graphically in the anointment of kings; legislatively in Carolingian capitularies inspired by the laws of Moses; institutionally by
royal reform of monasteries and churches, of monks and churchmen.
When St. Odo of Cluny no longer perceived in his own day the political
order upheld by these ideas, he made sense out of the new men and the
new political forms that he did see by drawing upon and reinterpreting
these norms.

THE SIGNIFICANCE OF THE SAINTS

The ideal of kingship that developed in the Frankish empire was important for setting standards for the ruler. The king knew that he should follow the example of Old Testament kings, listen to his clergy, and adhere to his coronation oath. But all of these ideals pertained only to men born or elevated to the purple; they did not constitute an ethos for the general run of men.

The rest of society was offered a somewhat different set of standards: the lives of saints, which were patterned on an interpretation of the life and meaning of Christ. Unlike Christ, who was God as well as man, the saints were only human beings. Yet, unlike their fellow men, they could and did overcome the vicious human condition. They alone were given the grace by God to do what men were originally supposed to do. They were models of virtue.

The virtues that the saints' lives reflected were remarkably similar, cutting across geographical boundaries and spanning several centuries. St. Athanasius' *Life of Antony* was in the mind of Sulpicius Severus when he wrote the first example of Latin hagiography, the *Life of St. Martin.* [28] The model of St. Martin was, in turn, in the words of Wallace-Hadrill, "the foundation-stone of the art of ecclesiastical biography in the West."[29] It was particularly important to St. Odo of Cluny, who was dedicated to Martin as a child, and who left extant four hymns, two sermons, and twelve antiphons about that saint. The *Life of St. Martin* thus serves as a convenient starting point for talking about saints' virtues and for describing their effects.

The virtues that Sulpicius selected were not new even when he was writing. Martin's kindness, charity, patience, humility, and abstemiousness had their precedents in the virtues of Stoic sages. Martin's "perseverance in abstinence and in fasts, his capacity for vigils and prayers" had, by Sulpicius' time, become *topoi* in the accounts of early Christian ascetics.[30] All of these were appropriate to the world-rejecting stance that Sulpicius gave his saint.

Part of that stance was the rejection of the military life as incompatible with a religious vocation. The historical Martin had spent twenty-five years in the army, but Sulpicius reduced the term to a five-year stint.[31] He downgraded the military life: if Martin had been virtuous while a soldier, it had been despite his enlistment. "[Martin practiced so many virtues] that even at that time he was regarded as a monk rather than as a soldier."[32] Hence, Martin's famous ironic retort to Caesar: "I am Christ's soldier; I am not allowed to fight."[33]

The ideal of monastic withdrawal reappeared when Martin was made a bishop. Sulpicius was careful to point out that

> he remained, indeed, most constantly the same man as he had been before. There was the same humility in his heart, the same vileness in his clothing; and so, full of authority and grace, he satisfied the dignity of the bishop such that, even so, he did not forsake the way and the virtue of the monk.[34]

In the course of time, this ideal of withdrawal from the world—and the repudiation of the military life that went with it—entered a growing list of *topoi* in Western hagiography. Although there were variations in the *Vitae* due to the place and purpose of the hagiographer, nevertheless many patterns were established that persisted into the time of St. Odo.[35] Indeed, the *Vita S. Odonis,* written by John of Salerno, a disciple of Odo, within a year of Odo's death, is a good example of this.[36] It followed a well-traveled biographical course. Odo was predestined from birth to his life of godly dedication; he had a decisive conversion experience; he spent his life in saintly communion with similarly blessed men; and he was virtuous and inspired virtue in others.[37]

Models of virtue described by Sulpicius and John, though offered to everyone, did not provide most people with a workable religious ethos. The asceticism that such paradigms lauded, along with their concomitant ideal of withdrawal from the world, demanded the renunciation of ordinary walks of life. Germanic tribesmen had a traditional standard of behavior, but they did not have a positive Christian ethos to draw upon. That was reserved for men of the cloth (who were outside of society) and men of the purple (who were above it).[38]

By the same token, the common run of men could not expect to wield the power inherent in virtue. For the saints were not merely good; the proof of their goodness was in the miracles they could perform, the prophesies they could make, and the extraordinary acts they could carry off with ease. St. Antony fought the demons and won. St. Martin, whom Sulpicius was anxious to compare favorably to Eastern holy men, cured demoniacs, quenched fires through prayer, and, most wonderful of all, raised the dead.[39] Such powers became as commonplace as virtues in the *Vitae* of the saints.

Meanwhile, the very bones of the saints had taken on a mystique of their own. The relics of the saints were prized possessions because of the power they were believed to wield.[40] Gregory of Tours considered the saints permanent local protectors. When Clovis came to Poitiers, St. Hilary's bones made sure that his stay was a success.[41] When one of Clovis's men wrested some hay from a peasant in the Touraine, Clovis killed him instantly, saying "And where will be the hope of victory if we offend the blessed Martin?"[42] St. Martin had long been dead, of course, but his remains rested at Tours. Through the relics of the saints, if by nothing else, ordinary men were helped or thwarted by the extraordinary powers inherent in virtue.

Odo perceived his world through the lenses provided by these traditions. He was especially influenced by St. Augustine. Very early in his *Collationes* he invoked the argument that Augustine had made in the *City of God* concerning the political and social consequences of the Fall. But, in Odo's hands, the focus of the argument changed. In his exposition, the difference between the bad and the good—the damned and the elect—became precisely the difference between men who persecuted others, and men who were the objects of persecution. Augustine's typology of the generations of Cain and Abel pointed up the distinction for Odo. Whereas for Augustine the sin of Cain had been simply one example of the hatred that evil men feel towards the good, for Odo this first fratricide had every characteristic of a power confrontation. While Augustine had explicitly denied that "the one who killed [Cain] envied the other [Abel] because his dominion would be curtailed if both ruled,"[43] Odo, in contrast, identified the generation of Cain with a political class: the powerful *(potentiores)*.

It was, indeed, Odo's painful awareness of this class that constituted the starting point of his *Collationes.* He wrote them, he said, to console a bishop (Turpio of Limoges) who lamented that the peace of the community was being broken:

> Then suddenly I remembered [Odo wrote] that complaint of yours . . . about the perversity of bad men who, ever increasing in evil and inwardly condemning ecclesiastical censure, cruelly afflict weak men at whim.[44]

These evil, strong men oppressed their fellows because, according to Odo, they were inflamed by malice.

In the Christian lists of vices, malice played a relatively minor role. However, its cousins—anger, enmity, contention, dissension—ranked among St. Paul's fruits of the flesh (Gal. 5: 19–21). Gregory the Great mentioned malice when he spoke of the forms of the Leviathan. He used the term in its root sense, "absence of charity." Odo made the natural association to the Biblical pairing of charity and love of neighbor; in contrast, men inflamed by malice "oppress their fellow men."[45]

What is particularly important is that for Odo malice, unlike the other vices, "pertained to the violent" only.[46] This had not been Gregory the Great's point at all. But for Odo there was a distinct group of men, the *violenti,* who were by and large coterminous with the rich and the powerful.[47] While men poor and weak might be tempted by pride *(superbia)* and lust *(luxuria),* they had no opportunity to be tempted by malice.[48] Malice was the abuse of power.

Since it was the abuse of power, it had also to be the result of power, and thus be a vice of the powerful alone. Odo described the process of degeneration that was involved:

> The powerful, indeed, are accustomed to be proud, to rejoice in temporal things; and in order for them to hold on to what they lavishly use up, they are wont to desire other people's things. . . . But however harmless, he will be cupiditous, since clearly the holy Apostle compares cupidity even to idolatry. . . . And in order that they use only their own things and not another's, John the Baptist says to them: "Terrify no one, nor make a false accusation, and be content with your pay" (Luke 3:14).[49]

In short, Odo was describing a retrogressive sequence in which wealth and power led to pride, pride to avarice, and avarice to malice.

Thus, the lines were drawn between those who were in a position to succumb to malice and those who were not: "You see the humble and weak and poor oppressed, afflicted, and unjustly hurt by the proud and powerful and rich."[50] Among the poor Odo numbered the church itself; the characteristic it shared with the oppressed was its vulnerability.[51] Similarly, Odo termed the oppressed, interchangeably, the weak, honest, quiet, just, and good.[52] Because the poor man was downtrodden and defenseless, he could not begin to ascend the ladder of vice—the first rung of which was pride—as easily as the rich man. "The poorer men are, the more rarely do they come into the abomination [of pride] but indeed the rich hardly ever discover the sacrifice [of humility]."⁵³ This is why Odo was able to alternate the terms "the good" and "the poor" indifferently and to identify both with the generation of Abel.

The equivalence between good and poor did not imply that poor people were consciously virtuous. They simply could not oppress their oppressor even if they wanted to. By their relative powerlessness, they were virtuous automatically and unwittingly, but this sort of viceless-ness was due to necessity. True, people who reluctantly bore injuries from others were, as it were, forced on the road to virtue: "Plunderers, therefore, who afflict the poor in things temporally seem . . . truly to impel them, although unwillingly, to seek celestial things for their salvation."⁵⁴ But these poor men were imperfect. The ideal response was to welcome the scourge:

> [Through the Scriptures God] reveals many examples of suff-erings to counter our impatience. . . . If the saying, "Be patient in tribulation" (Rom. 12:12) is hard, Paul, who is not only patient but also glorifies replies with "I will gladly glorify" (2 Cor. 12:9).⁵⁵

Christ's life provided the model: "He bore the jeers of contumely, the jabs of derision, the torments of the passion and death so that humble God might teach men not to be proud."⁵⁶ Aware of his sinful nature, the just man restrained his self-will: he did not murmur. In this way, Odo pointed up the virtue of patience—the welcoming of afflictions— in the world. We shall return to it, for it was the very essence of the monastic life for the early Cluniacs.

It would seem that the members of the generations of Cain and Abel would be easy to distinguish: one would simply note who was in a position to oppress whom. In a miracle that Odo related "about the persecutors of the poor," he described some men taking pigs to market *(negotiatores)* who, seeing some men on horseback *(equites)* approach them, fled to the shelter of a church for protection. Their fears were justified; the horsemen took the pigs and rode off in triumph. But miraculously the robbers were unsuccessful, notably when one of them fell off his horse.⁵⁷ There was no question in this story who belonged to which generation. Men on horseback were suspect.

But Odo thought that in real life the lines were not so clearly drawn.⁵⁸ When he spoke theoretically of evil men who afflicted others, he used the positive form *potentes.* But when he came to look at social reality, he used the relative form, *potentiores*.[59] These men, the "rather powerful," were the princes and the nobles.[60] They were not inherently more malicious than other men, but they were, as has been noted, in a position open to temptation. If they succumbed to malice, Odo called them *raptores*, plunderers.[61] Their victims were, theoretically, the *pauperes*. But, in reality, even poor men might find a way to exercise malice. For example, they might become dependents *(clientelae)* of someone more powerful than themselves, and gain the opportunity to coerce others on their lord's behalf. These men were not really powerful; indeed, they were "quite poor":

> Those who are richer are always zealous to augment their riches. . . . with which they would subject poorer men to themselves, whom these haughty men would hold as their obsequious dependents. Poorer men themselves subject themselves freely to them for the sake of their satiety.[62]

Then the dependents were able, on borrowed power, to oppress others. They also acted like the *potentes* in their drinking, playing, vomiting, abandon, and dancing.[63] Because of their ambiguous position as both afflicters and afflicted, Odo could not be satisfied with a purely dualistic model of society: the *pauperiores* who succumbed to the temptation of malice while being maliciously treated themselves belonged to the "less perfect" members of the generation of Abel.[64]

Thus, two absolute attributes, *potens* and *pauper*, defined the ends of a continuum in which men in the world had a relative social and spiritual position.[65] Odo's view of society might be schematized as follows:

decreasing wealth and power	Social Position	Probable Spiritual Position
	potentes (divites)	oppressor/not oppressed
	potentiores (ditiores)	oppressor/oppressed[66]
	pauperiores (humiliores)[67]	oppressed/oppressor
	pauperes (humiles)	oppressed/not oppressor

When Odo spoke of the violence inflicted by men of malice, he referred to two things: plundering and killing on the one hand, harming by bad example on the other.[68] In his eyes, both were equally destructive. The evil *potens*, who lived on rapine, was in the first place guilty of "killing his own brothers," because "not only the plunderer but also the defrauder of money is said to be equal to a murderer." In fact, some men slaughtered their fellows outright: "[evil men] despoil good men of property or even kill them."[69] But, in the second place, and no less terrible, was the harm done to the *pauperiores* who were enticed into becoming dependents of the rich. Their oppression was spiritual: "subject to the favor [of the wicked potentate], oppressed by his example, they remain strangers to the light of truth."[70]

But what alternative did they have? How could a man of power—whether a lord or his client—avoid malice? The Frankish kings had a way to reconcile their power with virtue: they were anointed by priests and blessed by God during the coronation ceremony. But Odo was not speaking of or to kings. He was speaking to men who ruled over other men simply because they had the opportunity and the power to do so. In his perception of the world, it was not a king but rather an entire generation of men who exercised real coercive power.

On this point, at least, Odo's perception was not so very different from the modern one discussed in Chapter 2. Already in Odo's lifetime the disintegration of Carolingian institutions and the advent of both self-made men and their deliberate or inadvertent victims had begun. The question for Odo was how to make these men morally responsible. He could not look to a king to control them; their rise was due largely to the weakness of royal power. He could not look to the papacy; the family of Alberic, which controlled Rome, controlled the papacy as well. He could not look to individual churchmen; these, as his *Collationes* made clear, were often corrupt, seduced by the standards of their lay counterparts, and they were impotent in any case. The church, as has been noted, was counted part of the "poor." This left Odo with saints on the one hand and powerful men on the other. Neither of these categories was, as Odo found them, adequate to his needs. The point is clear with regard to the powerful; they tended to be malicious. The inadequacy of the saintly category requires some comment.

The saints were models for the virtuous. But the example of the saints led to a rejection of the world. They avoided the problem of abusing coercive power because they gave it up altogether. It is true that, at the same time, the saints' unworldliness gave them new and greater powers. But nothing here provided guidance for a man still on the battlefield or exercising his power in the law courts.

The escapist moral of the lives of saints had its effect: the pattern was repeated in early Cluniac texts. At the same time, attempts were made to formulate a new model combining piety with coercive power. John of Salerno's *Vita Odonis,* which was much more concerned with the monastic world than with the world at large, contained a whole cast of powerful characters struggling with the problem of being virtuous in the world. According to John, Odo's father, Abbo, was a powerful man. He presided over a court, and "if ever a dispute would have arisen in any manner between parties . . . everyone from everywhere would hasten to him."[71] Abbo was a good man, combining his power with both wisdom and virtue. He knew the "ancient histories and the *Novella* of Justinian by heart," and his speech was "evangelical."[72] He celebrated the great festivals and the saints' days with vigils lasting "throughout the night." He taught his son, Odo, how to combine this rigorous schedule with the duties of a warrior.[73] He practiced sexual abstinence and attributed Odo's birth to his fervent prayers to "God, in the name of the Virgin birth" on the vigil of Christmas. Yet, in John's account this vision of a pious potentate eventually gave way to the old model: Abbo was pictured as retiring from the world to become a monk and save his soul.[74]

In John's account, Count Fulk of Anjou figured above all as a rich man; he tempted others to avarice as he succumbed himself.[75] He was destined to suffer for this sin. After taking some vessels from St. Martin's church, Fulk fell deathly ill. Only when he promised to return the vessels was he cured. But even though he made good his appropriation, regained his health, and showed that his conduct was truly reformed, Odo wanted him to "leave the world."[76] Fulk refused, and we hear no more of him; but John went on to describe Adhegrinus, a man in Fulk's retinue as

> vigorous in arms and wise in counsel, who soon repented in his heart. . . . And so, after he laid aside the hair of his head and worldly warfare, he became forthwith a soldier of Christ.[77]

John's account of Odo also bore the marks of the traditional paradigm. Odo, sent to the court of William of Aquitaine to learn how to fight, saw with the help of God how evil a vocation this was. Then began the series of events that led to Odo's eventual monastic profession.

A few Cluniac charters from the period of Odo's abbacy reveal the influence of the same paradigm. Monastic charters are not generally very rich sources by which to measure human motivation for a number of reasons. First, they were often drawn up by monks, so they do not necessarily reveal the motives of their subjects. Second, the writers generally used all-purpose phrases to cover the multitude of sins of those who were intending to enter the monastery. Finally, the charters were rarely precise about the entrant's previous style of life. Yet a few were. For example, when Letbald (whose family we have met in connection with land at Verzé) entered the monastery, his charter read:

> I, the aforesaid Letbald, uncinching the belt of war and shaving the hair of my head and my beard for the love of God, arrange to receive the monastic habit in the aforesaid monastery, with the help of God.[78]

What is important here is not how well such a formulation described Letbald's true perception of the step he was about to take but rather how well the traditional paradigm was thought to describe—hence explain—the essential point of Letbald's change.

Only in the case of Abbo, and perhaps of Fulk, do any of these texts suggest the possibility of reconciling piety with power. Odo's texts, in contrast, spoke directly to the issue. If the *Collationes* focused on the problem of malice, the solution to the problem was presented in the *Vita Geraldi*. A crucial passage in the *Collationes* provides a connecting link.

Towards the end of the *Collationes* (which reads almost unrelievedly as a harangue against evil people in general and malicious people in particular) Odo, in a brief hiatus, suddenly stopped short and wrote a "sermon to the *potentiores*." He took this sermon, almost verbatim, from two sources: from a sermon delivered by Gregory of Nazianzen to "those who preside in positions of power" and from Gregory the Great, who devoted part of his *Moralia in Job* to the subject of powerful men. The critical passage from Odo is as follows:

> Remember, therefore, [in the words of Gregory of Nazianzen] how great a debtor you are to God, who has given you power over equals. [Odo then adds this admonition]: Do not think of what you can do but what you ought. For [again, as Gregory says] you bear the sword at His direction not to wound but to threaten. Would that you restore it unpolluted to Christ, your commander, who has given power from heaven for this reason, that [paraphrasing Gregory the Great] He might crush by [your] assistance those whom the authority of the holy church by its own strength does not suffice to restrain from oppressing the poor.[79]

This, then, was Odo's conception of the proper use of coercive power. It was to be used in alliance with the earthly church, whose duty it was —in this case at least—to help the poor. The potentate was to assist with temporal force when the church's spiritual sanctions proved ineffective. There was no question that violence was involved: Odo borrowed from Gregory the Great the view that crushing the wicked and powerful was one good use of worldly power. On the other hand, the passage also reflected the pacific sentiments of Nazianzen, who hoped that the mere threat of armed force would keep the peace. "Would that" the sword never be used, Odo wrote, echoing his source. In the *Collationes,* the passage was left without happy resolution; the use of the subjunctive made the whole idea a condition contrary to fact.

In the *Vita Geraldi,* the ideal was realized. Gerald was explicitly set forth as a model for the *potentiores:* "Since truly we believe this man of God to have been given as an example to the powerful, let them see how they themselves may imitate him, as a man brought forth to them out of [their] neighborhood and from their own order."[80] Indeed, Odo noted the efficacy of Gerald's life in this regard already: the inhabitants of Aurillac "used to have very ferocious habits, but gradually by the example and the reverence of the holy man they seem to be better."[81]

Gerald was rich *(dives)* and powerful *(potens)* and a warrior *(pugnator).* He was also a man on the rise, who had taken the title of count. Given Odo's view of the dangers of power, it might be expected that Gerald would have to resist constantly the vice of malice and, in the process, refrain from using his power. But in Odo's formulation, power—indeed force—was the key to Gerald's virtue. It gave Gerald the opportunity to exercise virtue superior to most; his military might made charity possible. We have seen that for the powerless, the crucial virtue was patience, accepting and welcoming the afflictions that grew out of a lowly social position. But inadvertent patience was not charity, and the poor man had to be content with his limitations. The man of power, on the other hand, had no such restraint; here lay his weakness and his strength. He was sorely tempted to use his power selfishly, to help himself and to resist his afflictors. In this case, he was neither patient nor charitable. But Gerald was both. When it came to helping himself, he acted like a weak man; he "permitted himself to be injured by persons of low degree as though he were powerless."[82] Like a poor man or (as will become clear) a monk, Gerald was a willing victim, a practi-

tioner of patience. Although a potentate, Gerald belonged to the generation of Abel:

> It was necessary that malicious Cain had exercised the just
> Abel in patience. Gerald too, like Job, . . . was often attacked
> by certain men of his provinces.[83]

In this passage lay an extraordinary literary and conceptual conflation.
Odo inserted the fighter Gerald into Augustine's generational scheme.
At the same time, he fit him into the Gregorian teaching on Job, who
was understood as a figure for tormented and patient Christ. In his
Moralia in Job, Gregory had set up a whole series of associations—
spiritual, typological, historical—for Job. With one sentence, Odo made
the figure of Gerald reverberate with Job's many meanings.

Yet, Gerald was not always patient. When others were victimized,
charity subsumed patience; impatience became holy. As Odo put it, "if
he had been inactive because of indolent patience, he would have
seemed to neglect the precept concerning the care for the poor."[84] This
combination of patience and charity was the perfect realization of the
virtue of justice *(justitia)* for Odo. It involved nothing less than the full
panoply of powers inherent in the magnate's high position. For, in the
first place, the excellence of the powerful man's voluntary patience was
made clear by contrast to his strength, and in the second place, the full
measure of care for the poor was made possible only by the use of that
same strength.

When Gerald sat as judge in his law court and heard a case in which
a poor man was brought before a more powerful man, Gerald, "thirsting
for justice," always saw to it that "he upheld the weaker just enough
that he crushed the stronger without hurting [him]."[85] The law court,
no doubt, offered the man of power a forum for victimizing others,
should he succumb to the temptation of injustice. Moreover, the law
courts could legitimately be used to order bloody punishments; such
was the norm. Gerald pointedly refrained from killing or maiming anyone.[86] But the court was not the only nor even the most opportune place
for using or abusing power. The battlefield gave a far wider range for
the expression of malice. In the *Collationes,* Odo had been content with
the hope that coercive force might never be used. Now, in the *Vita
Geraldi,* he outlined an entire program of battlefield behavior that, in its
own way, "upheld the weak without hurting the strong."

Gerald went to battle only when he realized that "it is better that audacious men be suppressed by the force of war than that the rustics [?] and unarmed be oppressed unjustly by them."[87] He never used his power for his own selfish ends. He did not revenge himself on the *dux,* the *comes,* or the *vassi* who persecuted him.[88] He waited until his dependents pleaded with him before taking action: "he habitually was persuaded—incited not by the attack but by reason—to have mercy and to give help."[89]

The battle itself was a *psychomachia,* a war between virtue and vice. It was not men, but "insatiable malice" that "jeered at peaceful men," wasting the district.[90] Gerald, for his part, "did not want to attack his enemies themselves but only to drive their audacity crazy."[91] Charity confronted malice on the battlefield, and won.

The victory was miraculous; no one was hurt. Gerald and his men fought hilt forward, grasping the sword by the blade![92] Like Quixote with the windmills, they looked ridiculous; like Quixote's foolishness, theirs was a holy folly.[93] It was an unvarying fact of the battle that no blood was shed. Odo called it "a new kind of fighting which was mingled with piety."[94]

The piety was a fact of war. Gerald "whom piety conquered at the very moment of battle," could not have been virtuous if he had refused to fight.[95] In fact, in line with Odo's argument in the *Collationes,* Gerald would have been justly condemnable:

> Those who feast themselves on the rapine of the poor ought to be opposed very severely. For, in truth, even those who do not afflict the poor but nevertheless do not care to resist such afflicters, are seriously sinning in any event.[96]

Only men of power could battle vice by force of arms. Odo thought that churchmen could and should resist oppressors of the poor through "excommunications or admonitions."[97] As a monk writing about the punishment in store for *raptores,* he followed his own injunctions. But churchmen, who had theoretically given up their wordly power, i.e., their arms, could not promote the full measure of justice, precisely because they were ineffective.[98] Stronger medicine was needed. With Gerald, Odo broke the old mold of the saint. Gerald wanted to be a monk, and indeed, he became one, but he hid his tonsure under his cap and continued to function as a *potens.* This was a radical redefinition of the virtuous life. According to Odo it was the best way to perform the work of God:

For what way of life could he show more pleasing to God than that in which he neither neglected the general good nor diminished any of the perfection of his own life-style? Indeed, what life-style has shown itself so very valuable and so very useful to many, yet was known to God alone?[99]

Concern for the general good was a corollary of the biblical injunction of charity; the perfection of life was the norm of Christ and the saints. The animating principle of Gerald's life-style as Odo conceived it was scrupulous adherence to such models and directives. Had Odo himself made our observation in Chapter 2—that many in Gerald's position were men unused to their new status and their power—his injunctions could not have been more apposite. Odo countered normlessness with discipline (disciplina); its essence for Odo was lawfulness.[100] Every act was determined by (or rather understood as determined by) a divine directive. The laws existed primarily in the Old and New Testaments, but Odo thought that they might be found in any place God chose—in miracles, in customs, in nature, in history, and biography —all properly understood, of course.[101] In the *Collationes,* Odo spoke of the disciplinary effects of Scripture—"the Lord's precepts . . . by their own laws curb us from evil deeds"—and also of the reassurance men needed that an obedient life was possible: "It is demonstrated to be easy by the examples of the fathers."[102] Gerald was cast in their mold: "The law of the Lord always resounded in his mouth," Odo wrote, and "he seemed to do everything in the name of the Lord."[103]

Odo meant this literally. He conceived of every aspect of Gerald's life as being regulated by divine law. There was no question that Gerald had deviated from the usual "warrior of Christ"; contemporaries might complain that Gerald was in fact deviating from a divinely appointed norm. On the contrary, Odo argued:

> Truly, no one ought to be worried because a just man sometimes makes use of fighting, which seems incompatible with religion.[104]

The fact is, Odo continued, there was a different, equally divinely inspired model that Gerald was following to the letter, namely, the just men of the Old Testament. These men went to war, but only in order to defend those who could not defend themselves:

> Indeed, some of the fathers, although they had been the most holy and the most patient, nevertheless used to take up arms

manfully in adversities when the cause of justice demanded, as Abraham, who destroyed a great multitude of the enemy to rescue his nephew.[105]

If Gerald's battles were on behalf of others, then this was because, by heeding the cry of the poor, Gerald did the work of the Lord.[106] Such was the testimony of Scripture—"as long as you did it to one of these my least brethren, you did it to me," says Christ in Matthew—and it was the lesson of St. Martin as well: "Therefore that night, after [Martin] had given himself up to sleep, he saw Christ clothed in the part of his cloak, with which he had covered a poor man."[107]

In the case of Gerald's strange way of fighting, Odo quoted no source. He may have considered that the avoidance of bloodshed was an injunction that went without saying. But the necessary precedent existed in Sulpicius Severus' St. Martin, a model that Odo knew.[108] In this *Vita,* after St. Martin declares himself "Christ's soldier" and therefore unwilling to fight the enemy, a military victory ensues anyway, precisely because of Martin's sensibilities:

> The enemy sent ambassadors of peace, giving up themselves and all their things. Hence who can doubt that this had truly been a victory of the blessed man, to whom it was granted lest he be sent to the battle unarmed? And although the good Lord could have saved his soldier even among the swords and javelins of the enemy, still, lest [Martin's] holy gaze be violated by the deaths of others, He removed the necessity for battle. For Christ was bound not to grant any other victory for his own soldier than that, since the enemy were beaten bloodlessly, no man should die.[109]

If one considers that wielding a sword hilt forward has the net effect of not wielding a sword at all, even Gerald's weaponry recalls the example of Martin. But this need not be—and probably was not—the only source for Odo. We have already mentioned Nazianzen's sentiment that the sword remain unpolluted by blood. Odo's realization of this hope in Gerald as much as turned the words of the Greek father into an order fulfilled.

The scrupulous adherence to set and presumably divinely inspired standards ran like a *leitmotif* through the *Vita Geraldi.* The wellspring, not only of the principles of Gerald's behavior but also of their very form, was external law. For the most part the law was biblical, but other sources, some of them perhaps lost to us or at least unfamiliar, were also invoked. An example of the way law determined form may be seen in Gerald's zeal for sobriety: "the blessed prince, who ate at the right time for restoration and not for pleasure, used to observe that precept of Scripture [i.e., the precept to be sober]."[110] It was not the general spirit of the law that Odo had in mind. Rather, in Odo's account, Gerald understood the precept literally and gave it a concrete and unvarying meaning in his life. Sobriety meant specifically not eating before the third hour on ordinary days and observing fast days by postponing the meal until the ninth hour.[111] And when, because of other responsibilities, Gerald varied his routine and, for example, observed a fast on an alternate day, Odo was quick to explain that this was proper because "it was allowed a layman, especially one so just, to use licitly those things which are not licit to those whose profession forbids them."[112] Gerald did not, therefore, break the law but rather adhered to the one proper for his station: "But if a fast had occurred on a Sunday, he did not at all break it nor omit it for the occasion, but he kept the solemnity of the fast on the preceding Saturday."[113]

Behaviors justified and presumably determined by these norms were incorporated into a complex and orderly routine of daily living. It is not surprising that elements of church liturgy became a regular part of Gerald's schedule, because these were already ritualized expressions of piety. Every day Gerald completed the Divine Office, recited the entire psalter, and attended mass.[114] He set out food for the poor and heard the *lectio divina* at his own table.[115] After he took the tonsure, he intensified his liturgical activities:

> For he was so intent on listening alternately to readings and prayers—now with others, now alone—that it is a marvel how he could have so much zeal for these things and also want to finish so great a number of psalms.[116]

Every act of Gerald's life came to be—and was depicted as such with approval by Odo—an act of devotion. Gerald found the laws that turned banal activities of everyday necessity into pious ritual:

> He had noted to himself certain holy words which seemed to fit bodily duties. Thus, before he began to speak in the morning he said: "Set a watch, O Lord, before my mouth and a door round about my lips" (Ps. 140:32) and there were other sayings of this sort which he adapted to particular actions, for

example when he awoke, when he got out of bed, when he put on his shoes, when he took up his clothes, or his belt, or certainly when he began a journey or anything else.[117]

Thus, all of Gerald's acts became part of a quasi-liturgical sequence. They were always planned, and they became invariable as well: "He so held to this manner of living in his external way of life that his servants knew how he would act at every season of the year."[118] Even the unpredictable was anticipated and managed by a predetermined plan:

> He never incurred a nocturnal emission without grieving. For, however often that misfortune of humanity happened to him while sleeping, a chamber servant used to bring him privately, in an adjoining place, of course, a change of clothes always prepared for this, and a towel and a vessel of water.[119]

Thus the expedient became, through use, a law of its own, taking its place among the many *regulae* which Gerald followed.

For Odo, therefore, virtue was demonstrated and maintained by constraints. The poor man was constrained, by his very position, to the life-style of humility enjoined by the Bible. The powerful man was not constrained by circumstance, but by knowledge. It was no accident that Odo depicted Gerald as a lover of Scripture, for in Scripture he would find the laws he needed to follow. These would "bridle the beast." In his "sermon to the powerful," Odo had spoken of the purpose and the limits of power. Now in the *Vita Geraldi,* he connected both of these to *disciplina,* that is, lawfulness. The passage by Gregory the Great that had inspired Odo's sermon in the *Collationes* was a comment on Job 39:10: "Will you bind the rhinoceros to the plow with your thong, or will he break the clods of the valleys behind you?" The rhinoceros, Gregory had explained, was an earthly prince; the thong was the bond of faith; the clods were unbelievers, including haughty men who violently afflicted the humble.[120] Now, in the *Vita Geraldi,* Gerald became the rhinoceros who, voluntarily limiting the use of his own power so that he could prevent the misuse of power by others, aided the church:

> [Gerald knew] that the rhinoceros, that is, any powerful man, is bound with a thong so that he may crush the clods of the valleys, that is, the oppressors of the humble. . . . It was allowed, therefore, to a layman belonging to the order of

fighters to carry the sword, so that he might defend the unarmed masses . . . and so that he might check either by the
judgment of war or by the force of the judiciary those whom
ecclesiastical censure was not able to subdue.[121]

The constraints on Gerald's power—the thongs that bound him—
were, as the examples above have shown, the laws belonging to the
order of fighters. Odo could not have made the pivotal position of the
law more explicit. He equated Gerald with Noah, "a man of God who
lived according to the law."[122] Yet a modern perspective cannot help but
notice an important difference. Noah's law had been "God's way,"
enjoined on all believers. Gerald's laws were at once more specific in
object and more diverse in origin. As to object, Odo was careful to
distinguish the laws proper to the order of fighters from the laws applicable to other *ordines* in human society.[123] As to origin, some of the laws
Odo spoke about derived from Scripture, some from pious custom,
some from the model of the Fathers and the saints. Yet for Odo the
difference was only apparent. God was the ultimate and unitary source
of all righteous laws. Hence Gerald's life, reflecting its creator, blended
seemingly diverse directives into the harmonious and orderly whole
proper for all men.

The result of this strictly regulated, lawful, and godly behavior was
success. Gerald and his followers were always victorious. In one incident, Gerald conquered by reciting a psalm; in another his opponent,
miraculously lured from a fortified position, sued for peace. In yet
another miracle, his adversaries overestimated his troops and retired.[124]
When forced to fight, Gerald's enemies went down to defeat in the clear
manner of a prizefight: Gerald "broke the teeth of the wicked."[125]

Gerald not only thrived militarily, but he also amassed a greater
fortune than his fellow magnates, and inadvertently impoverished his
enemies:[126] "Whoever had hurt him, as if he had committed a sacrilege,
was certain not to allow himself to prosper."[127] Gerald maintained his
independence against potential overlords, holding himself a servant of
God alone.[128] The relationship between Gerald and God was, of course,
the key to Gerald's success, which extended into the eternal order as
well: Gerald's salvation was certain. Thus, Gerald's discipline won him
life after death and power in the world. It was an unbeatable combination, and as Odo asked, "What life-style could be more valuable?"

It was Gerald's lawfulness that made his power work for him.
Theoretically, every sort of power came from God. If a powerful man,

a worldly *potentior,* oppressed others, he was still, unknowingly, using his power to carry out the predestined plan. On the other hand, his temporal power would not save him eternally; his success was ephemeral; his power was partial and weak. Gerald's power was real, the result of God's grace. In this way, Gerald was the equal of an anointed king.

The primitive Germanic king had been the guarantor of prosperity, his key attributes being strength and success. Later, as we have seen, he acquired the additional power of protecting the church and carrying out Christ's precepts on behalf of the weak. Those who were not kings, however, had no such essential ecclesiastical function. With Gerald of Aurillac, Odo ascribed royal duties and royal powers to an independent fighter. He compared Gerald to kings David, Ezechias and Josias—"were they not powerful and bellicose?" he queried—thus in one stroke leveling kings with warriors.[129] There was another basis for the comparison: Odo likened Gerald to "Oswald, king of the English, whom God glorified by signs [because] he was zealous to glorify God by observing His commands."[130] The emphasis was no longer on anointment; it was on obedience. Adherence to divine laws was Odo's only hope for reordering the human condition, making it amenable to the working of God's grace even as it witnessed to that grace. There need be no essential difference between strong men and kings. Power was delegated directly by Christ, the Commander. He gave the orders. It was up to the strong men to listen and to carry them out.

Most men did not do so, and for them the very model of Gerald was meant to be salvific. Gerald, rising above the ineluctable hold of sin, could obey God's laws and therefore call upon the powers inherent in God's might. Through him, others would learn:

> And let [Gerald's unruly neighbors] not think the observance of the commands of God hard or impossible since in fact it is seen that they were observed by a lay and powerful man.[131]

That most people did not learn went without saying; it was inevitable, given human nature. If the commands were to be followed, they would have to be imposed. Hence if Gerald's first redemptive function was as a paradigm for fighters, his second was as a rhinoceros trampling them down.

As caught in the prism of the charters, the world outside Cluny presented much the same unregulated features as it did in Odo's writings. There we see the same laments about the human condition, about sin, and, above all, about the need for redemption. Most of the deeds involved land transactions with the monastery, connected indissolubly with questions of salvation according to the testimony of the charters. It was clear that one form of spiritual discipline was gift-giving. There was nothing unique about the sentiments expressed in the Cluniac charters. They contained the same *formulae* as those which paraded through the extant cartularies from the Merovingian and Carolingian periods and through the charters of monasteries contemporary with Cluny. The gift set up a bond between the donor and monks. At Cluny, to be more precise, it set up a link between the donor, the monks, and SS. Peter and Paul, to whom the monks at Cluny were dedicated. In 928, for example, Bertasia, the step-mother of that Letbald who later entered Cluny, gave three *curtiles* to Cluny:

> For the salvation of the soul of my lord [husband] Warulf, and my own, and for the souls of all our relatives and of all Christians, through the intercession of blessed Peter and Paul and other saints. May the good Lord deign to free our souls from the punishments below.[132]

Toward the end of the tenth century, new and more stringent forms of discipline were perceived to be necessary. When old institutions of law and order in Cluny's immediate locale were disintegrating, the Cluniac abbot, in concert with other ecclesiastic officials, in effect proclaimed some of the laws they thought appropriate for the different grades of men in the vicinity. We have already discussed some of the implications of this Council of Anse of 994.[133] The series of positive injunctions and negative prohibitions that it drew up was based indifferently on biblical precepts, canon laws, and defunct Carolingian legislation. The cleric was not allowed to hunt. The layman was enjoined to observe the sabbath and go to mass. The count was forbidden to enter Cluny's "holy precincts." Men of "higher secular and military authority" or those living next to Cluny were forbidden to make off with Cluny's property. Each special station in life brought with it special laws. The ordinary layman was simply required to go to mass, but the highly placed layman had to honor Cluny's liberty as well; after all, he was the only one in a position to be tempted to violate it. Disobedience carried with it the threat of anathema. Obedience, on the other hand, merited blessings, including those of a very tangible nature: powerful men were given some of Cluny's outlying lands to protect.

Thus, in Cluniac eyes, the world was unruly in the root sense of that term: ungoverned by rule. Unwittingly, of course, all was going according to God's plan. But for individuals to survive and surmount this well-merited and almost insurmountable disorder, there had to be a knowledge of and adherence to God's many laws. Keeping in mind the changes outlined in Chapter 2, we may say that the Cluniac emphasis on restraint, on lawfulness, on prescribed and ritual behavior, was the antidote to the social and political transformations of the tenth century. In Chapter 5, we shall argue that Cluniac discipline was, in fact, a response to—and the antithesis of—anomie. The Cluniacs saw men gaining new positions of power, institutions of peace and order changing, and the poor victimized. Their prescribed remedy was scrupulous adherence to norms that, in their view, were uniquely enduring. The Lord's precepts were thongs, restraining untutored wills.

If the Cluniacs rejected the world for the monastery, it was because the monastery offered just such harnesses. The following chapter will demonstrate the ways in which this idea informed the Cluniacs' perception of their own monasticism.

4 | LOOKING IN: *The Cluniac Perception of the Monastery*

In the face of change in the world, Odo stressed enduring norms. The monastery was not so different from the world. True, the monastery was a rejection of the worldly community, but it was also a subset of that community. Monks, like all men, partook of the fallen human condition, and the society they formed had within it the same potential for disorder and wickedness as society at large. On the other hand, the monastery took advantage of something that was available to the world but was more difficult to institute there: the reinterpretation and redirection of temporal institutions in the light of Christ's coming and his message of redemption. Christians, who loved God, were to have institutions and laws regulated by divine principles. The monastery was an exclusive club of Christians. It could claim, as St. Benedict did in his *Rule,* to be a "school for the service of the Lord."[1] This meant that it was somewhere between an alternative society of the elect, on the one hand, and a mirror of the society of evil men, on the other. It was, in short, a training ground for eternal life. Because of its small size and the small number of institutions—laws, forms of knowledge, forms of behavior —necessary to keep it going, the monastery was presumably capable of being ordered more in accordance with God's original plan for man than society at large. Therefore, the way in which the Cluniacs viewed their own brand of monasticism should be complementary, and add nuance, to our understanding of their view of the world. At the same time, it should help us to understand what the world saw in Cluny.

Apart from a short sermon written by Odo on the feast of St. Benedict, there is only one source from the tenth century that directly bears upon Cluny's monastic ideal: John of Salerno's *Vita Odonis,* written within a year of Odo's death in 942.[2] Very little is known about John.[3] He reports that he had been a canon at Rome when he met Odo, probably in 938.[4] With Odo's encouragement he became a monk— Arnaldi thinks at St. Paul's in Rome[5]—and was taken on by Odo as a companion.[6] It seems that he was with Odo primarily during Odo's Italian trips. Just before Odo's death, Baldwin, who had been abbot of St. Paul's, became abbot of Monte Cassino. Arnaldi postulates that it was at this time that John moved to a monastery in Salerno, where he probably became either an abbot or a prior.[7]

This, then, is the sum of our knowledge about John's life. Happily, from his biography of Odo, we know a good deal more about his ideals. Near the beginning of the *Vita Odonis,* John made an inventory of his subject's virtues:

> Now let me pass more quickly to the contempt of things. Let those who wish praise the exorcisers of demons, the raisers of the dead, and other men famous for miracles. I, the least of all, shall praise the first virtue of my Odo, namely patience; then his contempt of things; after this [his] wealth in souls; [his] restoration of monasteries; [his] clothes, and food for monks; [his] peace for churches; [his] bringing together kings and princes; his guardianship of all [right] ways; his promptness in commands, his perseverance in vigils and prayers; his care for the poor, his correction of youths; his honor toward the aged; his emendation of morals; his love for virgins; consolation of the continent; mercy for the miserable; his perfect observance of rules; in the end the specimen of all virtues.[8]

Some of these qualities, such as Odo's restoration of monasteries and the institution of regulation clothes and food for monks, were without question linked to a monastic ideal. But it will become apparent that all of these virtues were consistent with, indeed dependent upon, one another. Most striking is the place of patience in John's list, given the role of patience in Odo's writings about the outside world. If Odo was concerned with disorder without, John saw the same thing within the monastery. When Odo first came to Baume (St. Berno's first monastery, and presumably the model for Cluny), wicked monks, bent on turning Odo from his vocation, warned him about Berno's cruelty:

Do you know the custom of abbot Berno? . . . Oh, oh, if you knew how harshly he knows how to treat the monk. In truth, lashes follow his correction, and then those he beats he binds with fetters, tames with incarceration, afflicts with fasts. And when the miserable [monk] has suffered all these things, even so he is not able to get his pardon.[9]

Here the monks were ascribing to Berno (falsely, of course) the very misuse of power that (as we have seen) was the antithesis of justice in the outer world. There powerful men succumbed to malice and had to be subdued by other powerful men, who were themselves restrained from wrongdoing by the precepts of the Lord. In the final analysis, however, it was not the power of men but rather the power of justice within them—if anything—that kept the peace. The monastery presented an analogous situation, as John showed. In the monastery, the abbot was in a powerful position and, like the powerful layman, was meant to be restrained by divine precepts.[10] In John's view, Berno and Odo constantly allowed themselves to be hurt by those weaker than themselves, just as did the powerful men we have met in Odo's writings. Vice, on the other hand, flourished at a lower level, among the brethren. Theirs was not the vice of malice since they, like the poor and weak in the world at large, were not in a position to be truly malicious; that belonged to the violent and the powerful only.[11] Instead, the brethren persecuted Odo with verbal injuries and false accusations. The antidote for these men was precisely the antidote for all murmurers who found fault and complained: patience. If Gerald had been a model for the *pugnatores* in his justice, so Odo was a model for his fellow monks in his patience:

> But truly Odo, the peaceful man, used to take them aside, and innocent [but] as if guilty, he used to prostrate himself at their feet begging pardon; not, however, out of human fear but out of fraternal love, doubtless so that his patience might correct those whom he saw were incurring divine punishment. In the end they were sometimes restrained by his patience; but in the manner of running water, they reverted right back to their own vices. And him who they should have imitated, on the contrary they reproached.[12]

John was consistent when he sought to praise patience as Odo's first virtue. In the context of the monastery, patience effected (as much as anything could effect) the emendation of morals. In the lay world, with its vicious *potentiores,* justice was the other prime virtue. Both of these virtues were forms of charity. John, who wanted to demonstrate that Odo "opened his hand and extended his palm even to his persecutors" (hence was perfectly patient), told about a "certain rustic who wanted to kill Odo for a small bottle of water." The man was stopped before he could do any mischief, and Odo, instead of punishing the malefactor, gave him some money. When the local strong man in the region—Alberic, the prince of Rome (see pp. 49–50)—wanted to cut off the peasant's hand, Odo "begged him very strenuously not to do it, and he dismissed the peasant safe and sound."[13] In the many other instances of Odo's charity to the poor, John always made clear that, in addition to giving something to the poor, Odo actually took on the poor man's condition. For example, when Odo came upon a feeble old man who carried as his dinner a rancid-smelling sack of garlic, onions, and leeks, Odo put the man on his horse and took the sack himself. John was disgusted by the smell of the food, but he realized that in carrying the sack, Odo was showing himself to be the "true poor man of Christ."[14]

The question immediately presents itself: in this view of things, was justice, insofar as it involved the use of armed force, proper only to the lay world (and, within this group, only to the lay *potentiores*)? There is no doubt that in Odo's mind there was a real distinction between the duties and the virtues of those who belonged to the lay and ecclesiastical orders. It was the place of the powerful layman to pick up where the church stopped, precisely at the point where armed force had to be used. Yet, on another level, it was a distinction without a difference. Gerald can hardly be said to have used his arms. His real power came from God; his real coercive strength had its basis in his virtue, not in his sword. The same was true of the monk Odo. Without picking up arms, he kept the peace between princes. Through his patience he kept the peace of the monastery. Through his virtue he imposed his brand of monasticism on other houses whose monks were often (originally) hostile to him. Thus, for example, through his humility Odo "conquered" Fleury:

> When the brethren [of Fleury] heard about [Odo's and his followers'] coming, some, after putting on their swords, went up to the roof of the buildings, as if they were about to strike their enemies with stones and missiles from the sky. Others, protected by shields and putting on their swords, took guard at the entrance to the monastery, saying that they would die before they would allow those men to enter or receive an abbot

from another order. . . . But a short time later Father Odo, unknown to everyone, mounts an ass's colt and quickly starts to go to the monastery. The bishops and those who were associates with them together with their own companions were running after him shouting: "Where are you going, Father? Are you perhaps looking for death? Don't you see that they are ready to kill you? Indeed, at the hour you reach them you will die. Do you want to give them joy at your death and give us deathly sorrow?"—sending these and words of this sort after him. But, as Scripture says, "The just man, bold as a lion, shall be without terror" (Prov. 28.1); Once the journey began, they could not stop him in any way. I am about to say a marvelous thing: when he approached and was recognized by those who knew him before, those who were resisting then were immediately moved and changed, so that I can say without doubt: "This is the change of the right hand of the most High" (Ps. 77.11). In fact, after they threw down their arms, they quickly went out to meet him and his feet were embraced.[15]

In this passage were all the elements of the Geraldian battle. Odo's enemies went at him with armed force, but the divine power, the right hand of the most High, intervened and turned Odo's foolhardy act into an effective maneuver. It was, moreover, an act of justice; indeed, John was reminded of the scriptural simile between the just man and the lion. The virtue that subsumed both patience and justice was charity, and just as Gerald was interested in quashing not his enemies but their vices, so Odo's real ambition was to save the souls of the monks at Fleury.[16] As will later become clear, that goal was inextricably bound up with Odo's monastic reforms. When, not quite a century later, Abbot Odilo's biographer, Jotsaldus, stressed Odilo's justice, his selfless conduct on behalf of others, he was not at all contradicting John of Salerno's emphasis on patience.[17] The difference was that Jotsaldus's Odilo, unlike John's Odo, had many responsibilities in the outer world to attend to: he had to protect widows and orphans as well as monks. When, at the Council of Anse in the late tenth century, the Cluniacs took over judicial and peace-keeping functions in the area immediately contiguous to the monastery, they were—from their point of view—simply making explicit some of the notions of power implicit in the perception of reality they already held.[18] Power, derived from God, was shared out amongst many. Social *ordo* was less crucial than *virtus.*

Virtue was God's alone, but men might, by grace, participate in it. In Odo's Gerald, this participation was expressed and proved by linking every element in his life literally to a divine commandment and viewing the sequences of these now symbolic acts as pious rituals. This same interpretation of obedience was implied in John's ideal of monastic life. If one recalls that Christ entered Jerusalem on an *asellus,* as ass's colt, then even the passage just quoted may be an example of literal adherence to divine—in this case Scriptural—precept. John's picture, which used such concrete elements of symbolic significance as the *asellus,* linked Odo's ride to Fleury with Christ's ride to the place of his execution.

But an emphasis on scrupulous adherence to divine law at Cluny may be inferred from more than a close reading of the symbolic imagery of the *Vita Odonis.* Indeed, if this were the only proof, it might well show a mentality not so much of literal obedience as of imitation or, indeed, of typology. Clearly Odo's arrival at Fleury was understood as a figure for Christ's arrival at Jerusalem. But the purpose of Odo's journey was something different—it was to demand literal obedience from the monks. Odo (and the bishops who supported him) were determined to impose the Benedictine *Rule*—as they understood it—on the monastic *ordo* of Fleury. The *Rule* was both a constitution and a series of precepts, and the question of its interpretation at Cluny is crucial for understanding Cluniac literalism. Indeed, in one way or another, this is the primary issue of the present chapter, and must be introduced by a word or two on the place of the *Rule* in monasteries before Cluny's day.

Although a few textbooks still claim the contrary, scholarly opinion is now generally agreed that the *Rule,* written in the sixth century by St. Benedict of Nursia, was not normative in Gaul until the time of the Carolingian king, Louis the Pious (814–840). Louis's monastic reformer, Benedict of Aniane (who, significantly, adopted the very name of Benedict), organized, unified, and centralized the Carolingian monasteries under the aegis of the *Rule.* [19] He confronted the opposition of his contemporary abbots and monks, who were accustomed to a rather disorderly variety of monastic customs, styles, and idiosyncracies.[20] In the end, Benedict of Aniane compromised a bit. In the crucial realm of the liturgy, for example, he allowed certain psalms and an Office of the Dead to be added to the *opus Dei* (the liturgical round) provided in the *Rule.* [21] The chaotic conditions of the ninth century prevented any long-term or systematic imposition of Benedict's reforms, but his reputation as the promulgator of an ideal monastic *ordo* persisted. It surfaced, in fact, in the *Vita Odonis,* where John claimed that the customs instituted by Benedict of Aniane were kept by the monks at Baume under Berno.[22] But, as we shall see, the *Rule* was not for the Cluniacs—as it was for Benedict of Aniane—an exclusive and essentially complete norm.

There is no question, however, that the *Rule* was highly esteemed in early Cluniac circles. Indeed, as might be expected, the Cluniacs' obedience to the *Rule* was in some cases so scrupulous as to border on literalism. John described Odo as following the *Rule* even before he became a monk:

> It happened meanwhile that, while [Odo] was reading volumes of various books, he had come to the *Rule* of blessed Benedict. And when he wanted to go through it quickly, he struck upon that place in which is the precept that monks ought to sleep clothed. But not understanding the meaning clearly, he lay down clothed [in his day clothes] for three years. Thus not yet a monk, he bore gently the yoke of monks. He took care to obey the precepts of that saint [Benedict].[23]

The care to obey in this case was misplaced, for John's words indicate that Odo later realized that the *Rule* provided for both day and night tunics.[24] But John did not imply that Odo's response was misguided. On the contrary, he pointed out that Odo had thereby taken on the yoke of monks. He knew how to obey the precepts; he had only to get the precepts right! Later, when Odo was a monk and an abbot, he obeyed the *Rule*'s injunction to keep the head bowed with such perfect literalism that he never looked up. His brethren dubbed him "the digger."[25]

When Odo took in hand the reform of other monasteries, he considered it his job to institute the provisions of the *Rule* as he understood them. His experience at Fleury is a reminder that the imposition was not always welcome. At Fleury, Odo insisted on (among other things) the prohibition against eating the flesh of four-footed animals, but the brethren wanted to eat meat.[26] It was not the need for discipline in the ordinary sense that inspired Odo to insist on his position; it was the need for discipline in the Cluniac sense of adhering to the laws because of their divine origin. John reported on the dire consequences that Odo knew were preordained for monks who ate any animal meat. The food would stick in their throats and they would die a horrible death.[27] Similarly, Odo instituted a ritual washing of shoes to precede the *mandatum*, the ritual washing of feet called for in the *Rule*.[28] At least one monk at a house undergoing reform found this practice unprecedented and unnecessary. John of Salerno, turning to his readers as he defended the practice, said that it was proper and essential, especially since it fulfilled the provisions in the *Rule* concerned with caring for the sacred vessels and the property of the monastery.[29] Similarly, John took so seriously the *Rule*'s injunction to silence that he triumphantly told a miracle about some monks who refused to speak even when captured and questioned by Viking marauders. These law-abiding monks merited to see their own release and the death of their captors.[30]

It was, in fact, the lawlessness of the monk who doubted he had to wash his shoes that most incensed John. The monk had spoken up during the period when the *Rule* imposed silence. He was, in John's words, one of those men who "do not know how to live legally according to the law [and] are not afraid to turn their face away from its precepts."[31] The very same conception of the *Rule* as law is to be found in Odo's sermon on St. Benedict. There the *Rule* is called the work of a "legislator." But this was no secular lawmaker: he was God's amanuensis. Benedict was a new Moses for a new audience: instead of giving the Jews the laws of the Old Testament, Benedict gave the monks the *ordo* of the Holy Spirit.[32]

Thus far the Cluniac view seems to parallel the Anianian. But in the very identification of the *Rule* with God's law, the Cluniacs opened the door to an entirely different—because not exclusive—appreciation of the place of the *Rule* in the monks' lives. In that passage on the laudable muteness of the captured monks, the *Rule* functioned simply as John's initial ammunition. He had a virtual arsenal of precepts to defend his position on the importance of silence. In the style of a *florilegium* were invoked the laws of the Old Testament patriarchs and prophets, the example of Christ, and the exhortations of the evangelists, the Apostles, and Fathers Antony and Hilary. These sources were not invoked to show merely their compatibility with the *Rule;* rather the *Rule* was invoked as one of the many sets of God's laws.[33] Odo's sermon on St. Benedict presented the same idea. There had been, in the course of human history, a number of men who had decreed God's rules; some of these had given the particular commands suitable for monks; among these St. Benedict had been preeminent.

In point of fact, the standard of virtue at Cluny was not established only by the Benedictine *Rule* but also by divine commands from any number of sources. A typical example is Odo's penance as a young monk at Baume.[34] Odo's first act had been one of humility in the face of his unfair accusers. It was clearly a moment of the *imitatio Christi.*

Peter had established the general principle of Christ's patience long before:

> What is the glory if you allow yourself to be boxed on the ears while you are sinning? But if you bear up patiently while doing well, this is grace before God. For you are called to this, because Christ also suffered for us, leaving you an example, so that you might follow his footsteps. He did not sin nor was guile found in his mouth (Isa. 53:9); when he was cursed he did not curse; when he suffered, he did not threaten, but he handed himself over to those judging unjustly (1 Pet. 2:20–23).[35]

Such a passage did not require outright mimicry, but John was so anxious to show the association between Odo and Christ that he made the patterning literal. Thus, in a second episode of persecution by his brethren, Odo threw himself down in the posture of penance before abbot Berno, even though he was innocent, because (in the words of John) Odo "had come to follow Him who 'when he suffered did not threaten'."[36] And Odo's actions were not adhering solely to the injunctions of St. Peter. John reported that Odo was also thinking of the psalms, or rather of two particular lines from the psalms. The first was, "I have acted like a beast before You; and I am always with You" (Ps. 72:23).[37] These were the words which the psalmist applied to himself, the weak man who doubted God's justice and envied the tranquility of sinners. It was, in effect, Odo's recognition of his own sinfulness, despite the injustice of the immediate situation. The second line John quoted was "You have laid tribulations on our back, you have set men over our heads" (Ps. 65:11–12).[38] Here the psalmist recounted the ways in which God tested the Jews and brought them to triumph in the end. They were the very lines used in the *Rule* of St. Benedict in his discussion of patience.[39] John explicitly made the connection when he noted that Berno—who in this instance excommunicated Odo at the behest of the brethren—was being harsh with Odo precisely to test his patience. The net effect of all these precepts was to validate Odo's behavior through biblical injunctions and, in this particular case, through the *Rule* as well. Indeed, the chapter on patience in the *Rule* contained a slight digression: the lines from the Psalm "You have set men over our heads" was incidentally interpreted as biblical proof for the necessity of an abbot. The abbot himself, therefore, existed by divine command. With typical literalism, John's Odo understood Berno's order that Odo be excommunicated "so that he might not ask pardon from him any more that day" to mean that, although he personally might not beg pardon, he could ask the other monks to intercede with Berno on his behalf. Thus, the binding effects of divinely inspired commandments from many sources—the Bible, the *Rule,* the abbot—allowed Odo to test and prove his patience.

The evocation of all these complementary sources takes us far from Benedict of Aniane's conception of the monastic ideal. The disintegration of the Carolingian political world had its parallel in notions of monastic discipline. We can see how far things had changed by looking at John's interpretation of what Benedict of Aniane had done. Benedict, John said, "dedicated himself completely to the rules and institutions of the blessed Fathers, selected diverse customs from these authorities, and collected them into one volume."[40] John was referring to the *Concordia Regularum,* a pastiche of important passages from various monastic rules. Benedict of Aniane had written this book (his contemporary biographer tells us) in order to demonstrate "that nothing frivolous or empty had been put forth by St. Benedict."[41] For John, however, the volume was important for precisely the opposite reason: it lent the authority of Benedict of Aniane's name to a rich diversity of customs. It conveniently gathered together the many sacred directives that, taken as a whole, were the basis for the ideal monastic life.

The theoretical syncretism implied by this view found its concrete application in the Cluniac's perception of their daily life. John did not describe a liturgical round that adhered to the *Rule* alone, but one that took practices from many other sources. He described it with the satisfied air of a man who thought that the Cluniacs had done wisely and well. He pointed with pride to the debt that Baume (and presumably also Cluny) owed to Benedict of Aniane. He then went on to talk about monastic customs under Berno and to note that they had changed somewhat in his day. Under Berno, the monks had two daily masses, two litanies, and sang 75 psalms per day on ordinary days. On feast days the number increased to 138. But at Salerno in 943, the psalmody was a little different:

> we subtracted fourteen [from the 138 psalms] for the sake of weak souls, but that does not count the special prayers which our brethren repeat, which clearly seem to exceed the length of the psalter [150 psalms]. Similarly [that does not count] two masses and constant litanies.[42]

Whence these customs? Many may be traced to a monastic precedent. The special psalms were used under Benedict of Aniane. He, in
turn, was responding to prior custom. The daily recitation of a number
of psalms equivalent to the psalter had long predated him in numerous
monasteries. If the Cluniacs were, in effect, going back to those practices, they certainly were not deviating from indigenous historical tradition. The celebration of two masses per day was likewise nothing new:
such had been the practice at St.-Riquier, for example, in the early ninth
century.[43] But more important than finding precedents for each practice
at Cluny, Baume, and Salerno, is to know the animating principle of
choice, of incorporation, and of change for these practices. The constitu-
ent parts—though not the sequence in which they were arranged or,
necessarily, the particular significance ascribed to them—were drawn
from the stock-in-trade of Christian piety as it had developed over the
centuries. The psalmody went back to Jewish worship. The *Rule* had
incorporated these psalms into a daily ritual that was followed, in addition to other psalmody, at Cluny. The legislation of Benedict of Aniane
provided other pieces of the Cluniac lifestyle. Fragments of the liturgy
from past and contemporary houses were integrated into their round.
The animating principle of this eclecticism was a passion for ritualizing
divine commandments.

Custom itself could be part of divine law for the Cluniacs. John's
Odo told a cautionary tale about the monks at Tours who

> began to abandon their way [of life] and customs and to cor-
> rupt their life and purpose according to their own desires. For,
> abandoning their native and accustomed dress, they began to
> carry around cowls and tunics [that were] colored and flowing
> and ornamented with a cloak. . . . They were doing these and
> many similar things against the laws of the *Rule.*[44]

The result was God's wrath and the death of the entire community, save
one to tell the story. In this case, the *Rule* did indeed enjoin custom: it
stated that the monks should wear a habit that is "appropriate to the
place where the brethren live and is of moderate cost."[45]

This may have been one textual foundation for the Cluniacs' tendency to transform what was customary into law itself. But of course no
text was necessary; in the Cluniac view, whatever existed did so—
directly or indirectly—by divine decree. Custom, when associated with
a venerable institution or with clearly virtuous men, was divinely in-

spired. The point was made in the context of the miraculous. There was, for example, a custom at Berno's monastery in which the monks collected and ate all crumbs before the end of dinner. It was observed as scrupulously as the precepts of the *Rule* or the commands of the abbot. If zeal flagged, divine mercy drove the point home. One day a monk demonstrated the fate of the careless; he cried out on his deathbed that the Devil was testifying against him before God because he had let some crumbs fall from the table.[46] On another occasion, Odo was tardy in putting the crumbs into his mouth. Recognizing his fault, Odo prostrated himself in penance at Berno's feet. Then the miraculous happened: the crumbs were turned into pearls.[47] It was a pretty anecdote, but implicitly, it told the monks what had to be done. By the same token, miracles about the terrible deaths of monks who did not follow the *Rule* resulted, John's Odo said, in the restoration of monasticism according to the *Rule;* the punishment taught the lesson.[48]

It was not the particulars of the practices but their presumed source in divine decree that was important to the Cluniacs. This did not rule out change. On the contrary, change and divergence were virtually built into the system. For the Cluniacs, the important question was what the divine directives were, and the divine commands, in their view, were constantly being revealed and refined for men by God, thus necessitating the creation of new forms and (sometimes) the putting aside of old forms. John of Salerno could speak of new practices at his monastery without implying anything scandalous.[49] When St. Benedict appeared in a vision to a monk at Fleury, Odo instructed the brethren there to spend that day "in spiritual hymns and prayer."[50] Evidently he was asking them to do something out of the ordinary, but it was, after all, a response to an extraordinary event. At the end of the tenth century, Abbot Odilo, for similar reasons, instituted a new, yearly festival of All Souls.[51] New practices could be created as long as they expressed God's laws.

It is clear that God's laws were to be found not only in Scripture, in the fathers, and in the *Rule,* but also in visions, miracles, customs, and of course, the lives of saints. That all of these were to be obeyed was (and is) a precept of any Christian life. But the Cluniacs took it literally; they meant to live a legislated life. This was the substance of Odo's words concerning St. Benedict's *Rule.* This was the import of John's marshalling legions of authoritative precepts in the *Vita Odonis* to justify practices at Cluny. It is quite possible that, from our point of view, John was simply clutching at whatever appropriate commandments he could find to suit his purposes. But John gave no evidence of seeing the matter that way. Like a new Matthew describing his Savior's every act as a fulfillment of prophecy, so John considered everything Odo did as obedience to God's commandments. The most minor incident was occasion enough for John to make the point. Did Odo turn off the road to Rome in order to consult his friend Adhegrinus (the knight-turned-monk we have already met) about the restoration of St. Paul's? John did not justify the detour on its particular merits. He told the reader that Odo visited Adhegrinus "so that he might do what is written: 'Do everything with counsel, and you won't regret it after you have done it' " (Ecclus. 32:24).[52]

With this emphasis on life monitored by law, it is not surprising that there should be a new phenomenon in Western monasticism—the customary—nor that Cluny should be among the first to produce such a book.[53] The two earliest Cluniac customaries probably date from c. 1000–1015 and c. 1000–1030 respectively.[54] It is important to note their tone. They were not written as descriptions of the everyday life of the monastery, though they may provide a glimpse into that life. Rather, they were written in the subjunctive and/or imperative modes. They told the monks how things—mainly liturgical things but much else besides—ought to be done. In short, they were paradigms, not portrayals. Doubtless a good deal of the specific content in these customaries is not germane to the tenth century; we have seen that ritual could change at Cluny. But they are useful to illustrate at least a process: the process of legislative expansion. We know, from John, that a similar process of accretion went on in the tenth century at Salerno. Moreover, the first customary could not have sprung forth fully blown between 1000 and 1015. It must reflect at least some practices from the tenth century. The second customary is based on the first. Thus, they may be used as supplementary evidence. One example may serve to illustrate the way in which behavior at Cluny was prescribed ever more explicitly, regulating hitherto unregulated time.

In the first customary, the time just before None during an ordinary winter day was described as follows:

[Near the time of None] let them then celebrate mass. After Mass let the hebdomadaries and the cellarer and the reader go into the refectory to receive a snack. But let the other brothers sit in the choir and let the little signal sound again and let them chant None.[55]

In the next revision of Cluniac usages (1000–1030), the details of essentially the same series of events were made part of the legislation:

> When it is nearly the time for None, let the sacristan sound [the signal] and after the prayer is completed, let a child begin the litany and let the hebdomadaries go to dress themselves. When the litany is finished let them say mass. After this let the sacristan sound [the signal] again, and let them say a prayer and let them sit in the choir and read until the priest has taken off his vestments. Meanwhile, let the hebdomadaries and the reader receive a snack in the kitchen. But when the priest has returned to the others in the choir, let the sacristan sound the bell for the third time and let them chant None.[56]

Thus, the time before None had its set of prescriptions. We do not know why these particular ones were chosen; the most probable explanation is that they were simply convenient customs and then came to be considered necessary. John had already interpreted the collecting of crumbs as an example of this sort of evolution. By incorporating such seemingly incidental matters as the sounding of the signal into an account of the ordinary and ferial rites at Cluny, the customaries reveal the implicit ideal that all behavior be part of the divine worship. One is reminded forcefully of Odo's Gerald.

The customaries, the *Vita Geraldi,* and the *Vita Odonis* were of a piece in their view that the ritualization of norms—divinely ordained norms —was the corrective to the human condition. The liturgy loomed large in all these works because it was already a ritual associated with devotion. But there were also parallels in these texts in the ritualization of daily tasks and in the association of these more banal acts with divine injunctions. The earliest Cluniac customary speaks in the same breath of prayers, lessons, offices, and of going to bed, putting on shoes, washing hands, eating, and (as in the passage above) taking snacks.[57] The *Vita Geraldi* describes how Gerald integrated his prayers with the other tasks in his life; his time was carefully scheduled; his actions—each linked to a divine command—were planned. Similarly, the *Vita Odonis* shows Odo's father, Abbo, teaching the young Odo how to mingle his warfare with liturgy. Abbo's suggestions—to alternate the hunt and armed exercise by day with vigils by night—did not satisfy Odo. But, in his own way, Abbo, too, tried to ameliorate sin through ritual. And, of course, Odo was an institutor of rituals and perfect in his observance of rules.

Gerald's rituals had been both a sign of his love for God and—because he was able to carry them out—a sign of God's love for him. Blessed by God, he wielded God's power. This power was exercised on two levels. On the first, the physical level, Gerald prospered, his word at the law court was obeyed, he conquered all his enemies, and he saved the lives and goods of his dependents. On the second, the spiritual level, Gerald set an example of virtue for his neighbors so that they might be saved. He overcame the malice of the violent. He freed the poor from the clutches of sinners. He conquered his own vices: he was a veritable "cedar of paradise."[58] Moreover, having performed many miracles in his own lifetime, his power continued to be demonstrated after his death: "It is not incredible that he now frees the possessed from the demons," Odo wrote.[59] Gerald's final power was to intercede on behalf of sinners back on earth. Odo was explicit about the divine participation involved in this:

> But since [O Lord] "Your eyes see the imperfection of the church" (Ps. 138:16) and "its stones shall have pity for the earth" (Ps. 101:15), we beg that those who are called "stones" on account of the solidity of their morals may deign to help us who are "earth" because of our wickedness. [We beg] that we who do not have the garment of justice may embrace the stones so that we might be able to cover our nakedness with their merits. Therefore, may this servant of Yours [i.e., Gerald] direct to us the love of mercy which Your charity put into him. And may he look down affectionately from that eternal court of the capitol in which he now resides among the consuls of the sky to this vale of tears which he has left. May he hear the prayers of each, and may he meet the necessities of all in Your presence, with the assistance of our Lord Jesus Christ, your Son.[60]

Of course, the power of the saints—including their ability to bring about miracles in the physical world, their saving of souls, their conquest of the demons—was one of the common and traditional points of hagiography. Traditional, too, was the conception of the virtues that rooted them in well-known norms (such as ascetic withdrawal) believed to be founded on the *imitatio Christi*. What was new in Cluniac sources was the legalistic interpretation of that imitation. In the *Vita Geraldi*, Gerald showed his virtue by obeying all the appropriate, divinely ordained precepts. Along with this obedience came power. John's view of virtue in the *Vita Odonis* was similarly literal. It remains, therefore, only to show that for John, too, obedience to the commands of God was accompanied by power.

Several examples from John's book make the point explicitly. One of these has already been mentioned (p. 91). Monks captured by the Vikings observed the customary period of silence even in the face of a brutal attack by the barbarians' leader. John explained the monks' seeming obstinacy: "This was being done by them not in any sort of deceit but rightly and in observance of the holy *Rule* under which they clearly wanted to die and to live and never to deviate from it."[61] The power of their obedience was instantaneously manifested in the practical results:

> But the hand of the Almighty immediately turned [the Viking's] excited spectacle into grief. As soon as the barbarian came close to [the monks], the horse on which he was sitting sprang back sideways and threw and dashed his own rider to the ground. Immediately a deadly fever followed the blow.[62]

The rule of silence was evidently a test case for John. He maintained that: "The life of a monk is something only to the extent that he is zealous to be under silence. But with that lost, whatever he will have thought he does well or honorably will be nothing, according to the teaching of the fathers."[63] In another of John's tales, a monk who maintained silence when confronted by a thief merited that the thief be frozen in his tracks until the period of silence was ended.[64]

The moral—insofar as these experiences may be said to stand for the outcome of literal obedience in general—was the potency of virtue. The same principle applied when Odo was obedient to the injunction to give to the poor:

> Because [Odo] used to give himself to all who asked, all things used to be supplied to him by the will of God. He always had that precept of Tobias before his eyes: "Do not turn your face from any poor man and give to all who ask of you" (Tob. 4:7).[65]

Power and piety, in conclusion, were linked at Cluny as in the world at large. In both instances power, understood to be divine in origin, was tapped through scrupulous adherence to laws, also understood as divine. The particular acts legislated by those laws were different at different times, for different social orders (e.g., laymen as opposed to monks), and for different positions of power (e.g., abbots as opposed to brethren; rich as opposed to poor). Integrated into a daily round, these acts became ritualized, and since they were devotional, they became almost part of the liturgy. Cluniac legalism evolved naturally into a more and more highly organized way of life, as the customaries show. Such a life-style had symbolic significance. While much of the world outside the monastery was in disorder, Cluny was predictable. While much outside was new, Cluny held on to old-fashioned norms and tied new ones to the most revered source people knew: the Divinity itself. We have seen that people supported Cluny precisely when their own conditions of life changed. The conjunction between the circumstances of Cluny's supporters and Cluny's spirituality is the subject of Chapter 5.

5 | LOOKING AT CLUNY IN CONTEXT

From what has been said thus far, the Cluniac ideal may be summed up fairly neatly as a form of legalism. Our understanding of the context which fostered that ideal is less tidy. In Chapter 2, the observation was made that many of the men and women who supported Cluny had experienced a shift in status and fortune. But the significance of that observation was not—and is not—immediately apparent. Comprehending its meaning, then, is the first task of this chapter.

It is at this point that the insights of modern sociology are of help. Where medievalists—following the metaphors of the times they study —may see the revolution of Fortune's wheel, sociologists may see the experience of anomie. The concept of anomie is useful here for three reasons. First, it links together the seemingly disparate experiences of those Mâconnais allodists who were rapidly descending the social ladder with would-be or newly constituted kings, dukes, counts, and castellans. Second, the concept immediately opens up to us a large corpus of literature on the causes and consequences of the anomic condition.[1] Of course, this generally pertains to the modern world; sociologists have not, certainly, explored the issue in the Middle Ages. But that does not mean it is inapplicable to that period. Although associated with (indeed considered endemic in) industrial society, the idea of anomie is not dependent on one particular historical situation. Industrialism is a potent, but not the only, context for sudden swings in status. Third, the concept of anomie allows us to make comparisons: in particular, it allows us to set against the modern responses to anomie—which, by and large, sociologists have connected to the most deleterious social ills—at least one constructive manifestation in the early Middle Ages.

The pioneer in the use and elaboration of the term anomie for the modern social sciences was Émile Durkheim, who worked at the end of the nineteenth century.[2] Struck, as was Marx before him, with the boom-and-bust convulsions of Europe's newly industrialized economy, Durkheim, unlike Marx, did not propose a countervailing economic vision. Instead, he chose to concentrate on the effect of the one that existed, and among his discoveries was a correlation between sudden economic crises and the suicide rate. The peculiarity in this correlation was its irrationality: it was not simply that unhappy victims of economic depressions did away with themselves, but rather that the suicide rate jumped just as significantly for people riding the crest of a sudden economic boom.[3] In short, the decisive factor was "declassification": a sudden, unexpected, unprepared-for shift from any given *status quo* to any unknown, uncharted status. What was needed then was a new adjustment, a finding of new bearings, a discovery of new behaviors. What often happened instead of, or prior to, this optimal reorientation was a period of anomie, of disequilibrium, and of deregulation. People's behavior simply went haywire, for there was nothing to restrain them. Their passions went wild because they no longer knew how they must behave; their wants outstripped their needs because they no longer knew what they might reasonably desire. For some, the end result was suicide.

Implicit in Durkheim's argument were two assumptions: first, that human beings were passionate and greedy by nature, and were restrained and regulated only by social norms; second, that anomie was a condition of crisis. Both of these assumptions were challenged, at one blow, in a seminal paper by Robert Merton.[4] Industrial society, still a novelty in Durkheim's day, was, for the New Yorker Merton writing in 1938, a well-entrenched system. The same entrenchment was true of deviant behavior. Merton reasoned that something must be built into the system that could explain widespread dissatisfaction and deviance. Merton objected to Durkheim's assumptions about the naturalness of deviance. What Durkheim considered innate, Merton considered induced. For Merton, human nature was just as precisely determined by the social structure as restraining norms were for Durkheim. Retaining anomie as the explanation for non-normative behavior, then, Merton transformed Durkheim's scheme from human nature vs. normative crisis to a scheme of normative system vs. normative system. Specifically, Merton identified a disjunction between cultural goals (which, in American society at least, included the goal of success) and the ways that society provided to meet those goals. People conforming to the norm that told them to "get ahead" found few normative avenues by which to do so. But turning to alternative means meant abandoning social norms. Thus, the social structure, with its double set of ill-fitting norms, forced people to become social deviants and to live without norms.[5] Anomie was, therefore, not a state of mind for Merton but rather a condition of being. Indeed, the anomie was already built into the system, the disjunction itself being a form of anomie. The choice for the individual was, by and large, deviant behavior or retreat.[6]

Merton's discussion of anomie became the basis for most subsequent studies of the phenomenon in the modern world. His hypothesis was tested over and over again in the areas of alcoholism, drug abuse, juvenile delinquency, white-collar crime, and lower-class crime.[7] More recently, however, sociologists have fixed on functional responses to anomie. This will be discussed below.[8] It is necessary at this point to concentrate on the causes, not the consequences, of anomie. Merton's study has shown a way in which the social order may be understood to be the key to both norms and human aspirations. A human nature need not be postulated; it is necessary simply to look at the society men live in.

The society of the early benefactors of Cluny was, above all, structured for warriors. It had always been so. Duby has described warfare as the mainstay of the primitive Germanic economy: it provided the wealth that, redistributed in a round of obligatory gift-giving, held the society together.[9] Weapons were the carriers of symbolic significance. They may have been given upon the attainment of a man's majority;[10] they were most certainly buried with old men and even young boys.[11] Education, following suit, was primarily military.[12] But pillaging and plundering expeditions were not led by just any would-be mighty warrior; they were led by kings. Of course, the king had to be effective on the battlefield. If he was not, he might well lose his crown. Thus, in the eighth century, when the Carolingians took over royal power, they justified their usurpation by pointing out that the Merovingian line had lost its "vigor."[13]

The amalgamation of this warrior culture with the culture of the Romans served to enhance the authority of the king. His position as tribal leader had been ordinarily to lead the army, give generously of his share of plunder, and (through his magical and divine lineage) provide the tribe with luck and prosperity.[14] After settling in *Romania,* kings were newly confronted with the duties of Roman governors, the expectations of Roman-educated churchmen, and the model of Roman emperors.[15] There is no need to discuss the slow development of the notion of sovereignty here.[16] Suffice to say that by the time of Charlemagne the king saw himself, and was seen by others, as the upholder of public order and justice. Royal power was not just mighty; it was the human source of all other human power. In practical terms, that conception turned the king into an administrator. He set up legal, economic, and military institutions; he set up governmental functionaries, delegating his authority.[17]

As it turned out, these developments were confronted by the countervailing force of the family. Always the family had commanded at least as much loyalty as the king, but the two structures had worked together complementarily, both protecting and enriching the individual.[18] Now, however, the new goals of the monarchy were inadvertently transforming family relationships, ironically, not to the benefit of the monarch. Charlemagne tried to place his functionaries in parts of the empire separate from the areas where their ancestral lands lay. His plan was to assign these lands and offices as a temporary trust.[19] However, once ensconced in their new, lofty positions, the officials saw the advantages, and they tried to hold on to their trust as if it were a private possession.[20] The new lands and offices were incorporated into the family inheritance.[21] The Viking invasions and Carolingian dynastic wars served to encourage this process.[22] The ninth century saw inheritance, not appointment, as the primary way by which legitimate claim to lands, titles, and duties might be had.

As Duby has shown in the Mâconnais, the change from trust to inheritance did not necessarily lead to a breakdown in the structure of the Carolingian social order. Allodists and peasants remained independent, free men. Prior to the time of Otto-William, the count-by-inheritance of Mâcon (actually, originally from the viscomital family), continued to exercise his office as of old. He carried on essentially the same sort of functions in the same way, and with the same sort of general community cooperation, as the count-by-appointment had in the early ninth century. However, the situation was potentially unstable; new opportunities were present for an enterprising, powerful, or well-placed man. Otto-William was a newcomer to the region who married the widow of the last, childless, count. He began a new line of hereditary counts in the Mâconnais. While Otto-William engaged in wars over his claim to the duchy of Burgundy, the castellans in the region seized the moment to enhance their power. As has been seen, in some areas powerful men grasped at the chance sooner, perhaps because the opportunities were clearer. The south of France and Jurane Burgundy were loosened early from Carolingian hegemony, while Italy had never been firmly under its sway either institutionally or sentimentally.[23] At the same time, there were strong forces motivating men to grasp at power. There was, first, the warrior tradition, which tied success and leadership to conquest. Second, there was the family tradition, which demanded the expansion of the patrimony.[24] However built into the culture, these values and traditions were in conflict with the institutions and norms of the Carolingian state. That is, they flew in the face of royal appointment, of public office, and of the administrative district of *pagus* and county.

In Merton's terms, what has been described here are social goals (land, title, extended patrimony, power) that were induced by the norms of the social structure. At the same time, the normative opportunities available in this society to attain these goals were so limited as to produce a disjunction. Inheritance was indisputably a norm, as was appointment. Some men, however, took advantage of the decrepit monarchical system to take other avenues. They neither inherited nor were appointed to their new positions. For the most part, they got their new status by force or by its threat. The rise of the castellans is a clear case in point; their new powers were directly associated with a military fortification. Other men, willy-nilly, experienced the consequences of the new mobility passively; it often affected them, as in the Mâconnais, by depriving them of their independence and incorporating them into a network of personal ties, as either serfs or vassals. One might, of course, find instances of such social changes by these very means at any period of the early Middle Ages. What was different about the tenth century was, first, the sheer number of men and women involved in this mobility, and second, the depth of social levels—from peasants to nobles—affected by it. The world that these men forged looked forward to the feudal one of the eleventh and twelfth centuries, not to the Merovingian and Carolingian order of the past.

Finding themselves, then, on avenues open but unauthorized, these men sought to follow more clearly sanctioned paths as well. They took pains, as we have seen in Chapter 2, to legitimize their new positions. Those who would be kings—like Rudolf of Burgundy and Hugh Capet —sought election, certainly a norm in early Germanic society. Others appropriated titles: Alberic became prince of Rome; Lambert became count of Chalon. Moreover, many sought to justify their appropriation: Lambert attributed his new status to God; Geoffrey Greymantle claimed the grace of the duke of France as well.[25] These men wanted the blessings of the church. Raoul's penance at Reims is one example. The sponsorship of monasteries reformed by Cluny is another.

We have suggested that the support of Cluny was a socially constructive response to anomie. However, thus far, it looks as if it was constructive only in the negative sense of not being destructive. Support of Cluny was not suicidal, nor was it (in any immediately clear way, at least) deviant. On the contrary, Cluny was the model of the proper, traditional, hence normative monastery.

At this point, therefore, it is necessary to discuss briefly what some sociologists have already identified as functional responses to anomie.[26] These may be categorized under four general headings: normative reactions, quest for community, normalization, and adaptive social control. Normative reactions, as defined by Becker, is the attempt on the part of a group or institution to reaffirm old norms.[27] The quest for community is a way of circumventing the alienation engendered by anomie: it leads to subsocieties in which the anomie of the larger community is rendered less acute by the solidarity of the smaller.[28] Normalization, on the other hand, involves the attempt to turn deviation itself into a norm: new rules are elaborated that legitimize the hitherto illegitimate behavior.[29] Adaptive social control, as formulated by Nett, is less extreme than this: social institutions sometimes are able to integrate deviant behavior into the old norms. Close to this idea is that of Dubin's "typology of deviant adaptations" in which innovative substitutions for both norms and means are identified.[30]

In the context of its donors' anomie, Cluny answered each of these purposes, and with regard to the last point, Cluny's solution suggests a paradigm of adaptive social control somewhat different from that of either integration or substitution.

It is the normative reaction at Cluny that is most striking. People in new positions of status and power supported a monasticism devoted to mastering old traditions and adhering to manifold laws. They founded monasteries or renewed the endowments and religious lives of old ones. The Cluniacs imposed an *ordo* (their donors wanted them to do precisely this) that disciplined other monks to adhere to the exact rites that the Cluniacs themselves followed. Other monasteries followed idiosyncratic custom; at Cluny, custom was law. In this sense, Cluny's organization was the very antithesis of anomie.

If Cluny affirmed stability in the face of change, it also served to connect its donors with its solid bedrock of correct behavior. This association was implicit in any request the donor might make regarding prayers for his soul. In addition, the quest for community was explicitly met at Cluny, as at other monasteries, through systems of confraternities.[31] These gave the laymen and bishops who joined them a vicarious part in the observances and prayers of the monks, linking them both to the monastic community and to the community of saints. Confraternities evolved into a particularly well-developed institution at Cluny during the eleventh century.

These were functional responses, but they were not particularly socially constructive. They point to a formalism for its own sake, or for the sake of a tradition-seeking clientele. In this sense, Cluny's significance was to give the semblance of order to those experiencing disorder. However, there was more to Cluny's adherence to old laws than this. Cluniac writings and daily round presented the possibility and the realization of disorder turned into order. Implicitly, this served to justify the fragmentation of power. We must recall that the mobility of the ninth and tenth centuries resulted in the sharing out—or, at any rate, the dispersal—of power into many hands. The Cluniac model of order made a virtue of this disintegration. God's directives, even for the monastery, were not to be found in one place, one law, one man; they were refracted, like the sun's beams. The world, in its own way, also had many sources of borrowed light. Here God acted like a puppeteer, synchronizing and coordinating the efforts of seemingly independent strong men by the taut strings of His many laws.

Taken at face value, this is an example of normalization at its most self-serving.[32] It justified any seizure of power, any imposition of seigneurial rights, any appropriation of title, and any oppression engendered by these acts. But, as we have seen, this was not the point at all. The Cluniacs' form of legalism, both within and without the monastery, did not turn deviant behavior into the norm. Instead, it incorporated only certain, select aspects of the new behavior into a now transformed value system. In this way, the Cluniac life-style and ideology together provided an instructive example of adaptive social control. Within the monastery, rules did not legitimize just any behavior. Above all, rules were used to mitigate war: the individual, warring within himself, became virtuous; the monastic community, bickering within itself, became orderly; the society of professed monks, each adhering to a different standard, became unanimous.[33] Odo's patience, the touchstone of his obedience to God's precepts, put an end to petty feuds within the monastery and overcame the armed opposition of the monks at Fleury.

All this was behind the formalism at Cluny because the Cluniacs believed that human willfulness would lead to violence if uncontrolled by the harnesses of God's laws. On the other hand, if God's laws were followed, violence and injustice would be contained and virtue and patience fostered. The mode of containment was neither utterly repressive nor indiscriminately all-embracing, but rather was carefully delimiting. The Cluniacs tried neither to stamp out the problems they saw in human nature nor to justify everything as proper, but rather to control and channel behavior. Because of their view of God's creative role, they did not condemn anything outright; they saw positive possibilities inherent in all things. The trick was to discipline the negative aspects. The rhinoceros had to be bound. Thus, within the monastery, individual idiosyncracy was not tolerated as such, but it might well be incorporated into the daily round as law. Violence, too, was not allowed as such; but coercion was part and parcel of Cluniac reforming activities. The use of power was not stamped out but was allowed in certain prescribed circumstances, as when the monks of Fleury were forced— for their own good—to follow the Cluniac way of life.

This view of social amelioration was the more complete (and perhaps the more efficacious) because it promised a reward in the end: success. Cluniac legalism was perceived as the way to tap the powers inherent in the Christian cosmology. As we have seen, when the monks adhered to the law, they always triumphed.

All this is still more clear in the Cluniac teaching on the delimiting of armed power. Once again their legalism mitigated the extremes of wanton violence on the one hand and passive victimization on the other. In the Cluniac perception of the well-ordered world, fighting was not banned but was circumscribed by conventions of motive, time, place, and form. This had immediate practical effect on Cluny's supporters, for one salient fact of Cluniac monasteries was their immunity from lay domination.[34] The subtlety of this limitation on power may best be seen in the Mâconnais at the end of the tenth century, when the castellans, now with new seigneurial status, were forbidden by the Council of Anse to enter Cluny's central sanctuary but were given alternative, outlying lands to protect.[35]

Ambition, too, was delimited by considerations of charity, considerations that were discoverable in divine precepts, as the example of St. Gerald was meant to show. With both violence and ambition now tamed, illegitimate, uncertain, or innovative forms of power on the one hand, and loss of power on the other, found justification in a new scheme of things. For, in the Cluniac view, although there was divine origin in all power and in all lack of power, at the same time each condition had responsibilities attached to it. These responsibilities were not built into the social fabric, known by men because stable conditions and norms of behavior implied them. On the contrary, they were built into the divine order of things, knowable from books and traditions independent of any particular social or political organization. Gerald of Aurillac did not need to be the vassal of anyone but God, but there his obedience had to be complete. Social anomie was tamed by God's good laws. Once again, the final justification for the restraint demanded by this program of behavior was the success promised when it was properly carried out.

In Merton's terms, Cluny offered a new institutionalized means toward the goal of gaining new power. It neither integrated deviant behavior wholesale, nor substituted new behavior for it, but rather delimited deviation. This adaptation may be viewed as bipartite: it involved the rejection of certain forms of antisocial behavior along with the extraction and fostering of many aspects of these same behaviors.[36]

Sociological theory makes no claim, nor is it implied here, that this sort of process was deliberate or even conscious on the part of the Cluniacs or the clientele they served. The question of Cluny's significance—the problem of this book—is quite different from the question of Cluny's purpose—the problem of the monks and their patrons. Cluny's significance must be discovered from disparate kinds of written sources and an analysis of circumstances. The supporters of Cluny provide the connection between those circumstances and Cluniac ideals. These people admired and fostered Cluny's legalistic mentality when they called upon its abbots to reform the monasteries they set up. They demanded the Cluniac style of doing things. There is no reason to believe that they misperceived its message; the Cluniacs claimed, after all, to have found the formula for success. At the very least, its donors wanted to associate themselves with the keepers of this formula: they founded or endowed Cluniac monasteries for the salvation of their souls.

The importance of Cluny's ideas for reforming their donors is another question. The answer is not known. It is clear that the abbots talked to their supporters: Odo and Majolus were known for hobnobbing with kings, princes, and great men. It was for that reason that Brackmann called the Cluniacs political maneuverers. Odo gave sermons, and part of his *Collationes* was, as we have seen, in the form of an exhortation to the *potentiores.* He wrote the *Vita Geraldi* as a model for the men of Gerald's *ordo.* Clearly he did not think he was writing in a vacuum; indeed he (and others who wrote about him) thought that he was an effective force in the world. Moreover, Cluny's participation in the Council of Anse at the end of the tenth century is important. At that council were spelled out some of the delimiting rules for the clergy and laity that have been associated here with Cluny, but that may well have been shared in other circles.

Yet it would be wrong to equate Cluny's role with that of social reform as it is thought of today.[37] Inherent in the world-view of the Cluniacs was a basic belief in original sin and therefore in the impossibility of man effecting man's reform. On the contrary, Cluny provided an exhortatory paradigm, not a plan of action.[38] This is very different from—but not inferior to—the modern understanding of a constructive response to anomie. The Cluniacs rejected anomie literally with their lawfulness (*anomos* means without law); they held on to the old norms. At the same time, they elaborated a paradigm on which new and adaptive forms of behavior might be based for the new, non-Carolingian world. Cluny confronted problems of violence, oppression, and political disintegration. At one and the same time, it connected these issues to past traditions, justified certain aspects of them in the present, and reinterpreted them for the future. All of these problems, and their solutions, were related. For clarity let us distinguish them here.

1. VIOLENCE: Armed violence was part of the Germanic tradition. It was also part of the Christian *psychomachia,* but the *psychomachia* had nothing to do with men fighting men. Indeed, the rejection of worldly warfare was a *topos* in hagiography and a condition of monastic life.

However, Odo acknowledged the necessity of armed force in his discussion of the potentates and in his portrait of Gerald of Aurillac. He linked Gerald's fighting both to the hagiographical tradition of the bloodless victory and to the tradition of the *psychomachia,* where virtue fights vice. For Odo, violence was virtuous when it defended the poor, supported the excommunications of the church, and resisted the malicious. This was a reinterpretation of the significance of violence against men, for now delimited, human violence was in fact made an integral part of lay devotional life. Lay warfare (not just royal warfare) became an arm of the church. The Council of Anse, with its provision for lay protectors, made this explicit for Cluny.

2. OPPRESSION: The oppression of the poor by the rich was lamented in the Bible. In the Augustinian tradition, it was linked to God's grace as an earthly trial and purgative. The Cluniacs, like Augustine, justified oppression as a goad to patience. However, they delimited that patience by the corrective of justice. Hence, they reinterpreted oppression: the just man was to oppress oppressors. In the world at large, this meant that men in a position to impose their will had the duty to be vigilantes. In the monastery, this attitude justified the creation of a network of monastic houses reformed—by force if necessary—to behave in the proper way.

3. POLITICAL DISINTEGRATION:[39] The tradition here was in fact an ideal: one universal monarchy. It derived some of its force from the model of the Roman empire, some from the Old Testament kings of Israel, and some from the memory of Charlemagne. The Cluniacs connected the rise of new men and the dispersal of power into many hands to this tradition by looking to the theoretical source behind all power, namely the One God. Political disintegration was an appearance, not the reality; God ruled behind the scenes. The use of power by disparate men, howsoever risen to their position, was thus justified as right and proper, but this justification, once again, involved severe limitations. Power had to be exercised as Christ commanded and, in fact, had to be exercised as part of a life of obedience to Christ. The many laws that this involved were available to special men like Gerald of Aurillac through God's grace and through his study of the Bible. The laws were available to other men through the example of a man like Gerald, through the provisions of peace councils, such as the one at Anse, through the work

of men like Odo, through miracles, and through preaching the words of the Bible. In this way, the new political order was interpreted; it did not signify breakdown; it signified simply a more local mode in which God's power was now to be instituted. Reflecting that unitary source of order, men obeyed the same laws—God's laws—in every aspect of their lives. Hence, the Cluniac emphasis on ritual, both within and without the monastery.

In these ways the Cluniacs pointed one way to—and gave one model for—a chivalric code, the idea of the crusade, and government by responsible laymen. Hence, our final point: a case study of Cluny begins to suggest the enormous resourcefulness of the tenth century in dealing with changing conditions and the attendant problems of anomie, deviance, and disorder.[40]

Notes

NOTES TO THE INTRODUCTION

1. The charter is in A. Bernard and A. Bruel, eds., *Recueil des chartes de l'Abbaye de Cluny,* 6 vols. (Paris, 1876–1903) [hereafter *C*], 1 (no. 112): 124–28. Long dated 910, many recent scholars now date it 909.
2. The dates for abbatial tenure given here are only approximate. Most are based on the cartularies (n.1 above), which are unreliable and subject to a variety of interpretations. Most modern authors cite dates very close to those given here, varying by only one or two years; but see, for example,G. de Valous, "Cluny," *Dictionnaire d'histoire et géographie ecclésiastiques,* 13: 35–174, where the dates used are: Berno 909–27, Odo 927–42, Aymard 942–65, Majolus 948–994.
3. Urban II, *Epistola* 214 in *Patrologiae cursus completus. Series latina,* ed. J.-P. Migne, 221 vols. (Paris, 1844–88) (hereafter *PL*), 151: col. 486, echoing Matthew 5:14.

NOTES TO CHAPTER 1

1. M. Marrier and A. Duchesne, *Bibliotheca cluniacensis* (Paris, 1614). On the Maurists, cf. D. Knowles, *Great Historical Enterprises: Problems in Monastic History* (New York, 1963), pp. 32–62.
2. P. Lorain, *Histoire de l' abbaye de Cluny depuis sa fondation jusqu'à sa destruction à l'époque de la Révolution française* (1839; 2d ed., Paris, 1845); M. F. Cucherat, *Cluny au onzième siècle, son influence religieuse, intellectuelle et politique* (1850; 2d ed., Mâcon, 1873); J. H. Pignot, *Histoire de l'Ordre de Cluny depuis la fondation de l'abbaye jusqu'à la mort de Pierre-le-Vénérable (909-1157),* 3 vols. (Autun, 1868).
3. Lorain, *Histoire,* p. 5; he speaks of the "préjudices vulgaires" of the masses on p. i.
4. Cucherat, *Cluny,* p. 218.
5. Pignot, *Histoire,* 3: 508. Cf. Cucherat, *Cluny,* p. 168.
6. The importance of the leader was the organizing principle behind these histories of Cluny; the acts of its abbots served to define the role of the monas-

tery. Not surprisingly, the first modern biography of a Cluniac abbot derives from this period. Cf. A. L'Huillier, *Vie de St. Hugues, Abbé de Cluny, 1024–1109* (Solesmes, 1888).

7. Cucherat, *Cluny,* p. 172.

8. *C,* 1 [909]: 124–28.

9. Lorain, *Histoire,* p. 94; Cucherat, *Cluny,* p. 45; Pignot, *Histoire,* 3: 508.

10. The major seventeenth- and eighteenth-century collections of documents relating to Cluny were as follows: The writings and lives of the abbots, in Marrier and Duchesne, *Bibliotheca cluniacensis;* papal bulls relating to Cluny, in P. Simon, *Bullarium sacri ordinis cluniacensis* (Lyons, 1880); one of two customaries of Cluny from St. Hugh's time, Bernard's *Ordo cluniacensis,* in M. Herrgott, ed., *Vetus disciplina monastica* (Paris, 1726), pp. 134–364; the second customary, Ulrich's *Antiquiores consuetudines cluniacensis monasterii,* in L. d'Achery, ed., *Spicilegium; sive collectio veterum aliquot scriptorum,* 3 vols. (Paris, 1723), 1: 641ff.

11. Cf. . P. Gooch, *History and Historians in the Nineteenth Century* (London, 1913); D. Knowles, *Great Historical Enterprises,* pp. 63–98.

12. E. Sackur, *Die Cluniacenser in ihrer kirchlichen und allgemeingeschichtlichen Wirksamkeit bis zur Mitte des elften Jahrhunderts,* 2 vols. (Halle a.S., 1892–94).

13. The charters, in *C,* were later subjected to review and criticism by M. Chaume, "Observations sur la chronologie des chartes de Cluny," *Revue Mabillon* 16 (1926): 44–48; 29 (1939): 81–89, 133–42; 31 (1941): 14–19, 42–45, 69–82; 32 (1942): 15–20, 133–36; 38 (1948): 1–6; 39 (1949): 41–43; 42 (1952): 1–4. Before Sackur, the only specialized study of Cluny in German had concerned itself primarily with the Lotharingian monastic reform, attributing it to Cluny. See W. Schultze, *Forschungen zur Geschichte der Klosterreform im 10. Jahrhundert,* vol 1, *Cluniacensische und lothringische Klosterreform* (Halle a.S., 1883).

14. Sackur, *Die Cluniacenser,* 1: v.

15. On the reasons for his periodization, ibid., 1: vi.

16. On Cluny's role in the Gregorian reform, ibid., 2: 445ff.

17. J. Burckhardt, *Die Kultur der Renaissance in Italien, ein Versuch* (Basel, 1860).

18. Sackur, *Die Cluniacenser,* 1: 34–35. On the Viking invasions and their effects, ibid., 1: 9ff.

19. Ibid., 2: 438.

20. On Cluny's impact in Germany, ibid., 2: 449ff; in England, ibid., 1: vii; on its relations to the episcopacy, ibid., 2: 458.

21. Ibid., 1: 140. "Freilich gewährt die Durchführung der neuen Tendenzen ganz äusserlich betrachtet in den verschiedenen Reformbezirken ein unterschiedliches Ansehen; aber man darf nicht vergessen, dass diese Besonderheiten weniger durch eine innere der betreffenden reformatorischen Richtung innewohnende Kraft, als durch recht äusserliche und zufällige Umstände hervorgerufen wurden." His view was hotly debated in later historical studies. See below, pp. 17–19.

22. L. Chaumont, *Histoire de Cluny depuis les origines jusqu'à la ruine de l'Abbaye,* 2d ed. (Paris, 1911).

23. Cf. N. D. Fustel de Coulanges, *Histoire des institutions politiques de l'ancienne France,* 6 vols. (Paris, 1875–1892), 1: xi–xiv.

24. Chaumont, *Histoire de Cluny*, p. 52. Yet in 1923 Letonnelier, without acknowledging the new viewpoint argued by Sackur, wrote that Cluny's "grand idéal" had been "l'établissement du gouvernement pontifical de la théocratie." G. Letonnelier, *L' Abbaye exempte de Cluny et le Saint-Siège. Etude sur le developpement de l'exemption clunisienne des origines jusqu'à la fin du XIIIᵉ siècle* (Ligugé, 1923).

25. Académie de Mâcon, *Millénaire de Cluny*, Congrès d' histoire et d' archéologie tenu à Cluny, 10–12 September 1910, 2 vols. (Mâcon, 1910).

26. L. Lex, "Un office laïque de l'abbaye. La prévôté et crierie de Cluny," *Millénaire de Cluny*, 1: 404–15; A. Guépin, "La grande époque de Cluny. Ses causes. Sa fin au XIIᵉ siècle," ibid., 2: 211–30; P.-B. Egger, "Die Schweizerischen Cluniacenserkloester zur Zeit ihrer Bluete," ibid., 1: 374–86; L. Guilloreau, "Les prieurés anglais de l'Ordre de Cluny," ibid., 1: 291–373; M. Bauchond, "Un sermon de Saint Odilon (962–1049), cinquième abbé de Cluny," ibid., 2: 103–13; J. Virey, "Note sur un manuscrit du XIVᵉ siècle sur parchemin, provenant de l'Abbaye de Cluny," ibid., 1: 264–290.

27. An exception was Guy de Valous, who, by the 1920s was combining Sackur's thesis and approach with Fustel de Coulanges's analytic method on documents relating to economic questions. See Valous's discussion of the spread of Cluny in "Le domaine de l'abbaye de Cluny aux Xᵉ et XIᵉ siècles," *Annales de l'Académie de Mâcon* 3d ser. 22 (1920): 299–481, esp. 311–323; for a discussion of this article, cf. infra, Chapter 2, pp. 30–31. For Valous's major synthetic work, see infra, n. 47.

28. L.M. Smith, "Cluny and Gregory VII," *English Historical Review* 26 (1911): 20–33.

29. L.M. Smith, *The Early History of the Monastery of Cluny* (London, 1920).

30. L.M. Smith, *Cluny in the Eleventh and Twelfth Centuries* (London, 1930).

31. E. Tomek, *Studien zur Reform der deutschen Klöster im XI. Jahrhundert*, vol 1, *Die Frühreform* (Vienna, 1910).

32. Sackur, *Die Cluniacenser*, 2: 449ff. On Bertha, cf. infra, Chapter 2, pp. 51–52.

33. Sackur, *Die Cluniacenser*, 1: 160–61.

34. G. Schreiber, "Zur cluniazensischen Reform," *Gemeinschaften des Mittelalters. Recht und Verfassung. Kult und Frömmigkeit* (Münster, 1948), pp. 139ff (originally published in *Zeitschrift der Savigny-Stiftung für Rechtsgeschichte, Kanonistische Abteilung* 32 [1911]: 356–68); idem, "Kirchliches Abgabenwesen an französischen Eigenkirchen aus Anlass von Ordalien," *Gemeinschaften*, pp. 160ff (originally published in *Zeitschrift der Savigny-Stiftung für Rechtsgeschichte, Kanonistische Abteilung* 36 [1915]:414–83).

35. Schreiber, "Kirchliches Abgabenwesen," pp. 172–73.

36. Ibid., p. 179.

37. Cf. infra, n. 57.

38. P. W. Jorden, *Das cluniazensische Totengedächtniswesen vornehmlich unter den drei ersten Äbten Berno, Odo und Aymard (910–954). Zugleich ein Beitrag zu den cluniazensischen Traditionsurkunden* (Münster, 1930).

39. Ibid., p. 97.

40. K. J. Conant, "Mediaeval Academy Excavations at Cluny: The Season of 1928," *Speculum* 1–4 (1929): 3–26, 168–76, 291–302, 443–50. For a summary of Conant's recent conclusions, see idem, *Cluny. Les églises et la maison du chef d'Ordre* (Cambridge, Mass., 1968). Conant has also written a short paper on the tenth-century buildings at Cluny: "Cluny in the Tenth Century," *Medievalia et Humanistica* 9 (1955): 23–25. Before Conant's excavations, historians had to rely primarily on written descriptions. See, for example, R. Graham and A. W. Clapham, "The Monastery of Cluny, 910–1155," *Archaeologia* 80 (1930): 143–78. On Sackur's judgment of Cluny's place in the history of art, cf. Sackur, *Die Cluniacenser*, 2: 369ff.

41. A. Brackmann, "Die politische Wirkung der Kluniazensischen Bewegung," *Zur politischen Bedeutung der Kluniazensischen Bewegung* (Darmstadt, 1958), pp. 7–27. (Presented in August, 1928, at the International Congress of Historians in Oslo; first published in *Historische Zeitschrift*, 139 [1929]: 34–47.) All references here are to the Darmstadt edition.

42. Ibid., p. 13.

43. Ibid., p. 19.

44. P. Boissonnade, *Du nouveau sur la chanson de Roland* (Paris, 1923), pp. 11–12, 22; idem, "Cluny, la papauté et la première grande croisade internationale contre les Sarrasins d'Espagne. Barbastro (1064–1065)," *Revue des questions historiques* 3d ser. 21 (1932): 257–301.

45. S. Berthelier, "L'expansion de l'Ordre de Cluny et ses rapports avec l'histoire politique et économique de X^e au XIIe siècles," *Revue archéologique* 6th ser. 11 (1938): 324.

46. J. Evans, *Monastic Life at Cluny 910–1157* (London, 1931), p. vii.

47. G. de Valous, *Le monachisme clunisien des origines au XVe siècle. Vie intérieure des monastères et organisation de l'ordre*, 2 vols. (Ligugé, 1935). (A 2d, augmented edition was published in Paris in 1970.)

48. Cf. H. Talbot, "Cluniac Spirituality," *The Life of the Spirit* 2 (1945): 97–101, where Cluny represents a flight from the world. This notion contributed to the older, pre-Sackur view that Cluny had intrinsic importance as a national, French institution regardless of its significance within society at large. Thus, in the 1940s Dom G. Charvin published a series of articles on Cluny's history from the sixteenth through the eighteenth centuries in the *Revue Mabillon* (33 [1943]: 85–124; 34–35 [1944–45]: 20–28; 36 [1947]: 69–97; 38 [1948]: 61–99; 39 [1949]: 25–35, 44–58; 40 [1950]: 1–28, 29–42; 43 [1953]: 85–117; 44 [1954]: 6–29).

49. Cf. papers presented at the conference *A Cluny, Congrès scientifique. Fêtes et cérémonies liturgiques en l'honneur des Saints Abbés Odon et Odilon*, 9–11 July 1949 (Dijon, 1950), particularly G. Duby, "La ville de Cluny au temps de Saint Odilon," pp. 261ff; J. Evans, "L'Iconographie clunisienne," pp. 44ff; K. J. Conant, "Les églises de Cluny à l'époque de Saint Odon et de Saint Odilon," pp. 37ff. For further discussion of this conference, cf. infra, p. 27.

50. Evans, *Monastic Life.* Cf. also J.-F. Lemarignier, *Étude sur les privilèges d'exemption et de juridiction ecclésiastique des abbayes normandes depuis les origines jusqu'en 1140* (Ligugé, 1937), where Cluny is judged to have contributed only uncon-

sciously to the Gregorians by providing them unwittingly with a model of organization. Similarly idem, "L'exemption monastique et les origines de la Réforme grégorienne," *A Cluny,* pp. 293ff.

51. H. V. White, "Pontius of Cluny, the *Curia Romana* and the End of Gregorianism in Rome," *Church History* 27 (1958): 195–219. Cf. G. Tellenbach, "Der Sturz des Abtes Pontius von Cluny und seine geschichtliche Bedeutung," *Quellen und Forschungen aus italienischen Archiven und Bibliotheken* 42 (1963): 13–55.

52. C. Erdmann, *Die Entstehung des Kreuzzugsgedankens* (Stuttgart, 1935), pp. 63–65; English trans., *The Origin of the Idea of Crusade,* trans. and annotated by M. W. Baldwin and W. Goffart (Princeton, 1977), pp. 68–72. Cf. A. Harnack, *Das Mönchtum, seine Ideale und seine Geschichte* (Giessen, 1908).

53. G. Ladner, *Theologie und Politik vor dem Investiturstreit. Abendmahlstreit, Kirchenreform, Cluni und Heinrich III* (Baden bei Wien, 1936); G. Tellenbach, *Libertas, Kirche und Weltordnung im Zeitalter des Investiturstreits* (Stuttgart, 1936); English trans., *Church, State and Christian Society at the Time of the Investiture Contest,* trans. R. F. Bennett (New York, 1970). Already, in another connection, Marc Bloch had outlined some religious components of medieval kingship in *Les rois thaumaturges. Etude sur le caractère surnaturel attribué à la puissance royale, particulièrement en France et en Angleterre* (Strasbourg, 1924).

54. Ladner, *Theologie und Politik,* pp. 60ff.

55. Tellenbach, *Church, State,* p. 83. A somewhat different view was presented by A. Chagny, *Cluny et son Empire* (1934?, rev. ed., Lyon, 1938). Chagny did not cite Brackmann in his bibliography; and he argued, much as had pre-Brackmann historians, that Cluny's religious and civilizing mission necessitated its involvement—in spite of itself—in the politics of its day. But Chagny maintained that Cluny always was neutral, even during the investiture controversy (ibid., pp. 49–50). Like Evans and Valous, Chagny argued that the "principal objectif" (ibid., p. 58) of the Cluniacs was the *opus Dei.* He carried his history of the monastery from its apogee (10th–12th centuries), through its decline in the 13th century and thence to its destruction in the 19th century.

56. C. Erdmann, "Das ottonische Reich als Imperium Romanum," *Deutsches Archiv für Geschichte des Mittelalters* 6 (1943): 412–41.

57. G. Schreiber, "Cluny und die Eigenkirche. Zur Würdigung der Traditionsnotizen des hochmittelalterlichen Frankreich," *Gemeinschaften,* p. 84 (originally published in *Archiv für Urkundenforschung* 17 [1942]: 359–418).

58. Ibid., p. 135.

59. E. Werner, *Die gesellschaftlichen Grundlagen der Klosterreform im 11. Jahrhundert* (Berlin, 1953); K. Hallinger, *Gorze-Kluny. Studien zu den Monastischen Lebensformen und Gegensätzen im Hochmittelalter,* 2 vols. (Rome, 1950).

60. Werner, *Grundlagen der Klosterreform,* pp. 14–15.

61. Curiously, Werner argued that the Cluniac form of monasticism was not so much invented as imported—from Byzantium. Cf. Hallinger's reply to Werner in 1956, namely, that precedents and parallels for all Cluniac practices are to be found in indigenous Western monasticism. K. Hallinger, "Progressi e problemi della ricerca sulla Riforma pre-gregoriana," *Il monachesimo nell'Alto medioevo e la formazione della Civiltà occidentale,* Settimane di studio del Centro Italiano di

Studi sull'Alto medioevo, no. 4, 8–14 April 1956 (Spoleto, 1957), pp. 272ff (also published as "Neue Fragen der Reformgeschichtlichen Forschung," *Archiv für mittelrheinische Kirchengeschichte* 9 [1957]: 9–32). The point, though argued at length by Werner, does not seem essential to his view of the function of Cluniac monasticism in society.

62. The priory was a monastery dependent upon Cluny; its abbot was the abbot of Cluny; it was administered, in day-to-day matters, by a prior. For a morphology of the institution, cf. Valous, *Le Monachisme,* 2d ed., 1: 187–203; 2: 5–25, 67–69.

63. Werner, *Grundlagen der Klosterreform,* pp. 82ff.

64. Hallinger, *Gorze-Kluny,* p. 38.

65. Cf. supra, p. 9.

66. Hallinger, *Gorze-Kluny,* p. 40.

67. The corresponding issue of the relations between Cîteaux and Cluny, a subject of some attention in the thirties, was now revived. Cf., for example, D. Knowles, *Cistercians and Cluniacs: The Controversy between St. Bernard and Peter the Venerable* (London, 1955).

68. T. Schieffer, "Cluniazensische oder gorzische Reformbewegung (Bericht über ein neues Buch)," *Archiv für mittelrheinische Kirchengeschichte* 4 (1952): 24ff.

69. Ibid., p. 38. Cf. the reaction of Valous, "Cluny" (see supra, Introduction, n.2), pp. 41–42, who asserts in this article published in 1956 that all the monastic reform centers of the tenth and eleventh centuries followed fundamentally the same observances. Yet in 1935 he had argued that "la réforme lorraine, celle de Fleury, les tendances et la propagande d'un Guillaume de Volpiano en Italie . . . [etc.] n'ont que des rapports lointains avec le mouvement clunisien" (Valous, *Le Monachisme,* 1: x).

70. H. Dauphin, "Monastic Reforms from the Tenth Century to the Twelfth," *Downside Review* 70 (1952): 62–74.

71. J. Leclercq, "Cluny fut-il ennemi de la culture?" *Revue Mabillon* 47 (1957): 172–82; idem, "Y-a-t-il une culture monastique?" *Il monachesimo,* p. 342; idem, "Spiritualité et culture à Cluny," *Spiritualità cluniacense,* Convegni del Centro di Studi sulla Spiritualità medievale, 12–15 October 1958 (Todi, 1960), pp. 101–51; idem, "Pour une histoire de la vie à Cluny," *Revue d'histoire ecclésiastique* 57 (1962): 385–408, 783–812. Cf. idem, *L'Amour des lettres et le désir de Dieu. Initiation aux auteurs monastiques du Moyen âge* (Paris, 1957), English trans., *The Love of Learning and the Desire for God: A Study of Monastic Culture,* trans. C. Misrahi (New York, 1961), where the differences between Cluny and Cîteaux are also considered nuances within a common Benedictine tradition.

72. Leclercq, "Pour une histoire," pp. 389–93.

73. Ibid., pp. 393.

74. Necrologies are lists of the names of those departed faithful for whom the monks were pledged to say prayers. For a necrology of a Gorzian house that mentions a Cluniac abbot, cf. F. X. Kraus, "Nekrologium von St. Maximin," *Jahrbücher des Vereins von Alterthumsfreunden im Rheinlands* 57 (1876): 108–119, esp. p. 113, where Abbot Majolus of Cluny is listed. The significance of this docu-

ment for the Gorze-Cluny controversy was noted by J. Wollasch and reported by Tellenbach in G. Tellenbach, ed., *Neue Forschungen über Cluny und die Cluniacenser* (Freiburg, 1959), p. 7, n. 25. See also Wollasch's more recent "Les obituaires, témoins de la vie clunisienne," *Cahiers de civilisation médiévale* 22 (1979): 139–171.

75. Leclercq, "Pour une histoire," p. 386.

76. Even Hunt, who was to revive the old thesis that Cluny's internal ideals were undermined by its external activities, justified it on the new grounds: Cluny was not to be seen in a vacuum, and Cluny was not to be considered equivalent to Cluniac (N. Hunt, *Cluny under Saint Hugh, 1049–1109* [London, 1967], pp. ix–4). P. Schmitz described the liturgy at Cluny without claiming any implications for the practices of its dependencies. (P. Schmitz, "La liturgie de Cluny," *Spiritualità cluniacense,* pp. 83–99.) Hallinger in later publications limited his studies of Cluny's spirituality and liturgy to the mother house without attempting to extrapolate his conclusions to the whole order. See K. Hallinger, "Zur geistigen Welt der Anfänge Klunys," *Deutsches Archiv für Erforschung der Mittelalter* 10 (1953–4): 417–45. Abridged English trans. in N. Hunt, ed., *Cluniac Monasticism in the Central Middle Ages* (Hamden, Conn., 1971), pp. 29–55. See also K. Hallinger, "Klunys Bräuche zur Zeit Hugos des Grossen (1049–1109). Prolegomena zur Neuherausgabe des Bernhard und Udalrich von Kluny," *Zeitschrift der Savigny-Stiftung für Rechtsgeschichte, Kanonistische Abteilung* 45 (1959): 99–140. Cf. the study of Cluny's literary traditions and themes in P. Lamma, *Momenti di storiografia cluniacense,* Istituto storico Italiano per il Medio Evo. Studi storici, vols. 42–44 (Rome, 1961), pp. 12ff. All of these studies disregarded Werner's argument that Cluny's monasticism was Byzantine (cf. supra, n. 61), stressing instead the Benedictine tradition as the foundation of Cluniac life. But cf. the reaction of Violante, who warned that Cluny's particular form of monasticism, albeit Benedictine, nevertheless should be considered a "remarkable phenomenon" requiring explanation. (C. Violante, "Il monachesimo cluniacense di fronte al mondo politico ed ecclesiastico [Secoli X e XI]," *Spiritualità cluniacense,* pp. 158–59, n. 9.)

77. K. Schmid and J. Wollasch, "Die Gemeinschaft der Lebenden und Verstorbenen in Zeugnissen des Mittelalters," *Frühmittelalterliche Studien* 1 (1967): 365–405.

78. Cf. the introduction to L. Febvre, *A New Kind of History and Other Essays,* ed. P. Burke, trans. K. Folca (New York, 1973), pp. v–xii.

79. G. Duby, *La société aux XIe et XIIe siècles dans la région mâconnaise* (Paris, 1953). Cf. his addendum, "Lignage, noblesse et chevalerie au XIIe siècle dans la région mâconnaise," *Annales. Economies, sociétés, civilisations* 27 (1972): 803–23. English trans. P. Ranum, "Lineage, Nobility, and Chivalry in the Region of Mâcon during the Twelfth Century," in *Family and Society: Selections from the Annales. Economies, sociétiés, civilisations,* ed. R. Forster and O. Ranum (Baltimore, 1976); also in G. Duby, *The Chivalrous Society,* trans. C. Postan (Berkeley, 1977), pp. 59–80.

80. G. Duby, "Economie domaniale et économie monétaire. Le budget de l'Abbaye de Cluny entre 1080 et 1155," *Annales. Economies, sociétés, civilisations* 7 (1952): 155–71.

81. G. Duby and R. Mandrou, *A History of French Civilization,* trans. J. Atkinson (New York, 1964), p. 57; G. Duby, "Les laïcs et la Paix de Dieu," *I Laici nella "Societas christiana" dei secoli XI e XII,* Atti della terza Settimana internazionale di Studio Mendola, 21–27 August 1965 (Milan, 1968), pp. 448–61; idem, *The Making of the Christian West, 980–1140,* trans. S. Gilbert (Geneva, 1967), pp. 113ff.

82. J.-F. Lemarignier, "L'exemption monastique," pp. 293ff.

83. J.-F. Lemarignier, "Structures monastiques et structures politiques dans la France de la fin du Xe et des débuts du XIe siècle" *Il monachesimo,* pp. 357–400, esp. 393. This article was later revised and translated as "Political and Monastic Structures in France at the End of the Tenth and the Beginning of the Eleventh Century," in *Lordship and Community in Medieval Europe, Selected Readings,* ed. F. L. Cheyette (Huntington, N.Y., 1975), pp. 100–127. For historiographical purposes, the original formulation will be discussed here. But cf. infra, Chapter 2, pp. 31–32. For Hallinger's characterization of Cluny as antifeudal cf. *Gorze-Kluny,* p. 41.

84. Lemarignier, "Structures," p. 393.

85. F. Masai, responding to Lemarignier in discussion, in *Il Monachesimo,* pp. 520–21.

86. C. Courtois, responding to Lemarignier in discussion, ibid., p. 534.

87. Violante, "Monachesimo cluniacense," pp. 184ff.

88. For an excellent summary of the different definitions of feudalism and Cluny's relationship to it, cf. H. Hoffmann, "Von Cluny zum Investiturstreit," *Archiv für Kulturgeschichte* 45 (1963): 165–69. Hoffmann's personal position is close to that of Lemarignier.

89. Cf. Adalbero of Laon, *Carmen ad Rotbertum regem,* lines 130–81, in G.-A. Hückel, ed., "Les poèmes satiriques d'Adalbéron," in *Bibliothèque de la Faculté des Lettres, Université de Paris,* vol. 13 (Paris, 1901), pp. 142–47. I have been unable to consult the new edition by C. Carozzi (Paris, 1979).

90. Sackur, *Die Cluniacenser,* 1: 33ff; Jorden, *Cluniazensische Totengedächtnisswesen,* p. 13; Werner, *Grundlagen der Klosterreform,* passim.

91. G. Tellenbach, ed, *Neue Forschungen* (cf. supra, n. 74). Cf. also Tellenbach, "Zum Wesen der Cluniacenser," *Saeculum* 9 (1958): 370ff. On the related problem of tithes, cf. G. Constable, "Cluniac Tithes and the Controversy between Gigny and Le Miroir," *Revue Bénédictine* 70 (1960): 591–624, reprinted in idem, *Cluniac Studies* (London, 1980) and cf. idem, *Monastic Tithes from Their Origins to the Twelfth Century* (Cambridge, 1964).

92. J. Wollasch, "Königtum, Adel und Klöster im Berry während des 10. Jahrhunderts," *Neue Forschungen,* pp. 19–165. Cf. infra, p. 28. For Mager's contribution, "Studien über das Verhältnis der Cluniacenser zum Eigenkirchenwesen," *Neue Forschungen,* pp. 169–217.

93. T. Schieffer, "Cluny et la Querelle des Investitures," *Revue historique* 225 (1961): 51–52. The paper was first presented in October, 1959.

94. J. Fechter, *Cluny, Adel und Volk. Studien über das Verhältnis des Klosters zum den Ständen (910–1156)* (Stuttgart, 1966). Cf. infra, Chapter 2, pp. 32–33, where this work is discussed in detail. A more recent work dealing with the social origins of the lay (nonpriestly) monks and the lay brethren at Cluny is W.

Teske, "Laien, Laienmönche und Laienbrüder in der Abtei Cluny. Ein Beitrag zum 'Konversen-Problem,'" *Frühmittelalterliche Studien* 10 (1976): 248–322; 11 (1977): 288–339. Teske's findings are slightly different from Fechter's. He sees a mixture of all classes at Cluny in the eleventh century, with a shift under Peter the Venerable, in the twelfth century, to a monastic community made up exclusively of the upper classes *(milites)*, with the lower classes *(rustici)* now relegated to the lower status of lay brethren.

95. H.E.J. Cowdrey, *Cluniacs and the Gregorian Reform* (Oxford, 1970).

96. H.E.J. Cowdrey, "Unions and Confraternity with Cluny," *Journal of Ecclesiastical History* 16 (1965): 152–62.

97. Cowdrey, *Cluniacs,* pp. 139–41.

98. P. Pourrat, *La Spiritualité chrétienne,* 4 vols. (Paris, 1918–28). The periodical *Revue d'ascétique et de mysticisme* was launched in 1920. The subtitle of the *Dictionnaire de Spiritualité,* begun in 1937, reveals by implication a definition of spirituality: *Ascétique et mystique. Doctrine et histoire.*

99. B. Bligny, *L'église et les ordres religieux dans le royaume de Bourgogne aux XIe et XIIe siècles* (Grenoble, 1960), p. 6.

100. Lemarignier, "Structures monastiques," pp. 357–400 at the conference *Il monachesimo.*

101. Leclercq, "Spiritualité et culture à Cluny," pp. 101–51.

102. *Spiritualità cluniacense,* p. 5.

103. E. Delaruelle, "La vie commune des clercs et la spiritualité populaire au XIe siècle," in *La vita comune del clero nei secoli XI e XII.* Atti della Settimana di Studio Mendola, settembre, 1959, 2 vols. (Milan, 1962), 1: 142–73. For a critique of Delaruelle's approach, cf. J.-C. Schmitt, " 'Religion populaire' et culture folklorique," *Annales. Economies, sociétés, civilisations* 31 (1976): 941–53.

104. Cf. supra, n. 81.

105. L. Bouyer, et al., *Histoire de la spiritualité chrétienne,* 3 vols. (Paris, 1960–66). The new definition of spirituality is in vol. 1, *La spiritualité du Nouveau Testament et des Pères,* pp. 11–12. Leclercq wrote the sections dealing with the 6th–12th c. in vol. 2, *La Spiritualité du Moyen Âge,* pp. 11–272.

106. J. Leclercq, *Monks and Love in Twelfth–Century France: Psycho–Historical Essays* (Oxford, 1979). But see the critique of his psychological analysis by C. W. Bynum in *Speculum* 55 (1980): 595–97.

107. R. W. Southern, *Western Society and the Church in the Middle Ages* (Harmondsworth, 1970).

108. See A. Vauchez, *La spiritualité du Moyen Age occidental, VIIIe–XIIe siècles* (Vendôme, 1975). This takes the La Mendola point of view; it is a synthetic view of Christian spirituality, both lay and clerical. Vauchez uses acts, liturgy, and iconography as often as contemplative texts for his sources, for he sees spirituality as "l'unité dynamique du contenu d'une foi et de la façon dont celle-ci est vécue par des hommes historiquement déterminés," ibid., p. 7. So different were these responses that Vauchez sometimes uses the plural, "spiritualités," ibid., p. 6. See also A. Borst, *Mönche am Bodensee, 610–1525* (Sigmaringen, 1978) and L. K. Little, *Religious Poverty and the Profit Economy in Medieval Europe* (New York, 1978), both of which relate spirituality to social context. On spirituality (not simply religion) as a part of early medieval political life, see

C. B. Bouchard, "Laymen and Church Reform around the Year 1000: The case of Otto-William, Count of Burgundy," *Journal of Medieval History* 5 (1979): 1–10.

109. Hunt, *Cluny under St. Hugh,* p. 106.

110. Cowdrey, *Cluniacs,* pp. 162–71. The phrase heads a subsection of the book. A review of Cowdrey's book that deals at length with the question of Cluny's relationship to the papacy, is H. Jacobs, "Die Cluniazenser und das Papsttum im 10. und 11. Jahrhundert," *Francia* 2 (1974): 643–63.

111. A still more recent example is R. G. Heath, *Crux imperatorum philosophia: Imperial Horizons of the Cluniac "Confraternitas," 964–1109* (Pittsburgh, 1976). This touches on the tenth century, but it concentrates on the reigns of abbots Odilo and Hugh, arguing that Cluny was linked (by direct bonds of confraternity and by the indirect bonds of mutually held ideas) with the emperors of Germany until the very end of the eleventh century. At that time, Cluny was compelled by the success of the Gregorians to ally itself with the popes. See the review of Heath's book by Cowdrey in *Speculum* 53 (1978): 577–79.

A tenth-century gap should not be imputed to those works that focus on Cluny in the twelfth century. This is a topic with its own distinct (and distinguished) historiographical tradition. It is out of the question to discuss it here, but at least two relatively recent contributions must be mentioned: the collected articles by Giles Constable in *Cluniac Studies* (cf. supra, n. 91), and the collected papers of the Cluny congress of 1972, *Les courants philosophiques, littéraires et artistiques en occident au milieu du XIIe siècle, Pierre Abélard-Pierre le Vénérable.* Abbaye de Cluny, 2–9 July 1972, Colloques internationaux du centre national de la recherche scientifique, no. 546 (Paris, 1975).

112. A. Hessel, "Odo von Cluni und das französische Kulturproblem im früheren Mittelalter," *Historische Zeitschrift* 128 (1923): 1–25.

113. In *A Cluny* (supra, n. 49): J.-F. Lemarignier, "L'exemption monastique et les origines de la réforme grégorienne," pp. 288–340; J. Hourlier, "Cluny et la notion d'Ordre religieux," pp. 219–26; P. Cousin, "La dévotion mariale chez les grands abbés de Cluny," pp. 210–18; J. Leclercq, "L'Idéal monastique de saint Odon, d'après ses oeuvres," pp. 227–32; J. Laporte, "Saint Odon, disciple de Saint Grégoire le Grand," pp. 138–43.

114. C. Voorman, "Studien zu Odo von Cluny" (Dissertation, Rheinischen Friedrich-Wilhelms Universität, Bonn, 1951).

115. K. Hallinger, "Zur geistigen Welt," pp. 417–45. Cf. the review by G. Arnaldi, "La *Vita Odonis* di Giovanni Romano e la spiritualità cluniacense," *Spiritualità cluniacense,* pp. 245–49.

116. Introduction to *Spiritualità cluniacense,* p. 5.

117. R. Morghen, "Riforma monastica e spiritualità cluniacense," *Spiritualità cluniacense,* pp. 31–56, trans. in Hunt, *Cluniac Monasticism,* pp. 11–28.

118. O. Capitani, "Motivi di spiritualità cluniacense e realismo eucaristico in Odone di Cluny," *Spiritualità cluniacense,* pp. 250–57.

119. Schmitz, "La Liturgie de Cluny," *Spiritualità cluniacense,* pp. 83–89.

120. J. Wollasch, "Königtum, Adel und Klöster," *Neue Forschungen,* pp. 19–165.

NOTES TO CHAPTER 2

1. The charters have been used most successfully in social history. See Duby, *Société* (supra, Chapter 1, n. 79); idem, "Lignage, noblesse, et chevalerie" (supra, Chapter 1, n. 79); and most recently C. B. Bouchard, "Nobility, Church, and Reform in Eleventh- and Twelfth-Century Burgundy" (unpublished MS), which Dr. Bouchard was kind enough to let me see in draft. On the dating of the charters, supra, Chapter 1, n. 13.

2. Valous, "Le domaine" (supra, Chapter 1, n. 27), pp. 313ff.

3. M. Chaume, "En marge de l'histoire de Cluny," *Revue Mabillon* 29 (1939): 41–61; 30 (1940): 33–62. Chaume wrote partly in response to the suggestion that Cluny expanded along the boundaries of the ancient kingdom of Burgundy, put forth in S. Berthelier, "L'expansion de l'Ordre de Cluny" (supra, Chapter 1, n. 45).

4. Wollasch, "Königtum" (supra, Chapter 1, n. 92). Cf. Chaume, "En marge," 29 (1939): 55–60 (on Berno), 30 (1940): 36 (on Odo).

5. Lemarignier, "Political and Monastic Structures" (supra, Chapter 1, n. 83). Heath, *Crux imperatorum* (supra, Chapter 1, n. 111) adds another dimension to Lemarignier's idea that Cluniacs countered disintegration with centralization. For him both empire and Cluny were "universalizing" (hence, uniting) forces. See, e.g., his discussion of All Soul's Day, ibid., pp. 94–95.

6. Lemarignier, "Political and Monastic Structures," p. 114.

7. Fechter, *Cluny* (supra, Chapter 1, n. 94).

8. Duby, *Société*.

9. Fechter, *Cluny*, pp. 48–49.

10. Ibid., p. 47; cf. calculations in Sackur, *Die Cluniacenser* 2: 407.

11. Duby, *Société*, p. 118, n. 40.

12. Valous, "Le domaine," p. 371; E. Z. Tabuteau, "Transfers of Property in Eleventh-Century Norman Law" (Ph.D. dissertation, Harvard University, 1975). I am grateful to Dr. Tabuteau for sending me the relevant parts of her dissertation. The Benedictine *Rule* itself speaks of nobles making a donation and reserving the income for themselves. Cf. *Benedicti Regula* 59.5, in *La Règle de Saint Benoît*, ed. and trans. A. de Vogüé (hereafter *RB*), Sources Chrétiennes (hereafter *SC*), vols. 181–186a (Paris, 1972–77), 182: 634.

13. *C,* 1 [no. 747]: 704 (949): "eo tamen tenore ut, si michi necesse fuerit, de vestra substantia me adjuvetis." In point of fact, this donor does not seem to be very poor, for he is able to give Cluny land in three *villae.* Yet this is an example of the *Volk* cited by Fechter, *Cluny,* p. 47, n. 14. For Gauzfred, *C,* 1 [no. 446]: 434–36 (936).

14. All post-obit concessions to Cluny and the size of land involved are catalogued in A. Déléage, *La vie rurale en Bourgogne jusqu'au début du onzième siècle,* 3 vols. (Mâcon, 1941), 2: 1166–95, esp. from Mâcon, pp. 1168–83. Between 910 and 981, 225 donations to Cluny reserve the usufruct for the life of the donor (or, in a few cases, for an additional generation). Of these instances, 189 involve one to three *mansi* (one *mansus* is most frequent), 24 involve even less, and only 12 involve more substantial pieces of property. On this form of landholding, ibid., 1: 194–96, 598–609.

Examples of outright donations, taken from the early, middle, and later parts of the century: *C,* 1 [no. 202]: 190–91 (916), a manse and a field; *C,* 2 [no. 1033]: 126–27 (957), a vineyard in one village and more substantial holdings (probably equivalent to a manse) in another; *C,* 2 [no. 1392]: 454 (974), land in two fields and three slaves.

15. *C,* 2 [no. 883]: 2 (954): "consultum . . . primatum comitis, et etiam nostri et advocati Leotoldi"; *C,* 3 [no. 1957]: 176 (993): "comitis . . . nostri et advocati Aynrici." Cf. Duby, *Société,* p. 104, n. 70.

16. Duby, *Société,* pp. 57–58.

17. *C,* 1 [no. 248]: 239–40 (924–25); *C,* 2 [no. 1460]: 513–15 (978). For other such transactions, cf. *C,* 1 [no. 798]: 750 (951); *C,* 2 [no. 1087]: 180–81 (961); *C,* 1 [no. 793]: 744–45 (950–1); *C,* 1 [no. 802]: 754–56 (978); C, 2 [no. 1460] cited above. I have Constance Bouchard to thank for pointing out many of these references to me. For land granted outright by Cluny *in precaria* (involving no donation to the monastery), cf. Déléage, *Vie rurale,* 2: 1192–93.

18. P. Juénin, ed., *Nouvelle histoire de l'abbaïe royale et collégiale de Saint Filibert, et de la ville de Tournus,* 2 vols., bound as one (Dijon, 1733), 2: 116–17 for count Alberic, p. 119 for Henry.

19. M.-C. Ragut, ed., *Cartulaire de Saint-Vincent de Mâcon* (Mâcon, 1864). Examples of donations by the wealthy, p. 132 [no. 206] (928–36); gift from Count Alberic, p. 283 [no. 488] (c. 941); gift from Count Letald and his wife; cf. Déléage, *Vie rurale,* 2: 1186–87, 1194–95. For post-obit donations to St. Vincent, tables ibid., 2: 1184–85.

20. Duby, *Société,* pp. 98–100. See F. N. Estey, "The *Fideles* in the County of Mâcon," *Speculum* 30 (1955): 82–89.

21. On Otto-William, Duby, *Société,* pp. 137–39; C. B. Bouchard, "Laymen and Church Reform" (supra, Chapter 1, n. 108). See also infra, p. 54.

22. *C,* 3 [no. 2255]: 384–88 (994). The resolutions are discussed in Duby, *Société,* pp. 139–40; idem, "Recherches sur l'évolution des institutions judiciaires pendant le Xe et XIe siècle dans le sud de la Bourgogne," *Le Moyen Age* 52 (1946): 149–94; 53 (1947): 15–38. English trans. in *Chivalrous Society,* pp. 15–58. See also H. Hoffmann, *Gottesfriede und Treuga Dei,* Schriften der *Monumenta Germaniae Historica* (hereafter *MGH*), vol. 20 (Stuttgart, 1964), pp. 45–47.

23. Duby, *Société,* pp. 141–43.

24. On Hugh, Count of Chalon and Bishop of Auxerre, see infra, p. 53.

25. One uses the term "feudal" cautiously in the light of the issues raised by E. A. R. Brown, "The Tyranny of a Construct: Feudalism and Historians of Medieval Europe," *American Historical Review* 79 (1974): 1063–88. It is used here to indicate the rise of a network of personal, private, dependent relationships.

26. Duby, *Société,* pp. 65, 122 and passim. On the importance of the kin group see D. A. Bullough, "Early Medieval Social Groupings: The Terminology of Kinship," *Past and Present* no. 45 (1969), pp. 1–18.

27. Duby, *Société,* pp. 68–69.

28. Déléage has made the inventory of the possessors of parcels of land in these two communes, *Vie rurale,* 2: 1059–84, esp. 1063, 1079. On Cluny's becoming a major landowner after 980, Duby, *Société,* p. 68.

29. Duby, *Société,* p. 68, n. 95; p. 69.

30. For a rough estimate, note that between 909 and 981 there is an average of 14.8 charters per year in Cluny's collection of cartularies; between 981 and 1025 there is an average of 27.6 charters per year. This may be compared with St.-Vincent of Mâcon (proportionally, not in absolute numbers; St.-Vincent has a far less complete inventory than Cluny), where there are 3 charters per year between 910 and 981; 3.2 charters for the period 981–1025.

31. E.g., the lords of Beaujeu: Humbert and his wife gave land in Mâcon to Cluny, *C,* 3 [no. 1774]: 32–33 (987–96); the lords of Bâgé: Aremburg gave Cluny land and serfs in Lyon, *C,* 3 [no. 1958]: 177 (993); the lords of Brancion: Testa gave Cluny some land and a church, *C,* 1 [no. 517]: 502–3 (1000). I am indebted to Constance Bouchard for these references.

32. Duby, *Société,* pp. 69–70, 127, 141–45, 148; Fechter, *Cluny,* pp. 25ff.

33. A. Murray, *Reason and Society in the Middle Ages* (Oxford, 1978), p. 17.

34. Bouchard, "Nobility, Church" has shown that families sometimes supported a particular monastery over several generations.

35. C. B. Bouchard, "The Origins of the French Nobility: A Reassessment," *American Historical Review* 86 (1981): 501–32. I am grateful to Dr. Bouchard for letting me see this MS before publication.

36. Lemarignier, "Political and Monastic Structures," p. 106.

37. T. Evergates, review of M. Bur, *La formation du Comté de Champagne (v. 950–v. 1150)* (Nancy, 1977), in *American Historical Review* 83 (1978): 147–48.

38. Conclusions are listed here for each category in order of appearance in text and notes. Evidence of social mobility: Ebbo, Adelaide of Burgundy, Aimo and Turpio, Bernard I of Auvergne, Alberic, Stephen of Clermont, Boso of Arles, Bertha, Empress Adelaide, Otto I, Pope John XV, Lambert, Adelaide of Chalon, Geoffrey Greymantle, Hugh of Chalon, Otto-William, Odo I of Blois, Burchard, Hugh Capet; no evidence or evidence to the contrary: Bernard of Perigord, Elisiardus, Teotolo, the reformer of Sens, Gerald (sponsor of St.-Saturnin), Gaidulf, Henry of Burgundy; Lérins was reformed at the request of abbot Majolus himself.

39. This is the view of J. Calmette, "La famille de Saint Guilhem," *Annales du Midi* 18 (1906): 145–65; adopted by L. Auzias, *L'Aquitaine Carolingienne* (Toulouse, 1937), pp. 37, 519–25; reaffirmed (after the challenge of Levillain [see infra, n. 40]) by J. Dhondt, *Etudes sur la naissance des principautés territoriales en France (IXe–Xe siècle)* (Bruges, 1948), pp. 293–313.

40. L. Levillain, "De quelques personnages nommés Bernard dans les Annales de Saint-Bertin," *Mélanges dédiés à la mémoire de Félix Grat,* 2 vols. (Paris, 1946), 1:169–202. There is, in addition, a third lineage proposed by M. Chaume, who traces William's ancestry to Gerald I, count of Auvergne. See his genealogical table in *Les origines du Duché de Bourgogne,* 2 vols. (Dijon, 1925), 1: 531.

41. The documents show that William from the very first had authority as count or marquis in these regions. Cf. C. Devic and J. Vaissette, *Histoire générale de Languedoc,* 15 vols. (Toulouse, 1872–92), 3: 47–51. See also Auzias, *Aquitaine,* pp. 424–60. On the significance of the terms *dux* (more important than a count)

and *marquis* (the count of a march), cf. J. Dhondt, "Le titre du marquis à l'époque carolingienne," *Archivum latinitatis medii aevi. Bulletin du Cange* 19 (1948): 407–17.

42. F. Prinz, *Frühes Mönchtum im Frankenreich. Kultur und Gesellschaft in Gallien, den Rheinlanden und Bayern am Beispiel der monastischen Entwicklung (4. bis 8. Jahrhundert)* (Munich, 1965), pp. 122ff.

43. For the text of the charter, *C,* 1 [no. 112]: 124–28 (910 [now dated 909]).

44. Cowdrey, *The Cluniacs,* pp. 3–15. Vézelay, another Burgundian monastery, was founded in 858–59 and dedicated to SS. Peter and Paul. See *Monumenta Vizeliacensia,* ed. R. B. C. Huygens, Corpus Christianorum. Continuatio Mediaevalis (hereafter *CCCM*), vol. 42 (Turnhout, 1976), 244–48. It was placed under the jurisdiction of the papacy in 863, ibid., pp. 249–58. Cf. R. Berlow, "Spiritual Immunity at Vézelay (Ninth to Twelfth Centuries)," *Catholic Historical Review* 62 (1976): 573–88.

45. See infra., Chapter 4. Note that Vézelay was founded so that "per evum pro omnibus fieret communis oratio." *Monumenta Vizeliacensia,* p. 245.

46. On Ebbo, cf. G. Devailly, *Le Berry du Xe siècle au milieu du XIIIe. Etude politique, religieuse, sociale et économique* (Paris, 1973), pp. 123–27; Wollasch, "Königtum," pp. 70–74. Another castellan in the region, Aymard, lord of Bourbon l'Archambault, also a *fidelis* of Duke William, had already given Cluny the monastery of Souvigny in 915. However, it was given as a simple donation without mention of reform. Aymard's son reappropriated the property and in 954 redonated it to Cluny, again with no word of reform. *C,* 1 [no. 217]: 206–7 (920 [now dated 915]), *C,* 1 [no. 871]: 824–26 (954).

47. On Ebbo's grandfather, Devailly, *Berry,* p. 123, n. 5.

48. Ibid., pp. 168–76. Note, however, that Ebbo was a nominal *fidelis* of William's successors (cf. ibid., p. 165) and when they died (in 927), he became a *fidelis* of King Raoul.

49. Wollasch, "Königtum," pp. 89–92. The charter is printed in M. Bouquet, *Recueil des historiens des Gaules et de la France* (Paris, 1738–1786), 9: 713–15.

50. The codicil is not dated, but must be prior to 927. It is published in Sackur, 1: 381: "Monachos . . . obtestamur, ut secundum propositum monasticae professionis vivant, et si non melius vel ad exempla istorum, quos ibi Berno venerabilis et reverendus abbas primitus posuit quique successores conversentur, eandem psalmodiae quantitatem, eandem hospitalitatis humanitatem, eandem ab omni carne praeter piscium perpetuam abstinentiam tendant." Cf. the foundation charter in Bouquet, *Recueil,* 9: 714: "Monasterium regulare construatur, ibique Monachi juxta Regulam S. Benedicti viventes congregentur . . . ita duntaxet ut ibi venerabile orationis domicilium votis ac supplicationibus fidelium frequentetur, conversatioque coelestis omni desiderio et amore intimo perquiratur et expetatur . . . sintque ipsi Monachi cum omnibus rebus praescriptis sub potestate et dominatione Bernonis Abbatis."

51. On Rudolf, see R. Poupardin, *Le Royaume de Bourgogne (888–1038)* (Paris, 1907), pp. 10–28. Rudolf's Burgundy (in the Transjurane) is to be distinguished from the kingdom of Burgundy created by Boso (879–887), brother of Richard

le Justicier, which was centered in Provence; cf. R. Poupardin, *Le royaume de Provence sous les Carolingiens (855–933?)* (Paris, 1901), pp. 96–141. For Rudolf's acts, T. Schieffer, ed., *Die Urkunden der burgundischen Rudolfings* (Munich, 1977).

52. Carloman, *Diplomata* 1 (an. 880), in Bouquet, *Recueil,* 9: 418. On Richard's career see Chaume, *Origines*, 1: 361–90.

53. E.g., three counts witnessed Richard's donation to St.-Bénigne of Dijon; cf. E. Bougaud and J. Garnier, eds., *Chronique de l'abbaye de Saint-Bénigne de Dijon* (Dijon, 1875), p. 113; five counts witnessed his judgment in favor of Montiéramey; cf. diploma printed in H. D'Arbois de Jubainville, *Histoire des ducs et des comtes de Champagne,* 6 vols. (Paris, 1859–1886), 1 [no. 17]: 450. Other examples are in Chaume, *Origines,* 1: 370, n. 4.

54. For example, as reported in the *Series abbatum Flaviniacensium, MGH, Scriptorum Tomus* (hereafter *SS*) 8: 502–3. Cf. also R.-H. Bautier and M. Gilles, ed. and trans., *Chronique de Saint-Pierre-le-Vif de Sens, dite de Clarius (Chronicon Sancti Petri vivi Senonensis)* (Paris, 1979), p. 96. Other examples in Chaume, *Origines,* 1: 372–73.

55. *Annales sanctae Columbae Senonensis* (an. 895), *MGH, SS,* 1:104; cf. Chaume, *Origines,* 1: 374, with more examples of Richard's impact on comital personnel, and Dhondt, *Etudes,* pp. 159–163.

56. E.g., Walo, *Testamentum,* in Bouquet, *Recueil,* 9: 716. Cf. other citations in Chaume, *Origines,* 1: 385, n. 1.

57. On Raoul, Chaume, *Origines,* 1: 396–414. I have been unable to consult the new edition of his acts in J. Dufour, ed., *Recueil des actes de Robert Ier et de Raoul, rois de France (922–936)* (Paris, 1978).

58. Flodoard, *Annales* (an 924), ed. P. Lauer (Paris, 1905), p. 23.

59. Flodoard, *Historia Remensis ecclesiae* 4.22, *MGH, SS,* 13: 579: "At Rodulfus rex Remis veniens, ubi Karolus custodiebatur, pacem fecit cum illo, humilians se ante ipsius presentiam et reddens illi Atiniacum fiscum."

60. *C,* 1 [no. 379]: 359–60: "Monachi vero inibi consistentes modum conversationis istius, quae nunc ad informandum eos qui futuri sunt, de Cluniaco transfertur, ita conservent, ut eundem modum in victu atque vestitu, in abstinentia, in psalmodia, in silentio, in hospitalitate, in mutua dilectione et subjectione, atque bono obedientiae, nullatenus inminuant."

61. For Aurillac, *Breve Chronicon Auriliacensis abbatiae,* ed. J. Mabillon in *Vetera Analecta* (Paris, 1723), p. 349. For Tulle, Sackur, *Die Cluniacenser,* 1: 78–79. I have been unable to consult E. Baluze, *Historiae tutelensis libri tres,* 3 vols. (Paris, 1717), which Sackur cites. The Cluniacs were also confirmed in the possession of Charlieu at this time (932) by the pope, but there is no mention of reform: John XI, *Privilegium* 2, *PL,* 132: cols. 1058–59.

62. John of Salerno, *Vita S. Odonis* 1.37, *PL,* 133: col. 60; Odo of Cluny, *Collationum libri tres,* epist. nunc., *PL,* 133: cols. 517–20.

63. E.g., the foundation of St. Augustine; the charter is published in *Gallia Christiana,* 16 vols. (Paris, 1715–1865) 2: instr. cols. 167–68. On Turpio cf. J. Becquet, "Les évêques de Limoges aux Xe, XIe et XIIe siècles," *Bulletin de la société archéologique et historique du Limousin* 104 (1977): 63–90; sources on Turpio are culled and translated on pp. 75–82.

64. Adémar, *Historiarum libri tres* 3.25; in *Adémar de Chabannes, Chronique,* ed. J. Chavanon (Paris, 1897), p. 147. For what follows on the viscounts, cf. R. de Lasteyrie, *Etude sur les comtes et vicomtes de Limoges antérieurs à l'an 1000* (Paris, 1874), pp. 57–69, esp. 69, n. 3.

65. Lasteyrie, *Etude,* p. 61. The document is the foundation charter of St.-Augustine, infra, n. 68. It also mentions Adémar of Turenne, but not specifically as viscount.

66. J. Boussard, "Les origines de la vicomté de Turenne," *Mélanges offerts à René Crozet,* 2 vols. (Poitiers, 1966), 1: 101–9.

67. Adémar, *Historia* 3.23, in Chavanon, *Adémar de Chabannes,* p. 145. Cf. A. D. Anselme, *Histoire généalogique et chronologique de la maison royale de France,* 9 vols., 3d ed. (Paris, 1726–33), 3: 123.

68. The charter is in *Gallia Christiana,* 2: instr. col. 495.

69. Sackur, *Die Cluniacenser,* 1:83, citing E. Baluze, *Histoire généalogique de la maison d'Auvergne, justifiée par chartes, titres, histoires anciennes, et autres preuves authentiques,* 2 vols. (Paris, 1708), which I have been unable to consult.

70. See the extended discussion of the fate of the ducal title in Auzias, *Aquitaine,* pp. 472–90.

71. H. Doniol, ed. *Cartulaire de Brioude. Liber de Honoribus Sto. Juliano collatis* (Clermont-Ferrand, 1863) [no. 299], p. 305 (c. 983). I am grateful to Dr. Michael Sherman for making a copy of this document available to me. On the family of Robert I, infra, p. 50.

72. The foundation charter is in *Gallia Christiana,* 2: instr. cols. 323–24.

73. Aimo of Fleury, *Miracula Sancti Benedicti* 2.4 in *Les miracles de Saint Benoît,* ed. E. de Certain (Paris, 1858), pp. 100–101: "Odo, ex monasterio sancti Giraldi quod Aureliacium dicitur adveniens."

74. John of Salerno, *Vita Odonis* 3.8, *PL,* 133: col. 81: "Per illud tempus vir Elisiardus, qui tunc erat comes illustris, nunc vero in monastico degit habitu, audiens infamiam horum monachorum, praedictam abbatiam a Rodulfo rege Francorum petiit et accepit, acceptamque patri nostro tradidit." See infra, Chapter 4 on the reform of Fleury.

75. For the donation, M. Prou and A. Vidier, eds., *Recueil des chartes de l'abbaye de Saint-Benoît-sur-Loire,* 2 vols., bound as one (Paris, 1900–1912), 1 [no. 47]: 120–22 (941). Elisiernus mentions his son, Joseph, and his daughter, Elisabeth. The bottom of the charter has the signature of *Joseph acolitus* as well as the signatures of several counts, including Hugh the Great and Fulk the Good of Anjou. Chaume has speculated in "En Marge," 30 (1940): 49 that this demonstrates that the donor is a relative of the Angevin counts and father of the Joseph who was archbishop of Tours in 947. *Gallia Christiana,* 14: cols. 51–52 says the sources for Joseph are scanty; it does not mention his parentage.

76. Leo VII, *Epistola* 8, *PL,* 132: col. 1076. The reform is termed "recent" *(nuper).*

77. Charters of Teotolo's endowments to St.-Julien are published in C. de Grandmaison, "Fragments des chartes du Xe siècle, provenant de Saint-Julien

de Tours, recueillis sur les registres d'état civil d'Indre-et-Loire," *Bibliothèque de l'Ecole des Chartes* 46 (1885): 373–429. On Teotolo, cf. *Gallia Christiana,* 14: cols. 47–51.

78. Clarius, *Chronicon* in Bautier, *Chronique,* p. 76: "Cui successit sanctus Odo, abbas primus Clugniacensis cęnobii; accersiens igitur idem Odo Willelmum archiepiscopum, cum consensu monacorum Sancti Petri, prefecit eidem cęnobio Arigaudum abbatem, religiosum et timentem Deum, monachum sancti Benedicti."

79. For the historical background here, P. Toubert, *Les structures du Latium médiéval. Le Latium méridional et la Sabine du IX ^{e} siècle à la fin du XII ^{e} siècle,* 2 vols. (Rome, 1973), 2: 936–97.

80. On Alberic, in addition to Toubert, see G. Falco, *La Santa Romana Repubblica,* 4th ed. (Milan, 1963), pp. 191–210; G. Arnaldi, "Alberico di Roma," *Dizionario biografico degle Italiani,* 1: 647–56; G. Antonelli, "L'opera di Odone di Cluny in Italia," *Benedictina* 4 (1950): 19–40; B. Hamilton, "The Monastic Revival in Tenth-Century Rome," *Studia Monastica* 4 (1962): 35–68; G. Arnaldi, "Profilo di Alberic di Roma," *Atti, Academia nazionale di Scienze morali e politiche* 68 (1957): 138–58.

81. Falco, *Santa Romana Repubblica,* p. 203.

82. U. Balzani, ed., *Destructio Monasterii Farfensis,* in *Il Chronicon Farfense* (Rome, 1903), pp. 39–40: "[Alberic] eum [Odo] archimandritam constituit super concta monasteria Rome adiacentia, suamque domum propriam ubi ipse natus est Rome," i.e., St. Mary, St. Paul, Monte Cassino, and Farfa. The reform of St. Elias is mentioned in John of Salerno, *Vita Odonis* 3.7, *PL,* 133: cols. 79–80.

83. For St. Elias, John of Salerno, *Vita Odonis* 3.7, PL, 133: cols. 79–80. For Monte Cassino, Balzani, *Destructio,* p. 40; for Farfa, *ibid.*

84. *C,* 1 [no. 792]: 743–44 (c. 950). On Stephen, cf. *Gallia Christiana,* 2: cols. 255–56. Also from Aymard's time is the foundation charter of St.-Saturnin-du-Port (now Pont-Saint-Esprit), dated 945. The sponsor, who gave St.-Saturnin's direction over to Cluny, was one Gerald, who identified himself as *archiepiscopus* at the beginning of the charter and as *episcopus* at the end; cf. Devic and Vaissette, *Languedoc,* 5 [no. 81]: cols. 196–97. One can only speculate as to who this Gerald is. The annotators of Devic and Vaissette think that he might have been bishop of Apt, but, to account for the appelation archbishop, they suggest that he was archbishop of Aix-en-Provence. *Gallia Christiana,* 1: cols. 303–4 lists Odolric as archbishop of Aix from 928 to 947. Devic's annotators think this is too long a period, and they suggest inserting Gerald in what are now the last few years of Odolric's tenure; Devic and Vaissette, *Languedoc,* 4: 128. The identification of Gerald is too tenuous to be useful here.

85. M. Guérard, ed., *Cartulaire de l'abbaye de Saint-Victor de Marseille,* 2 vols. (Paris, 1857), 1 [no. 29]: 40: "filii Rothboldi quondam." On Boso, Poupardin, *Bourgogne,* pp. 283–84; Devic and Vaissette, *Languedoc,* 4: 59–62.

86. *Gallia Christiana,* 1: instr. no. 33, 103.

87. Bouquet, *Recueil,* 9: 700.

88. Guérard, *Saint-Victor,* 1 [no. 598]: 590. On William and Roubaud's authority, cf. Devic and Vaissette, *Languedoc,* 4: 62–65. William rid Le Freinet of the Saracens after Majolus's ignominius but brief capture by them. He and Majolus were involved in mutual gift giving: *C,* 3 [no. 1837]: 80–81 (993), in this charter William gives back property once given to him by Majolus, reserving the usufruct for his lifetime.

89. For Lothair, *C,* 2 [no. 1067]: 160–62; for Conrad, *C,* 2 [no. 1052]: 146–47.

90. The reform of St.-Marcel-lès-Sauzet (also known as St.-Marcel-de-Fellines) is a later example of the work of Lambert, count of Valence, a self-made grandee in the kingdom of Burgundy. Lambert's family was obscure, and it is not known how he succeeded to the comital office, which he was able to hand down to one of his sons, while another son became bishop of Valence. The foundation charter for St.-Marcel is in *C,* 2 [no. 1715]: 735–38 (985), as is its confirmation by King Conrad of Burgundy, *C,* 2 [no. 1716]: 739–40 (985). Sackur, *Die Cluniacenser,* 1: 232, attributes its reform to Majolus's influence, while Poupardin, *Bourgogne,* p. 338, numbers it among Majolus's reforms. However, the charters, while certainly providing for a Benedictine reform of the monastery, make no mention of Majolus. The foundation charter mentions two monks, Odoinus and Durannus, who are to effect the reform, but it does not say that they come from Cluny. St.-Marcel was later (1037) given to Cluny by Lambert's son, Adémar, count of Valence, because, according to the charter, it was neglecting its religious duties, *C,* 4 [no. 2921]: 122 (1037). It is possible that the two earlier documents came into Cluny's possession at this time.

91. On the rise of Henry I and Otto I to kingship from relative obscurity, see K. J. Leyser, *Rule and Conflict in an Early Medieval Society: Ottonian Saxony* (Bloomington, 1979), p. 11.

92. Poupardin, *Bourgogne,* pp. 392–413 calls into question—but does not decide against—Bertha's role in the foundation. His edition of the foundation charter is on pp. 408–13. Further discussion is in A. Hofmeister, "Die Gründungsurkunde von Peterlingen," *Zeitschrift für die Geschichte des Oberrheins,* n.s., 25 (1910): 217–38.

93. Liudprand, *Antapodosis* 4.14, in *Die Werke Liudprands von Cremona,* ed. J. Becker, 3d ed. (Hanover, 1915), p. 111.

94. Odilo, *Epitaphium domine Adelheide auguste* 9, in *Die Lebensbeschreibung der Kaiserin Adelheid von Abt Odilo von Cluny,* ed. H. Paulhart, pt. 2 of *Festschrift zur Jahrtausendfeier der Kaiserkrönung Ottos des Grossen,* vol. 2 (Graz, 1962), p. 36. For Conrad, *C,* 2 [no. 1127]: 217–19. Conrad was first prisoner, then ally, of Otto I; with his sister's marriage to Otto, his relations with the Empire became even closer. On this period in Burgundian history, F. Baethgen,"Das Königreich Burgund in der deutschen Kaiserzeit des Mittelalters," *Mediaevalia. Aufsätze, Nachrufe, Besprechungen,* vol. 1 (Stuttgart, 1960), pp. 25–50, esp. 31–32.

95. The possibility is advanced by Poupardin, *Bourgogne,* pp. 395–97.

96. Odilo, *Epitaphium,* in Paulhart, *Lebensbeschreibung,* pp. 1–45.

97. On Otto's ambitions, H. Büttner, "Der Weg Ottos des Grossen zum

Kaisertum,"*Das Kaisertum Ottos des Grossen*, ed. H. Beumann and H. Büttner (Constance, n.d.), pp. 55–80, pub. orig. in *Archiv für mittelrheinische Kirchengeschichte* 14 (1962): 44–62.

98. Odilo, *Epitaphium* 9, in Paulhart, *Lebensbeschreibung*, p. 36: "Maiolo ordinandum regulariter tradidit."

99. Syrus, *Vita Sancti Maioli* 2.22, *PL*, 137: col. 764: "[Majolus] ad beati Benedicti instituit tramitem ibique suum ordinavit abbatem."

100. Cf. *MGH, Diplomata*, 1 [no. 410]: p. 558 (972). Archbishop Honestus is quoted in this diploma as praising Otto for restoring the monastery. The diploma itself confirms the property of the monastery.

101. The documents, including the court judgment, the sale, and the donation, are in *C*, 2 [nos. 1228 and 1129]: 310–17 (967).

102. John XV, *Bull* (an. 987), in *Historiae Patriae Monumenta*, 22 vols. (Turin, 1836–1955), 13: col. 1461.

103. Gregorio di Catino, *Il Regesto di Farfa*, ed. I. Giorgi and U. Balzani, 5 vols. (Rome, 1879–1914), 3 [no. 401]: 104. Cf. B. Hamilton, "The Monastery of S. Alessio and the Religious and Intellectual Renaissance in Tenth-Century Rome," *Studies in Medieval and Renaissance History* 2: 277–78.

104. D'Arbois de Jubainville, *Histoire*, 1 [no. 20]: 452. On Lambert, see Bouchard, "Origins," p. 516–17. Some of the references for the Burgundian monasteries mentioned here and below were brought to my attention by Dr. Bouchard in private communications.

105. U. Chevalier, ed., *Cartulaire du Prieuré de Paray-le-Monial* (Paris, 1890), [no. 2], pp. 2–3: "Igitur postquam per dispositionem Dei, ante saecula praescientis omnia et que 'vocat ea quae non sunt tanquam ea quae sunt,' nobilissimus strenuissimusque Lambertus, filius Rotberti vicecomitis, Ingeltrude matre ortus, obtinuit comitatum Cabilonensem primus, assentante rege primoribusque Franciae; cogitans erga se Dei cara beneficia." The document gives the dates of the house's foundation and consecration.

106. A. Bertrand de Broussillon, ed., *Cartulaire de Saint-Aubin d'Angers* (Paris, 1903), 1 [no. 2]: p. 5. On Geoffrey's ancestry, see K. F. Werner, "Untersuchungen zur Frühzeit des französischen Fürstentums (9.-10. Jahrhundert)," *Die Welt als Geschichte* 18 (1958): 264–66.

107. There is an eleventh-century account of the reform of St.-Marcel in *C*, 4 [no. 3341]: 429–31. See also M. and P. Canat de Chizy, eds., *Cartulaire du prieuré de Saint-Marcel-lès-Chalon* (Chalon, 1894), [no. 6], pp. 11–12, also from the eleventh century, which names Adelaide and her new husband as the sponsors of reform by Majolus. On Geoffrey Greymantle, see Bouchard, "Origins," pp. 514–17 and n. 46.

108. *C*, 3 [no. 2484]: 562–66. For Orval, see also Chevalier, *Paray-le-Monial* [no. 14^1], p. 12.

109. *Gallia Christiana*, 12: col. 284; *Gesta pontificum Autissiodorensium* 49, in L.-M. Duru, ed., *Bibliothèque historique de l'Yonne*, 2 vols. (Auxerre, 1861), 1: 386–87. See the chapter "Hugh of Chalon" in Bouchard, "Nobility, Church," and M. Chauney, "Deux évêques bourguignons de l'an mil: Brunon de Langres et Hugues Ier d'Auxerre," *Cahiers de civilisation médiévale* 21 (1978): 388–92.

110. On Gerberga's family, Poupardin, *Bourgogne,* pp. 414–19.

111. *Gesta pontificum Autissiodorensium* 47, in Duru, *Bibliothèque historique,* 1: 382–83; M. Quantin, ed., *Cartulaire général de l'Yonne,* 2 vols. (Auxerre, 1854–1860), 1 [no. 82]: 157–59.

112. On Otto-William, Chaume, *Origines,* 1: 463–91, and supra, p. 36.

113. E.g., *C,* 3 [no. 2694]: 721–22 (c. 1015); [no. 2736]: 759–60 (c. 1020).

114. *Chronique de Saint-Bénigne,* p. 130: "Maiolus dedit ei duodecim monachos ex omni congregatione electos, disciplinis sancte religionis instructos." See also the obituary for Bruno, which speaks of Otto-William's role in the reform of St.-Bénigne, in G. Chevrier and M. Chaume, eds., *Chartes et documents de Saint-Bénigne de Dijon, prieurés et dépendances des origines à 1300* (Dijon, 1943), 2: 48–49. On William of Dijon, the man chosen by Majolus to become abbot of St.-Bénigne, and who became a reformer in his own right, N. Bulst, *Untersuchungen zu den Klosterreformen Wilhelms von Dijon (962–1031)* (Bonn, 1973). On Bruno of Langres, see Chauney, "Deux évêques," pp. 385–88.

115. There is considerable controversy about the noble vs. non-noble origins of Thibaud le Tricheur. See the bibliography in A. Chédeville, *Chartres et ses campagnes, XIe-XIIIe siècles* (Paris, 1973), p. 251, n. 1. However, it is clear that his father was originally only a viscount. On the family's extension into Berry, Devailly, *Berry,* pp. 129–35.

116. Richer, *Historiarum libri quatuor* 4.97, in *Histoire de France (838–995),* ed. and trans. R. Latouche, 2 vols. (Paris, 1937), 2: 306–310. On Odo's career, see R. T. Coolidge, "Adalbero, Bishop of Laon," *Studies in Medieval and Renaissance History,* 2 (1965): 43–44, 55–57; Bur, *Champagne,* pp. 114–25. On the date of the plot to get the title *dux Francorum,* Coolidge, "Adalbero," p. 56, n. 115.

117. E. Mabille, ed., *Cartulaire de Marmoutier pour le Dunois* (Châteaudun, 1874), [no. 92], p. 80 (1096), where Stephen II, count of Blois, mentions the people involved in the restoration of the monastery.

118. Richer, *Historia* 4.74, in Latouche, *Histoire* 2: 268.

119. Burchard used to be identified as brother of Geoffrey Greymantle of Anjou (Bouquet, *Recueil,* 10: 350), but C. Bourel de la Roncière has argued effectively against this attribution in his edition of Odo of St.-Maur-des-Fossés, *Vita Domni Burcardi* in *Eudes de Saint-Maur, Vie de Bouchard le Vénérable* (Paris, 1892), pp. i–ix. The background for Burchard given here is Bourel's. On Burchard's advancement by Hugh Capet, see Odo of St.-Maur-des-Fossés, *Vita Domni Burcardi* 1, in ibid., p. 6 (and see Bourel's comments, pp. x–xiv).

120. Odo of St.-Maur, *Vita* 2–3, in Bourel, *Eudes,* pp. 7–9.

121. Hugh Capet, *Diplomata* 7 (an. 989), in Bouquet, *Recueil,* 10: 555.

122. Syrus, *Vita Maioli* 3.19, *PL,* 137: col. 776. One other reform by Majolus needs to be mentioned. Lérins had been held by the papacy but was given to Majolus at his own request by Benedict VII in 978, cf. Benedict VII, *Epistola* 2, in Bouquet, *Recueil,* 9: 245.

NOTES TO CHAPTER 3

1. Odo of Cluny, *Collationum libri tres, PL,* 133: cols. 517–638; idem, *De vita Sancti Geraldi, PL,* 133: cols. 639–704. On the date of composition of the *Collationes,* cf. John of Salerno, *Vita Odonis* 1. 37–38, *PL,* 133: col. 60. The *Vita Geraldi* has been questioned regarding both the authenticity of the text and the date of composition. Briefly, the issues are as follows: There are two versions of this work: A, the longer (edited in *PL*); B, the shorter, printed in G.-M.-F. Bouange, *Histoire de l'Abbaye d'Aurillac,* 2 vols. (Paris, 1899), 1: 370–97. Hauréau has argued for the authenticity of B, with A as a later forgery (B. Hauréau, *Singularités historiques et littéraires* [Paris, 1894], pp. 162–65); Poncelet has argued for A, with B as its resumé (A. Poncelet, "La plus ancienne Vie de S. Gérard d'Aurillac," *Analecta Bollandiana* 14 [1895]: 91). The latest commentator argues that the version of A in *PL* is a corrupt text of the authentic *Vita,* cf. V. Fumagalli, "Note sulla 'Vita Geraldi' di Odone di Cluny," *Bullettino dell'Istituto storico italiano per il Medio Evo* 76 (1964): 217–40.

On the date of composition, Poncelet argues for 923–25 in "La plus ancienne Vie," pp. 104–7, based primarily on the notion that contemporaries of Gerald of Aurillac, whom Odo consulted for the *Vita,* could not have lived much beyond 925. Fumagalli argues for 909 in "Note sulla 'Vita Geraldi,'" pp. 234–35, because the *Vita Geraldi* so lauds lay life that Odo must have been a layman when he wrote it. (However, it should be noted that Odo had entered Baume by 909!) The most reasonable guess places the writing at 930–31, when Odo was reforming Tulle (cf. supra, Chapter 2); this is the date mentioned by G. Sitwell, ed. and trans., *St. Odo of Cluny. Being the Life of St. Odo of Cluny by John of Salerno and the Life of St. Gerald of Aurillac by St. Odo* (London, 1958), p. 91, n. 1.

2. For a study of the problem of tradition, cf. K. F. Morrison, *Tradition and Authority in the Western Church, 300–1140* (Princeton, 1969).

3. Cicero, *De Officiis* 1.5 et seq., ed. W. Miller, Loeb Classical Library [hereafter LCL] (New York, 1928), pp. 16ff. Ambrose, *De Officiis ministrorum* 1.24, *PL,* 16: col. 57. Plato introduces the virtues in his *Republic* 4.427, ed. P. Shorey, 2 vols., LCL (London, 1913), 1: 327. For a discussion of the tradition of the cardinal virtues cf. H. North, "Canons and Hierarchies of the Cardinal Virtues in Greek and Latin Literature," *The Classical Tradition. Literary and Historical Studies in Honor of Harry Caplan* (Ithaca, New York, 1966), pp. 165–83. I am indebted to Marcia Colish, of Oberlin College, for critical and bibliographic suggestions on the virtues and vices.

4. Horace, *Epistola* 1.1, in *Q. Horati Flacci Opera,* ed. F. Klingner (Leipzig, 1939), p. 241, altered here by changing Horace's adjectives into nouns. The original passage is quoted and discussed in M. Bloomfield, *The Seven Deadly Sins. An Introduction to the History of a Religious Concept, with Special Reference to Medieval English Literature* (East Lansing, Michigan, 1952), pp. 45–46.

5. Cicero, *De Officiis* 1.19, LCL, p. 64.

6. Ambrose, *De Officiis* 1.36, *PL,* 16: cols. 76–78.

7. Augustine, *Confessiones* 8.12, ed. P. Knöll, Corpus Scriptorum Ecclesias-

ticorum Latinorum (hereafter *CSEL*), vol. 33, sec. 1, pt. 1 (Vienna, 1896), pp. 193–96.

8. "Verumtamen Deo subjecta esto, anima mea, /Quoniam ab ipso patientia mea" (Ps. 61:6). All biblical quotes are my translations either from the Latin *Vulgate,* ed. A. Colunga and L. Turrado, 4th ed. (Madrid, 1965) or from the biblical text as it is quoted in a Cluniac or patristic text.

9. Prudentius, *Psychomachia,* ed. M. P. Cunningham, Corpus Christianorum. Series Latina (hereafter *CCSL*), vol. 126 (Turnhout, 1966), pp. 149–81. For a recent analysis of the poem, cf. M. Smith, *Prudentius' Psychomachia: A Reexamination* (Princeton, 1976), pp. 109–67.

10. Gregory the Great, *Moralia in Job* 31.45, *PL,* 76: cols. 620–21. In references to the *Moralia,* I shall use throughout the edition by M. Adriaen, *CCSL,* vols. 143, 143a (Turnhout, 1979) for Books 1–22 and, perforce, the *PL* edition for books thereafter.

11. Cf. *Homilia in Evangelia* 1.16, *PL,* 76: col. 1136 and *Homilia in Hiezechihelem* 2,7.17–19, *CCSL,* 142: 331–32. For other interpretations of the schema, see D. R. Howard, *The Three Temptations: Medieval Man in Search of the World* (Princeton, 1966).

12. Gregory the Great, *Moralia* 33.15, *PL,* 76: 691–92: "In eis quippe quos ad stultitiam luxuriae excitat, jumentum est; in eis quos ad nocendi malitiam inflammat, draco est; in eis autem quos in statu superbiae quasi alta sapientes elevat, avis est."

13. (Pseudo?) Odo of Cluny, *Epitome Moralium* 31, *PL,* 133: col. 475; ibid. 33: col. 492. Cf. René Wassèlynck, "Les compilations des 'Moralia in Job' du VIIe au XIIe siècle," *Recherches de théologie ancienne et médiévale* 29 (1962): 5–32. Serious arguments have been advanced against Odo's authorship of this particular abridgment of the *Moralia;* cf. G. Braga, "Problemi di autenticità per Oddone di Cluny: l'Epitome dei 'Moralia' di Gregorio Magno," *Studi Medievali* Ser. 3, 18, pt.2 (1977): 45–145, who, however, advances an alternative, unedited *Exceptio* of the *Moralia* as Odo's own work.

14. "Dimitte mortuos sepelire mortuos suos" (Matt. 8:22). "Regnum meum non est de hoc mundo" (John 18:36). For a discussion of this problem as it was worked out in the fourth century, cf. K. M. Setton, *Christian Attitude to the Emperor in the Fourth Century* (New York, 1941).

15. "Omnis anima potestatibus sublimioribus subdita sit: non est enim potestas nisi a Deo: quae autem sunt, a Deo ordinatae sunt. Itaque qui resistit potestati, Dei ordinationi resistit" (Rom. 13:1–2).

16. Hilary of Poitiers accused Constantine of enslaving the church. He looked back longingly to the days of the persecutions; *Contra Constantium* 4, *PL,* 10: col. 480f. Cf. K. F. Morrison, *Rome and the City of God: An Essay on the Constitutional Relationships of Empire and Church in the Fourth Century* (Philadelphia, 1961), p. 7. On the martyrs cf. W. H. C. Frend, *Martyrdom and Persecution in the Early Church: A Study of a Conflict from the Maccabees to Donatus* (New York, 1967), pp. 393–417. The epithet describing Constantine supra is from P. Brown, *The World of Late Antiquity, A.D. 150–750* (London, 1971), p. 87.

17. The summary of Augustine's thought here is much indebted to H. A.

Deane, *The Political and Social Ideas of St. Augustine* (New York, 1963), pp. 1–153. Cf. also P. Brown, *Augustine of Hippo: A Biography* (Berkeley, 1969), pp. 287ff. The fundamental primary source is Augustine, *De civitate Dei,* ed. B. Dombart and A. Kalb *CCSL,* vols. 47–48.

18. On Ambrose's attitude toward Theodosius and the civil power in general, cf. C. Morino, *Church and State in the Teaching of St. Ambrose,* trans. M. J. Costelloe (Washington, D.C., 1969), pp. 79–102. More generally, cf. Setton, *Christian Attitude,* pp. 109–51. For the argument that Theodosius was not, in fact, subservient to the clergy, acting instead out of his own notions of piety, cf. A. Lippold, *Theodosius der Grosse und seine Zeit* (Stuttgart, 1968), pp. 17–23, 33–37.

19. Cf. J. M. Wallace-Hadrill, *The Long-Haired Kings and Other Studies* (New York, 1962), pp. 49–71, 185–205.

20. Gregory of Tours, *Historiae Francorum* 5, pref., in *Grégoire de Tours, Histoire des Francs,* ed. H. Omont (Paris, 1886), p. 147: "Quid aliud sperandum erit, nisi cum exercitus vester ceciderit, vos sine solatio relicti atque a gentibus adversis oppraessi protinus conruatis?"

21. *Admonitio generalis* pref. *MGH, Legum* sectio 2: *Capitularia regum Francorum* (hereafter *Leg.* 2: *Capit. reg. Fr.*), 1 [no. 22]: 54. For Josias cf. 4 Kings 22:11–23, 25.

22. *Episcoporum ad Hludowicium imperatorem relatio* (829), *MGH, Leg.,* 2: *Capit. reg. Fr.* 2 [no. 196]: 47: "[Rex] debet primo defensor esse ecclesiarum et servorum Dei, viduarem, orfanorum caeterorumque pauperum necnon et omnium indigentium."

Coronations were not the only times kings confronted clerical standards; bishops were royal counsellors, and some of them composed "Mirrors of Princes." On this genre in the Carolingian period, cf. H. H. Anton, *Fürstenspiegel und Herrscherethos in der Karolingerzeit* (Bonn, 1968).

23. E.g., *Synodus Bellovacensis* (of Charles the Bald [845]), *MGH, Leg.* 2: *Capit. reg. Fr.* 2 [no. 292]: 387; *Capitula Electionis* (of Louis the Stammerer [877]), *MGH, Leg.* 2: *Capit. reg. Fr.* 2 [no. 283]: 364; *Karlomanni conventus Carisiacenis* (882), *MGH, Leg.* 2: *Capit. reg. Fr.* 2 [no. 285]: 370.

24. *Ordo LXXII,* in *Le Pontifical romano-germanique du dixième siècle,* ed. C. Vogel, 2 vols. (Vatican, 1963) 1: 256: "viduas et pupillos clementer adiuves ac defendas."

25. On these points, cf. K. F. Morrison, *The Two Kingdoms. Ecclesiology in Carolingian Political Thought* (Princeton, 1964), pp. 181ff. On the contractual and therefore limited power of the Carolingians cf. M. David, *La souveraineté et les limites juridiques du pouvoir monarchique du IXe au XVe siècle* (Paris, 1954), pp. 106–29.

26. *Odonis Regis promissio, MGH, Leg.* 2: *Capit. reg. Fr.* 2 [no. 288]: 376: "Promitto et perdono unicuique vestrum et ecclesiis vobis commissis, quia canonicum privilegium et debitam legem atque iusticiam conservabo et contra depredatores et oppressores ecclesiarum vestrarum et rerum ad easdem pertinentium deffensionem secumdum ministerium meum, quantum mihi posse Deus dederit, exibebo; et ius ecclesiasticum et legem canonicam vobis ita conservabo, et res ecclesiarum vestrarum, tam a regibus vel imperatoribus, quam a

reliquis Dei fidelibus collatas sub integritate et immunitate absque aliqua inonoratione permanere concedam, quas modo iuste et legaliter vestrae retinent ecclesiae; et eas augmentare et exaltare secumdum debitum uniuscuiusque servicium, prout scire et posse mihi Deus racionabiliter dederit et tempus dictaverit, studebo, sicut mei antecessores."

27. Carloman, *Capitula apud Vernis Palatium* (March 884), *MGH, Leg.* 2: *Capit. reg. Fr.* 2 [no. 287]: 372: "Nos vero praedamur fratres nostros, et idcirco pagani merito nos nostramque substantiam depraedantur. Quomodo igitur securi poterimus pergere contra inimicos sanctae Dei ecclesiae et nostros, cum rapina pauperis inclusa est in domo nostra?"

28. Sulpicius Severus, *Vita S. Martini,* ed. J. Fontaine, *SC,* vols. 133–34 (Paris, 1967–68); cf. also Sulpicius Severus, *Dialogus, CSEL,* 1: 97–89, where Martin is compared to Eastern holy men. On many of the following points, cf. B. H. Rosenwein, "St. Odo's St. Martin: The Uses of a Model," *Journal of Medieval History* 4 (1978): 217–31.

29. Wallace-Hadrill, *Long-Haired Kings,* p. 35.

30. Sulpicius, *Vita Martini* 2, *SC,* 133: 256, cf. also p. 312. On the Stoic virtues, cf. ibid., pp. 464–65; for *topoi* in general, cf. E. R. Curtius, *European Literature and the Latin Middle Ages,* trans. W. Trask (New York, 1953), pp. 79–105.

31. Sulpicius, *Vita Martini, SC,* 133: 82, n. 2; cf. P. Brown, *World of Late Antiquity,* pp. 123, fig. 86, 124.

32. Sulpicius, *Vita Martini* 2, *SC,* 133: 256: "Ut iam illo tempore non miles, sed monachus putaretur."

33. Ibid., 4, p. 260: "Christi ego miles sum: pugnare mihi non licet."

34. Ibid., 10, pp. 272–73: "Idem enim constantissime perseverabat qui prius fuerat. Eadem in corde eius humilitas, eadem in uestitu eius uilitas erat; atque ita, plenus auctoritatis et gratiae, inplebat episcopi dignitatem, ut non tamen propositum monachi virtutemque desereret."

35. Cf. F. Graus, *Volk, Herrscher und Heiliger im Reich der Merowinger* (Prague, 1965) and F. Prinz, "Heiligenkult und Adelsherrschaft im Spiegel merowingischer Hagiographie," *Historische Zeitschrift* 204 (1967): 529–44. Both these authors are especially interested in the change in the origins ascribed to saints. Unlike early *Vitae,* which speak of humble origins, the seventh- and eighth-century saints were portrayed as nobles. Graus and Prinz link this to the German aristocracy's striving for religious sanction and position in a newly Christianized milieu. For a typology of saints' lives, see R. W. Southern, *Saint Anselm and His Biographer: A Study of Monastic Life and Thought, 1059–c. 1130* (Cambridge, England, 1963), pp. 320–38.

36. John of Salerno, *Vita Odonis, PL,* 133: cols. 43–76. John describes Odo's death (942), and speaks of Odo having been in a certain monastery "last August" (praeterito isto mense Augusto), ibid., col. 72; therefore, it seems that he wrote the *Vita* before August 943.

37. On *topoi* in lives of saints, see C. W. Jones, *Saints' Lives and Chronicles in Early England* (Ithaca, N.Y., 1947), pp. 51–79; H. Delehaye, *The Legends of the Saints,* trans. D. Attwater (New York, 1962), pp. 49–78; Graus, *Volk, Herrscher,* pp. 74–86.

38. There are a few exceptions; they seem to prove the rule. The Merovingian *Vita Arnulfi, MGH, Scriptores rerum Merovingicarum* (hereafter *Script. rer. Mer.*) 2: 433 praised its hero's "potency in arms," but this was incidental to his religious conversion to the ecclesiastical life. Cf. Graus, *Volk, Herrscher*, pp. 268–69. The Carolingian *Vita Ermenlandi, MGH, Script. rer. Mer.* 5: 685 styled that abbot a "perfect soldier," but his saintliness came in spite of, not because of, his militancy. The various warrior-saints of the East either were not particularly popular in the West before the eleventh century, or they were popular for reasons other than their soldiering. Cf. Erdmann, *Origin* (supra, Chapter 1, n. 52), pp. 6, 14–15.

During the Carolingian period, "Mirrors of Laymen" began to appear. These cannot be said to have provided much of an ethos for lay living. For example, in his treatise (written c. 795) to Eric, marquis of Fruili, Paulinus of Aquileia warned of the dangers and temptations open to men of the world. Following the *topos* of the *Life of St. Martin*, he contrasted the *miles terrenus* (earthly warrior) with the *miles Christi*, ; cf. Paulinus of Aquileia, *Liber exhortationis* 20, *PL*, 99: cols. 212–14. Dhuoda's famous handbook, written for her son, William, in the mid-ninth century, enjoined on him the positive virtue of reverence toward his father, above all, and then toward King Charles the Bald (as the young boy's *senior*), the royal family, the great and small men of the realm, and the priests. But this was not meant to be—and was not—a program for the life of a responsible adult; cf. Dhuoda, *Manuel pour mon fils*, ed. P. Riché, *SC*, vol. 225. On this literature, see Anton, *Fürstenspiegel* (supra, n. 22); P. Riché, *De l'éducation antique à l'éducation chevaleresque* (Paris, 1968), pp. 41–47, and additional citations in idem, *Daily Life in the World of Charlemagne*, trans. J. A. McNamara (Philadelphia, 1978), pp. 81–83.

39. In Sulpicius' vocabulary, indeed, power *(potentia)* was the equivalent of virtue *(virtus)*: cf. *virtus* in the *index verborum et locutionum* in Sulpicius, *Dialogus, CSEL*, p. 278.

40. Cf. P. Geary, *Furta Sacra: Thefts of Relics in the Central Middle Ages* (Princeton, 1978).

41. Gregory of Tours, *Hist. Fr.* 2.27 (37), in Omont, *Grégoire*, p. 67.

42. Ibid., p. 66: "Et ubi erit spes victuriae, si beato Martino offendimus?"

43. Augustine, *De civ. Dei* 15.5, *CCSL*, 48: 458: "nec in hoc alter alteri invidit, quod eius dominatus fieret anustior, qui alterum occidit, si ambo dominarentur."

44. Odo, *Coll.*, epist. nunc., *PL*, 133: col. 519: "Cum subito recordatus sum illius vestrae querimoniae . . . de perversitate pravorum, qui semper in malum succrescentes et ecclesiasticam censuram penitus contemnentes, quoslibet invalidos crudeliter affligunt."

45. Ibid., 1.11, col. 528: "Per malitiam, qua suos proximos gravent." The origin of the association is biblical—Ps. 14:3, "Qui non fecit proximo suo malum."

46. Ibid., 1.13, col. 528: "Malitia ad violentos pertinet."

47. The terminology equating oppressors of the weak with *potentes (potenti-*

ores) goes back to the late empire. Cf. J. N. L. Myres, "Pelagius and the End of Roman Rule in Britain," *Journal of Roman Studies* 1 (1960): 21–36.

48. Odo, *Coll.* 1.3, *PL,* 133: col. 528.

49. Ibid., 3.25, cols. 608–9: "Solent enim potentes superbire, de temporalibus gaudere, et ut sit quod abundanter expendant, vel habeant, solent aliena concupiscere. . . . Nam quomodo innocens erit cupidus, quoniam videlicet cupiditatem Apostolus sanctus etiam idolis comparat. . . . Et ut suis tantum, et non alienis utantur, dicit eis Joannes Baptista: Neminem concutiatis neque calumniam faciatis, et contenti estote stipendiis vestris."

50. Ibid., 2.37, col. 584: "humiles et invalidos, atque pauperiores videas, a superbis et potentibus divitibusque comprimi, affligi atque injuste laedi."

51. For the church as the oppressed, cf. ibid., 3.34, cols. 616–17; 2.16, col. 563.

52. For *humiles* and *invalidi,* cf. supra, n. 50; for *honesti* and *quieti,* ibid., 2.37, col. 584; for *justi* and *boni,* ibid., 3.49, cols. 633–34. The identity of *pauper* with *humilis* is found in Gregory the Great, *Moralia* 26.27, *PL,* 76: col. 378: "Scriptura sacra plerumque pauperes, humiles vocare consuevit." Cf. also *Moralia* 21.16, *CCSL,* 143a: 1084; ibid., 6.22, *CCSL,* 143: 312; ibid., 16.46, *CCSL,* 143a: 833.

53. Odo, *Coll.* 2.21, *PL,* 133: col. 567: "Itaque superbia abominatio est, humilitas sacrificium. . . . Quanto autem quique pauperiores sunt, tanto in illam abominationem rarius incurrunt, at vero istud sacrificium divites vix inveniunt."

54. Ibid., 3.29, col. 613: "Raptores igitur, qui pauperes in rebus temporaliter affligunt, videntur . . . illos vero, licet nolentes, ad quaerenda coelestia salubriter impellere." The source is Gregory the Great, *Moralia* 26.13, *PL,* 76: col. 360: "Mali enim bonos magis ab hujus mundi desideriis expediunt, dum affligunt; quia dum multa eis his violenta ingerunt, festinare illos ad superna compellunt."

55. Odo, *Coll.* 1.3, *PL,* 133: col. 522: "quot patientium exempla contra nostram impatientiam exponit. . . . Nam si durum est quod dicitur: Estote in tribulatione patientes, occurrit Paulus, qui non solum patiens est, sed et gloriatur dicens: Libenter gloriabor."

56. Ibid., 1.34, col. 543: "Ad hoc contumeliarum ludibria, irrisionum probra, passionum tormenta mortemque toleravit, ut humilis Deus doceret hominem non esse superbum." Cf. Gregory the Great, *Moralia* 15.45, *CCSL,* 143a: 780: "Quia enim uia Dei in hac uita humilitas fuit, ipse hic Deus Dominus redemptor noster ad probra, ad contumelias, ad passionem uenit et aduersa huius mundi aequanimiter pertulit, prospera fortiter uitauit, ut et prospera doceret aeternae vitae appeti et aduersa praesentis uitae non formidari."

57. Odo, *Coll.,* 3.34, *PL,* 133: cols. 616–17.

58. The two generations passed their time on earth together, often mingling indistinguishably. Cf. Odo, *Coll.* 1.14, *PL,* 133: col. 529; 2.6, col. 552. The notion comes from Augustine, *De civ. Dei,* praef., *CCSL,* 47: 1: "gloriosissimam civitatem Dei sive in hoc temporum cursu cum inter impios peregrinatur ex fide vivens." Cf. also ibid., 18.49, *CCSL,* 48: 647. Odo calls the generations of Cain and Abel "duae civitates," Odo, *Coll.* 1.35, *PL,* 133: col. 543.

59. Odo, *Coll.* 3.24–25, *PL,* 133: cols. 607–9.

60. For *principes*, ibid., 3.34–35, col. 608; for *nobiles*, ibid., 3.30, col. 613.
61. Ibid., 3.26–27, cols. 609–11.
62. Ibid., 2.1, col. 549: "Quicunque autem ditiores sunt, student semper divitias augere . . . per quas pauperiores sibi subdant, quos ad clientelas sui fastus obsequentes habeant: quibus ipsi pauperiores causa saturitatis libenter se subdunt." Cf. Salvian of Marseilles, *De gubernatione Dei* 5.38–39, *MGH, Auctores,* 1:62.
63. Odo, *Coll.,* 2.1, *PL,* 133: col. 549.
64. Ibid., 2.2, col. 550: "Mos est autem non solum malorum, verum etiam bonorum, sed tamen minus perfectorum; ut . . . cum pravorum gloriam cernunt, eadem gloria delectentur." Cf. ibid., 1.38, col. 545: "Electorum quoque generatio in duobus generibus distinguitur," and ibid., 1.40, col. 547. Odo's scheme of the generations is actually quadripartite: good men may be perfect or imperfect; bad men may be lay or religious.
65. Cf. K. Bösl, "Potens und Pauper. Begriffsgeschichtliche Studien zur gesellschaftlichen Differenzierung im frühen Mittelalter und zum 'Pauperismus' des Hochmittelalters," *Alteuropa und die moderne Gesellschaft: Festschrift für Otto Brunner,* ed. A. Bergengruen and L. Deike (Göttingen, 1963), pp. 60–87. The dichotomy *potens-pauper* is, of course, biblical. Cf. Ps. 71:12, "liberabit pauperem a potente."
66. Cf. Gerald, a potentate who is oppressed by others, infra, pp. 73–74.
67. The comparative form of *humiles* does not occur in the *Collationes.*
68. Odo, *Coll.* 1.16, *PL,* 133: col. 530: "isti [the members of the generation of Cain] proximos aut damnis affligunt, aut exemplis necant." He goes on to say, in the words of Gregory the Great (*Moralia* 26.14, *PL,* 76: col. 360): "Calumniatores recte dicere possumus omnes iniquos, non solum qui exteriora bona rapiunt, sed etiam qui malis suis moribus, et vitae reprobae exemplo interna nostra dissipare contendunt."
69. Odo, *Coll.* 3.49, *PL,* 133: col. 634: "[Mali] bonos autem rebus exspoliant, aut etiam perimunt." Cf. ibid., 3.27, col. 611: "Quales ergo sunt Christiani raptores, vel quid merentur qui fratres suos occidunt, pro quibus animas ponere jubentur? Occidunt, inquam, dum affligunt, quoniam non solum qui rapit, sed qui mercenarium defraudat, par homicidae perhibetur."
70. Ibid., 2.1, col. 550: "subjecti favoris ejus exemplo depressi a lumine veritatis permanent alieni."
71. John of Salerno, *Vita Odonis* 1.5, *PL,* 133: col. 46: "Si quando lis quoquo modo inter partes fuisset orta, . . . undique omnes ad eum . . . proficiscerentur."
72. Ibid.
73. Ibid., 1.8–9, col. 47.
74. Ibid., 1.35, col. 58.
75. Ibid., 1.18, col. 51; cf. also ibid., 1.21, cols. 52–53.
76. Ibid., col. 53.
77. Ibid., 1.21–22: "Adhegrinum nomine, in armis strenuum, et in consilio providum . . . qui mox corde compunctur. . . . Deposita itaque capitis coma et saeculari militia, ex tunc Christi factus est agonista."

78. *C,* 1 [no. 802]: 756 (978): "Ego denique predictus Leotbaldus cingulum militiae solvens et comam capitis barbamque pro divino amore detundens, monasticum, Deo auxiliante, habitum in predicto monasterio recipere dispono." On Letbald's family, cf. supra, Chapter 2, n. 17.

79. Odo, *Coll.* 3.24, *PL,* 133: col. 608: "Memento igitur quantum Deo debitor sis, qui tibi super aequales tribuit potestatem. Noli attendere quid potes agere, sed quid debes. Ipsius enim dispositione gladium portas, non ut ferias, sed ut commineris, quem utinam impollutum restituas commendatori Christo, qui idcirco potestatem divinitus tribuit, ut quos sanctae Ecclesiae auctoritas propter propriam virtutem ab oppressione pauperum frenare non sufficit, per istorum opitulationem comminuat." (Cf. Gregory the Great, *Moralia* 31.5, *PL,* 76: col. 576, and Tyrannus Rufinus, *Orationum Gregorii Nazianzeni novem interpretatio* 6.9, *CSEL,* 46: pt. 1, p. 202.) For the elaboration of these ideas in the *Vita Geraldi,* cf. infra, n. 121.

80. Odo, *Vita Geraldi,* praef., *PL,* 133: col. 642: "Quoniam vero hunc Dei hominem in exemplo potentibus datum credimus, viderint ipsi qualiter eum, sicut e vicino et de suo ordine sibi praelatum imitentur." On the significance of the *Vita Geraldi,* cf. Erdmann, *Origin,* pp. 87–88, and J.-C. Poulin, *L'Idéal de sainteté dans l'Aquitaine carolingienne d'après les sources hagiographiques (750–950)* (Quebec, 1975). I have been unable to consult C. Carozzi, "De l'enfance à la maturité: étude d'après les Vies de Géraud d'Aurillac et d'Odon de Cluny," in *Etudes sur la sensibilité au Moyen âge,* vol. 2 of Actes du 102e Congrès national des Societés savantes, section de philologie et d'histoire jusqu'à 1610, Limoges, 1977 (Paris, 1979), pp. 103–16. On Gerald's political and social position in the Auvergne, cf. A. R. Lewis, "Count Gerald of Aurillac, and Feudalism in South-Central France in the Early Tenth Century," *Traditio* 20 (1964): 41–58.

81. Odo, *Vita Geraldi,* 4.8, *PL,* 133: col. 700: "Incolae autem regionis illius mores valde ferinos habere solebant, sed aliquantulum exemplo vel reverentia sancti hominis esse mitiores videntur."

82. Ibid., 1.24, col. 656: "qui se laedi ab infimis personis, tanquam impotens, permisisset." Cf. ibid., 1.7, col. 646.

83. Ibid., 1.32, col. 660: "oportuit ut justum Abel malitiosus Cain ad patientiam exercuisset. Geraldus quoque, sicut Job, . . . frequenter a quibusdam provinciarum lacessitus est."

84. Ibid., 1.8, col. 646: "si inerti patientia torpuisset, praeceptum de cura pauperum neglexisse videretur."

85. Ibid., 1.17, col. 654: "imbecilliorem ita sustentaret, quatenus fortiorem sine laesione fregisset."

86. Cf., the examples Odo gives in ibid., 1.19–20, cols. 654–55, a series that ends with Odo's conclusion: "Nunquam tamen auditum est ut se praesente quilibet aut moret punitus sit, aut truncatus membris."

87. Ibid., 1.7, col. 646: "Satius esse temerarios vi bellica premi, quam pagenses et inermes ab eisdem injuste opprimi."

88. Ibid., 1.32–39, cols. 660–66.

89. Ibid., 1.7, col. 646: "non assultu, sed ratione cohortatus, ad miserandum et subveniendum flectebatur."

90. Ibid., 1.8, col. 646: "inexplebilis malitia quorumdam pacificum hominem irrideret."

91. Ibid., col. 647: "non hostes ipsos vellet appetere, sed solam in eis audaciam dementare."

92. Ibid.

93. The word "ridiculum" is Odo's, ibid., col. 646.

94. Ibid., col. 647: "Novo praeliandi genere mista pietate."

95. Ibid.: "Geraldus, quem pietas in ipso praeliandi articulo vincebat."

96. Odo, *Coll.* 3.26, *PL,* 133: col. 609: "Illis vero qui rapinis pauperum pascuntur severius obviandum est. Nam et illi qui pauperes quidem non affligunt, sed tamen afflictoribus eorum resistere non curant, vehementer utique peccant."

97. Ibid., 1.19, col. 532.

98. On the subject of armed and unarmed clergy, cf. F. Prinz, *Klerus und Krieg im früheren Mittelalter* (Stuttgart, 1971).

99. Odo, *Vita Geraldi* 2.2, *PL*, 133: 671: "Nam quale genus conversationis Deo poterat gratiosius exhibere, quam istud, in quo neque commune solatium negligeret, nec sibi quidquam de conversationis perfectione minueret? Quae nimirum conversatio tanto pretiosior exstitit, quanto et multis utilior, et soli Deo cognita fuit?" Teske, "Laien, Laienmönche" (supra, Chapter 1, n. 94), 10: 319–21, argues that the notion of a "layman in monk's clothes," which was the position of the lay monks at Cluny, was the fulfillment of Odo's model of St. Gerald. However, Gerald was more precisely a "monk in layman's clothes." This is a transformation of the *topos* in Sulpicius' St. Martin, cf. supra, n. 34.

100. This was a conflation of at least two conceptually separate meanings of *disciplina*—as doctrine and as obedience—with a particularly legalistic interpretation of both. Cf. W. Dürig, "Disciplina: Eine Studie zur Bedeutungsumfang des Wortes in der Sprache der Liturgie und der Väter," *Sacris Erudiri* 4 (1952): 245–79.

101. God was the ruler of nature, and His laws were implicit in it. Cf. Odo, *Coll.* 1.3, *PL,* 133: col. 522.

102. Ibid.: "praecepta [Dominica] . . . suis nos jussis a malis actibus refrenant. . . . Patrum exemplis esse facilis demonstratur."

103. Odo, *Vita Geraldi* 2.15, *PL,* 133: col. 678: "in eodem ore semper lex Domini resonaret. . . . omnia in nomine Domini facere videretur."

104. Ibid., 1.8, col. 647: "Nemo sane moveatur, quod homo justus usum praeliandi, qui incongruus religioni videtur, aliquando habuerit."

105. Ibid.: "Nonnulli namque Patrum cum et sanctissimi et patientissimi fuerint justitiae tamen causa exigente viriliter in adversariis arma corripiebant: ut Abraham, qui pro eruendo nepote ingentem hostium multitudinem fudit." Gerald's cause was always the "causa Dei," a battle against "insensatos," fulfilling the precept in Wisd. 5:21, "et pugnavit cum illo orbis terrarum contra insensatos."

106. Ibid., 1.15, col. 652: "opus Domini non respiciunt [here Odo is speaking of evil *potentiores*], quoniam inter voces perstrepentium nec saltem clamorem pauperis audiunt."

107. Sulpicius, *Vita Martini* 3, *SC,* 133: 258: "Nocte igitur insecuta, cum se sopori dedisset, uidit Christum chlamydis suae, qua pauperem texerat, parte uestitum." Cf. Matt. 25:40.

108. Cf. Rosenwein, "St. Odo's St. Martin."

109. Sulpicius, *Vita Martini* 4, *SC,* 133: 260–62: "Hostes legatos de pace miserunt, sua omnia seque dedentes. Unde quis dubitet hanc uere beati uiri fuisse uictoriam, cui praestitum sit ne inermis ad proelium mitteretur. Et quamuis pius Dominus seruare militem suum licet inter hostium gladios et tela potuisset tamen, ne uel aliorum mortibus sancti uiolarentur obtutus, exemit pugnae necessitatem. Neque enim aliam pro milite suo Christus debuit praestare uictoriam, quam ut, subactis sine sanguine hostibus, nemo moreretur." Cf. Fontaine's comments, *St. Martin* 134: 537–38.

110. Odo, *Vita Geraldi* 1.13, *PL,* 133: col. 651: "Illud Scripturae praeceptum observabat beatus princeps, qui in tempore suo comedit ad reficiendum et non ad luxuriam." Cf. Prov. 13:25.

111. Ibid.

112. Ibid., 1.15, col. 653: "Licuit igitur homini laico, praesertim tam justo, licitis uti; quod non licet eis quibus id sua professio contradicit."

113. Ibid.: "Sin vero jejunium die Dominica evenisset, nequaquam illud solvebat, nec sub hac occasione praeteribat, sed praecedenti sabbato solemnitatem jejunii persolvebat."

114. Ibid., 1.11, col. 649–50.

115. For reading at table, ibid., 1.15, cols. 652–53; for charitable meals, ibid., 1.14, cols. 651–52.

116. Ibid., 2.9, col. 675–76: "Tantopere enim lectionibus audiendis, et vicissim orationibus, nunc cum aliis, nunc semotim erat intentus, ut mirum sit quomodo vel tantum studium in his habere potuerit, vel tantam psalmorum summam semper explere voluerit."

117. Ibid., 2.15, col. 679: "Nam sacra quaedam verba sibi notaverat, quae corporalibus officiis convenire videbantur. Ut est illud, mane priusquam loqui inciperet, dicebat: Pone, Domine, custodiam ori meo, et ostium circumstantiae labiis meis, et caetera hujusmodi quae ad singulos coaptabat, videlicet cum expergisceret, cum de lecto surgeret, cum caligas indueret, cum indumentum, vel cinctorium sumeret, sive certe cum iter, vel aliud quilibet inciperet."

118. Ibid., 2.16, col. 680: "Hunc etiam conversandi modum in exteriori conversatione tenebat, ut ministri ejus notum haberent, qualiter in singulis anni temporibus conversaturus esset."

119. Ibid., 1.34, cols. 662–63: "nocturnam illusionem sine moerore nullatenus incurrebat. Quoties namque illud humanitatis infortunium dormienti contigisset, consecretalis cubicularius afferebat ei seorsum, in competenti videlicet loco, vestes mutatorias, ad hoc semper paratas, et tomentum, et vas aquae."

120. Gregory the Great, *Moralia* 31.5, *PL,* 76: cols. 575–76.

121. Odo, *Vita Geraldi* 1.8, *PL,* 133: col. 647: "Non nesciens rhinocerotem, id est, quemlibet potentem, loro religatum, ut glebas vallium, id est, humilium oppressores confringat. . . . Licuit igitur laico homini in ordine pugnatorum

posito gladium portare, ut inerme vulgus . . . defensaret. Et quos ecclesiastica censura subigere nequit, aut bellico jure, aut vi judiciaria compesceret."

122. Ibid., praef., col. 641: "Noe . . . qui secundum legem vixerit."

123. On the notion of *ordines* in society, cf. G. Duby, *Les trois ordres: ou L'imaginaire du féodalisme* (Paris, 1979). Eng. trans. by A. Goldhammer, *The Three Orders: Feudal Society Imagined* (Chicago, 1980).

124. For conquest by a psalm, Odo, *Vita Geraldi,* 1.39, *PL,* 133: col. 666; by the miraculous lure, ibid., 1.40, col. 666; by faulty intelligence, ibid., 1.36, col. 664.

125. Ibid., 1.8, col. 646: "conterebat molas iniqui."

126. Ibid., 1.28, col. 658–59.

127. Ibid., 1.38, col. 665: "ut quisquis eum laesisset, quasi sacrilegium fecisset, non sibi in prosperum cedere certus esset."

128. Ibid., 1.35, col. 663. When Gerald refuses to become a vassal of William of Aquitaine, Odo comments: "Credo Mardocheum (Mordechai) vir iste meditabatur, qui superbo Aman se submittere, honoremque regibus a Deo collatum praebere contempsit." The issue raised here has an interesting historiography. F. Ganshof, *Feudalism*, trans. P. Grierson, 3d ed., rev. (New York, 1964), pp. 59–60, used it to illustrate mediatization (pressuring royal vassals to become vassals of local strongmen). Lewis, "Count Gerald," pp. 47–48, argues that Gerald held allods, not fiefs, from the king and maintained an independent position *vis-à-vis* royalty as well as *vis-à-vis* William. Odo's own understanding of the matter, however, was that Gerald was God's *fidelis*.

129. Ibid., 1.42, col. 668: "Annon potentes fuerunt et bellicosi rex David, Ezechias, et Josias?"

130. Ibid.: "rege Anglorum Oswaldo, quos Deus per signa glorificat, qui scilicet in observantiam mandatorum ejus illum glorificare studuerunt."

131. Ibid., praef., col. 641: "Nec observantia mandatorum Dei gravis aut impossibilis aestimetur, quoniam quidem haec a laico et potente homine observata videtur."

132. *C,* 1 [no. 359]: 336 (928): "pro remedium animas seniore meo Vuarulfo et mea et omnibus parentibus nostris, vel cunctum populum Christianum, per intercessione beati Petri et Pauli et aliorum sanctorum, pius Dominus animas nostras de penas inferni liberare dignetur."

133. *C,* 3 [no. 2255] (994). Cf. supra, Chapter 2, p. 36.

NOTES TO CHAPTER 4

1. *RB* prologue, *SC,* 181: 422 (cf. supra, Chapter 2, n. 12): "dominici scola servitii."

2. Cf. supra, Chapter 3, n. 36. For Odo's sermon, cf. Odo, *Sermo III: De Benedicto Abbate, PL,* 133: cols. 721–29.

3. On John of Salerno, cf. Sackur, *Die Cluniacenser* (cf. supra, Chapter 1, n. 12) 1: 107–12; 359–63; Sitwell, *Odo of Cluny* (cf. supra, Chapter 3, n. 1), p. 3, n.1 passim; H. Richter, "Die Persönlichkeitsdarstellung in cluniazensischen

Abtsviten" (Dissertation, Nürnberg, 1972), pp. 36–62; G. Arnaldi, "Il biografo 'romano' di Oddone di Cluny," *Bullettino dell'Istituto storico italiano per il Medio Evo e Archivio Muratoriano,* no. 71 (1959), pp. 19–37; idem, "La 'vita Odonis,'" *Spiritualità cluniacense* (supra, Chapter 1, n. 71), pp. 245–49.

4. John gives the date 939 in *Vita Odonis* 1.4, *PL,* 133: col. 45, but it has been disputed and changed to 938 by Sackur, *Die Cluniacenser,* 1: 359, and Arnaldi, "Il biografo," pp. 20–22.

5. Arnaldi, "Il biografo," pp. 35–36.

6. John of Salerno, *Vita Odonis* 1.4, *PL,* 133: col. 45: "me infelicem dignatus est sibi socium sumere."

7. Arnaldi, "Il biografo," pp. 35–36. Sackur thinks that John was a simple monk at Salerno, Sackur, *Die Cluniacenser,* 1: 362, but Sitwell, *Odo of Cluny,* p. 44, n. 3, argues that he was an abbot, while Arnaldi, "Il biografo," p. 25, allows for the possibility of either prior or abbot. John refers to himself as prior of his monastery; John of Salerno, *Vita Odonis* 2.4, *PL,* 133: col. 62.

8. John of Salerno, *Vita Odonis* 1.14, *PL,* 133: col. 49: "Nunc transcurram ocius ad contemptus rerum. Laudent ergo qui volunt expulsores daemonum, caratores cadaverum, caeterosque infamatos viros virtutibus. Ego inter omnes exiguus, Odonis mei primam patientiae laudabo virtutem deinde contemptum rerum, post haec animarum lucrum, restaurationem coenobiorum, vestimentum cibumque monachorum, pacem Ecclesiarum, concordiam regum et principum, custodiam viarum omnium, instantiam mandatorum, perseverantiam vigiliarum et orationum, respectus pauperum, correptionem juvenum, honorem senum, emendationem morum, amorem virginum, consolationem continentium, misericordiam miserorum, intemeratam observantiam regularum, ad postremum specimen omnium virtutum."

9. Ibid., 1.29, col. 56: "Nosti consuetudinum Bernonis abbatis? . . . Heu, heu, si sciretis quam dure scit ille monachum tractare. Correptionem vero suam sequuntur verbera, et rursum quos verberat compedibus ligat, domat carcere, jejuniis affligit: et haec omnia perpessus, nec sic suam potest miser impetrare gratiam."

10. Cf. *RB* 2.11–15, *SC,* 181: 444.

11. John called the brethren "childish" in *Vita Odonis* 1.34, *PL,* 133: col. 58: "fratres . . . mente et actione juvenes."

12. Ibid.: "At vero vir pacificus Odo seorsum eos ducebat, et innocens quasi reus eorum pedibus se prosternebat veniam petens, non tamen metu humano, sed amore fraterno, nimirum ut patientia corrigeret quos videbat divinam incurrere ultionem. Compescebantur tandem aliquando ab ejus patientia: sed more labentis aquae protinus ad propria revertebantur vitia. Illum namque quem imitari debuerant, econtra insequebantur."

13. Ibid., 2.8–9, *PL,* 133: col. 66: "persecutoribus suis manus aperiret et palmas extenderet. . . . Quidam rusticus voluit eum propter lagunculam aquae occidere. . . . Quo audito [i.e., that Alberic wanted to amputate the hand] domnus abbas Odo obnixius ne fieret exoravit, et rusticum illum incolumem atque indemnem absolvit."

14. Ibid., 2.6, col. 64.

15. Ibid., 3.8, col. 81: "Quorum adventu fratres cognito, sumptis gladiis alii ascenderunt aedificiorum tecta, quasi hostes suos lapidibus et missilibus coelorum jaculaturi. Alii muniti clypeis, accinctis ensibus monasterii observabant aditum, prius se mori fatentes quam eos introire sinerent, aut abbatem alterius ordinis susciperent. . . . At postmodum pater Odo cunctis ignorantibus ascendit asellum, et coepit ire concite ad praedictum monasterium. Episcopi vero et qui cum ipsis erant comites simul cum suis currebant post eum clamantes: Quo is, pater? an fortassis quaeris mortem? anne vides quia parati sunt te interficere? qua videlicet hora accesseris ad eos morte morieris. Velisne eis de tuo interitu facere gaudium, et nobis exitialem luctum? has et hujuscemodi voces post eum mittentes. Sed, sicut Scriptura ait: Justus ut leo confidens absque terrore erit; accepto itinere eum nullomodo potuerunt declinare. Mira dicturus sum. Appropinquante autem illo et agnitus ab his qui eum prius noverant, hi qui tunc resistebant protinus commoti sunt et immutati, ita ut proculdubio dicere possim: Haec est mutatio dexterae Excelsi. Revera extemplo projectis armis exierunt obviam ei, ejusque sunt amplexati vestigia."

16. On the new tenth-century combination of practical action and inward humility, see E. Auerbach, *Literary Language and Its Public in Late Latin Antiquity and in the Middle Ages,* trans. R. Manheim (New York, 1965), p. 163.

17. Jotsaldus, *De vita et virtutibus sancti Odilonis abbatis* 1.7, *PL,* 142: col. 902.

18. On the Council of Anse, supra, Chapter 2, p. 36, and Chapter 3, pp. 82–83.

19. On the nature of Carolingian monastic reform, cf. J. Semmler, "Die Beschlüsse des Aachener Konzils im Jahre 816," *Zeitschrift für Kirchengeschichte* 74 (1963): 15–82. On the historiography of the question, cf. B. H. Rosenwein, "Rules and the *Rule* at Tenth-Century Cluny," *Studia Monastica* 19 (1977): 307–20.

20. On Gallican customs before the Carolingian reforms, see the monastic customaries published in *Corpus consuetudinum monasticarum,* ed. K. Hallinger, vol. 1, *Initia consuetudinis Benedictinae* (Siegburg, 1963) (hereafter *CCM*), pp. 3–92.

21. For this interpretation of Benedict's reforms, cf. Semmler, "Beschlüsse," and Rosenwein, "Rules." Benedict's liturgy may be assessed from documents in the *CCM:* the Gradual psalms, p. 314; special psalms, p. 528; Office of the Dead, pp. 336, 518.

22. John of Salerno, *Vita Odonis* 1.23, *PL,* 133: col. 54.

23. Ibid., 1.15, col. 50: "Contigit interea dum diversorum librorum legeret volumina, ad beati Benedicti pervenisse regulam: et cursim eam cum vellet transire, impegit in eumdem locum, in quo praeceptum est monachis, ut dormire debeant vestiti; nam plane non intelligens eumdem sensum, per triennium jacuit vestitus, et necdum monachus, monachorum lene ferebat jugum. Istius sancti praecepta curabat obaudire." Cf. *RB* 22.5, *SC,* 182: 540.

24. Cf. *RB* 55.10, *SC,* 182: 620.

25. John of Salerno, *Vita Odonis* 2.9, *PL,* 133: col. 66: "Fossorium ludendo vocatus est." Cf. *RB* 7.63, *SC,* 181: 488.

26. John of Salerno, *Vita Odonis* 3.9, *PL,* 133: cols. 81–82. Cf. *RB* 39.11, *SC,* 182: 578.

27. John of Salerno, *Vita Odonis* 3.3, 4, *PL,* 133: cols. 78–79.

28. Cf. *RB* 35.9, *SC,* 182: 566.

29. For the episode and John's commentary on it, John of Salerno, *Vita Odonis* 2.23, *PL,* 133: cols. 73–76. Cf. *RB* 31–32, *SC,* 182: 556–61.

30. John of Salerno, *Vita Odonis* 2.12, *PL,* 133: cols. 67–68. Cf. *RB* 42, *SC,* 182: 584–86; on the spirit of silence, cf. ibid., 6, *SC,* 181: 470–72.

31. John of Salerno, *Vita Odonis* 2.23, *PL,* 133: col. 74: "quia legaliter nolunt vivere a legis praecepto non verentur faciem cordis avertere."

32. Odo, *Sermo III, PL,* 133: col. 723.

33. Cf. supra, n. 30. Collections of biblical and patristic writings on silence were common. Cf., for example, Defensor of Ligugé, *Liber Scintillarum* (written c. 700) 16, *CCSL,* 117: 73–77. Cf. also A. G. Wathen, *Silence: The Meaning of Silence in the Rule of St. Benedict* (Washington, 1973).

34. Cf. supra, p. 86.

35. "Quae enim est gloria, si peccantes, et colaphizati suffertis? Sed si bene facientes patienter sustinetis, haec est gratia apud Deum. In hoc enim vocati estis: quia et Christus passus est pro nobis, vobis relinquens exemplum ut sequamini vestigia eius: qui peccatum non fecit, nec inventus est dolus in ore eius: qui cum malediceretur, non maledicebat: cum pateretur, non comminabantur: tradebat autem iudicanti se iniuste."

36. The episode is recounted in John of Salerno, *Vita Odonis* 1.33, *PL,* 133: cols. 57–58.

37. "Ut iumentum factus sum apud te;/Et ego semper tecum" (Ps. 72:23).

38. "Posuisti tribulationes in dorso nostro;/Imposuisti homines super capita nostra" (Ps. 65:11–12).

39. *RB* 7.40–41, *SC,* 181: 482.

40. John of Salerno, *Vita Odonis* 1.23, *PL,* 133: col. 54: "Totum se dedit beatorum Patrum regulis et institutionibus; ex quibus nempe auctoritatibus diversas consuetudines sumpsit, unoque volumine colligavit."

41. Ardo, *Vita Benedicti, CCM,* p. 312: "ut ostenderet contentiosis nil frivola cassaque a beato Benedicto edita fore." For the *Concordia Regularum,* cf. *PL,* 103: cols. 713–1380.

42. John of Salerno, *Vita Odonis* 1.32, *PL,* 133: col. 57: "ex quibus (cxxviii psalmis) xiv nos dempsimus propter pusillanimorum animos, exceptis peculiaribus orationibus quas nostri frequentant fratres, quae videlicet modum psalterii videntur excedere. Similiter duabus missis identidemque litaniis."

43. Angilbert, *Institutio, CCM,* p. 293.

44. John of Salerno, *Vita Odonis* 3.1, *PL,* 133: col. 75: "coeperunt modum suum, consuetudinesque relinquere, ac propriis voluntatibus vitam suam propositumque corrumpere. Relinquentes namque nativa et assueta vestimenta, coeperunt fucatas, atque fluxas pallioque ornatas circumferre cucullas et tunicas . . . . Ista et harum similia multa contra regulae jura faciebant." On custom as law, cf. *C,* 2 [no. 181]: 1088 (960): "Mos est lex, licet non scripta." The charter authorized granting ecclesiastical property to a layman. Cf. Constable, *Monastic Tithes,* p. 4.

45. *RB* 55.1, *SC,* 182: 618: "Vestimenta fratribus secundum locorum qualitatem, ubi habitant vel aerum temperiem dentur."

46. John of Salerno, *Vita Odonis* 1.31, *PL,* 133: col. 56–57. For this and the following point, see Rosenwein, "Rules," pp. 315–16.

47. Ibid., 1.35, col. 58.

48. Ibid., 3.4, col. 79: "Horum tamen interitus multorum exstitit emendatio morum. Sic enim apud nos ordo monachorum cecidit; sicque et correctus fuit et frequenter multis prodigiis corrigitur, ut auctore Deo perseveret."

49. Cf. supra, n. 42.

50. John of Salerno, *Vita Odonis* 3.11, *PL,* 133: col. 83.

51. Jotsaldus, *Vita Odilonis* 2.13, *PL,* 142: col. 927.

52. John of Salerno, *Vita Odonis* 1.27, *PL,* 133: col. 55: "ut fieret quod scriptum est: Omnia fac cum consilio, et post factum non poenitebis."

53. Cf. Hallinger's remarks on *consuetudines* in *CCM,* pp. xlv–xlvii.

54. The first customary, F, is published in *Consuetudines monasticae,* ed. B. Albers, vol. 2, *Consuetudines cluniacenses antiquiores* (Monte Cassino, 1905) (hereafter *CM*), pp. 1–12; the second customary, S, is also in *CM,* pp. 31–61. On the dating, the latest assessment is Hallinger's, in his introductory notes in *CCM,* pp. xlv–xlvi.

55. F, *CM,* pp. 2–3: "[Ad horam nonam] et tunc celebrent missam. Post missam vero eant ebdomadarii et cellarius et lector in refectorium, ut accipiant mixtum. Alii autem fratres sedeant in choro et sonetur iterum signum minus et cantent Nonam."

56. S, *CM,* p. 33: "Cum fuerit Nonae tempus sonet secretarius et facta oratione unus infantum inchoet letaniam et ebdomadarii vadant se (se?) vestire; finita letania dicatur missa. Post quam iterum sonet secretarius et faciant orationem sedeantque in choro et legant donec divestitus sit sacerdos. Interim vero accipiant mixtum ebdomadarii quoquine et lector. Redeunte autem sacerdote ad alios in choro, sonet tercio secretarius et Nona cantetur."

57. Cf., for example, F, *CM,* pp. 2–3.

58. Odo, *Vita Geraldi* 1.9, *PL,* 133: col. 648: "cedrus Paradisi."

59. Ibid., 2.34, col. 690: "Incredibile non est quod nunc obsessos a daemonibus liberat."

60. Ibid., 3.8, cols. 695–96: "Sed quoniam imperfectum Ecclesiae vident oculi tui, et lapides terrae ejus miserebuntur, precamur ut hi, qui pro soliditate morum lapides vocantur, nobis, qui merito nostrae pravitatis terra sumus, subvenire dignentur: ut nos qui non habemus indumentum justitiae, lapides amplectamur, ut eorum meritis nostram nuditatem contegere possimus. Hic ergo famulus tuus affectum miserendi, quem eidem charitas tua invisceravit, in nos dirigat, et de illa sempiterna Capitolii curia, qua jam inter consules coeli residet, in hac convalle lacrymarum quam evasit pie respiciat; singulorum preces exaudiat, omniumque necessitates apud te expediat, praestante Domino nostro Jesu Christo Filio tuo."

61. John of Salerno, *Vita Odonis* 2.12, *PL,* 133: col. 67: "Et hoc non aliqua fiebat apud eos in delusione, sed jure observantiaque sanctae regulae, sub quo videlicet cupiebant mori et vivere, nunquamque ab ea declinare."

62. Ibid.: "Sed Omnipotentis manus eorum exhilaratum spectaculum protinus convertit in luctum. Mox ut ad eos barbarus appropinquavit, equus in quo residebat in obliquum, resilivit, sessoremque suum in terram stravit atque collisit. Quam collisionem statim febris lethalis secuta est."

63. Ibid., 2.11, col. 67: "Vita enim monachi usque adeo est aliquid, donec sub silentio esse studuerit. Eo vero remoto, quidquid bene vel honeste se agere putaverit secumdum institutionem Patrum nihil erit."

64. Ibid., 2.10, col. 66.

65. Ibid., 2.4, col. 62: "et quia se omnibus petentibus dabat, Dei nutu cuncta ei suppeditabant. Illud Tobiae praeceptum semper habebat in promptu: Vide ne avertas faciem tuam ab illo tempore [? mistake for ullo paupere], et omni petenti te tribue."

NOTES TO CHAPTER 5

1. Cf. S. Cole and H. Zuckerman, "Appendix: Inventory of Empirical and Theoretical Studies of Anomie," in M. B. Clinard, ed., *Anomie and Deviant Behavior: A Discussion and Critique* (New York, 1964), pp. 243–313. For bibliography after 1964, cf. S. Marcson, *Automation, Alienation, and Anomie* (New York, 1970), pp. 445–67; L. Coser, ed., *The Idea of Social Structure: Papers in Honor of Robert K. Merton* (New York, 1975), pp. 497–522.

2. E. Durkheim, *Le Suicide* (Paris, 1897). All references here will be to the English ed., *Suicide: A Study in Sociology,* trans. J. A. Spaulding and G. Simpson (New York, 1951), pp. 241–76. The concept of anomie was first mentioned by Durkheim, *De la division du travail social* (Paris, 1893); cf. English ed., *The Division of Labor in Society,* trans. G. Simpson (Glencoe, Ill., 1947).

3. Durkheim, *Suicide,* pp. 243–46.

4. R. K. Merton, "Social Structure and Anomie" (henceforth *SSA*) (orig. pub. in *The American Sociological Review* 3 [1938]: 672–82), in H. M. Ruitenbeek, ed., *Varieties of Modern Social Theory* (New York, 1963), pp. 364–401. Cf. also the additions to this theory in T. Parsons, *The Social System* (New York, 1951), pp. 256–67, and Merton's own reconsiderations, in "Continuities in the Theory of Social Structure and Anomie," *Social Theory and Social Structure* (New York, 1968), pp. 215–48; idem, "Anomie, Anomia, and Social Interaction: Contexts of Deviant Behavior," in Clinard, *Anomie,* pp. 213–42.

5. Pizzorno has called the problem a contradiction within the value system itself rather than a disjunction between means and goals, cf. A. Pizzorno, "Lecture actuelle de Durkheim," *Archives européennes de sociologie* 4 (1963): 1–36. Cf. also the notion of simple anomie in S. de Grazia, *The Political Community. A Study of Anomie* (Chicago, 1948), pp. 47–72.

6. Less important adaptations to disjunction are conformity (possible only for a relatively few privileged individuals), ritualism (the giving up of goals and the obsessive adherence to sterile means), and rebellion (the rejection of both means and goals); cf. Merton, *SSA*, pp. 374–90. Cf. also the fourteen categories of adaptations in R. Dubin, "Deviant Behavior and Social Struc-

ture: Continuities in Social Theory," *American Sociological Review* 24 (1959): 147–64.

7. Cf. Cole and Zuckerman, "Appendix," pp. 243–83, and contributions in Clinard, *Anomie,*, by J. F. Short, Jr., "Gang Delinquency and Anomie," pp. 98–127; A. R. Lindesmith and J. Gagnon, "Anomie and Drug Addiction," pp. 158–88; C. F. Snyder, "Inebriety, Alcoholism, and Anomie," pp. 189–212.

8. Cf. infra, p. 106.

9. G. Duby, *The Early Growth of the European Economy. Warriors and Peasants from the Seventh to the Twelfth Century,* trans. H. B. Clarke (Ithaca, N.Y., 1974), pp. 48–57.

10. Tacitus, *Germania* 13.1, in R. P. Robinson, *The Germania of Tacitus. A Critical Edition* (Middletown, Conn., 1935). pp. 290–91. Cf. P. Guilhiermoz, *Essai sur l'origine de la noblesse en France au Moyen Age* (Paris, 1902), pp. 403ff.

11. O. Doppelfeld, "Das Inventar des fränkischen Knabengrabes," *Kölner Domblatt* 21 (1963): 49–68; cf. the excavation of a warrior's tomb at Morken, the contents of which are in the Rheinisches Landesmuseum, Bonn; some photographs are in P. Lasko, *The Kingdom of the Franks. North-West Europe before Charlemagne* (New York, 1971), pp. 48–49.

12. P. Riché, *Education and Culture in the Barbarian West, Sixth through Eighth Centuries,* trans. J. J. Contreni (South Carolina, 1976), pp. 65–67, 230–46, 322–23.

13. Einhard, *Vita Karoli Magni* 1, in *Vie de Charlemagne,* ed. and trans. L. Halphen, 3d ed., rev. (Paris, 1947), p. 8. On the problem of legitimate and illegitimate accession to the throne, cf. the essays in E. Hlawitschka, ed., *Königswahl und Thronfolge in Fränkischer-Karolingischer Zeit* (Darmstadt, 1975).

14. Cf. J. M. Wallace-Hadrill, *Early Germanic Kingship in England and on the Continent* (Oxford, 1971), pp. 1–20; idem, *Long-Haired Kings,* pp. 148–63. W. Schlesinger, "Das Heerkönigtum," *Das Königtum, seine geistigen und rechtlichen Grundlagen* (Lindau, 1956), pp. 116–21; W. A. Chaney, "Paganism to Christianity in Anglo-Saxon England" (orig. publ. in *Harvard Theological Review* 53 [1960]: 197–217), in S. Thrupp, ed., *Early Medieval Society* (New York, 1967), pp. 67–83; idem, *The Cult of Kingship in Anglo-Saxon England. The Transition from Paganism to Christianity* (Berkeley, 1970), pp. 7–120.

15. J. M. Wallace-Hadrill, *The Barbarian West 400–1000,* 2d ed. (New York, 1962), pp. 31–32, 55–58, idem, *Early Germanic Kingship,* passim.

16. On this and what follows, cf. Wallace-Hadrill, *Early Germanic Kingship;* W. Ullmann, *Carolingian Renaissance and the Idea of Kingship* (London, 1969), pp. 43–124; Anton, *Fürstenspiegel* (supra, Chapter 3, n. 22). On the medieval notion of sovereignty, cf. David, *La souveraineté* (supra, Chapter 3, n. 25), pp. 7–86.

17. Of the vast bibliography on early Carolingian institutions, at least the following are essential here: W. Braunfels, ed., *Karl der Grosse,* 4 vols. (Düsseldorf, 1965), vols. 1 and 2; F. L. Ganshof, *The Carolingians and the Frankish Monarchy. Studies in Carolingian History,* trans. J. Sondheimer (Ithaca, N.Y., 1971); R. Latouche, *The Birth of Western Economy. Economic Aspects of the Dark Ages* (New York, 1966), pp. 143–90. Cf. also Duby, *Early Growth,* pp. 77–111.

18. Cf. B. Phillpotts, "The Germanic Kindreds," and L. Lancaster, "Kinship in Anglo-Saxon Society (7th Century to Early 11th)," both in Thrupp,

Medieval Society, pp. 3–41; M. Bloch, *Feudal Society,* trans. L. A. Manyon (Chicago, 1961), pp. 123–42.

19. On Charlemagne's use of the comital, ducal, and like offices, cf. Ganshof, *The Carolingians,* pp. 240–59. For the view that even under Charlemagne these officials were a largely independent, blood aristocracy, cf. K. F. Werner, "Bedeutende Adelfamilien im Reich Karls der Grossen," in Braunfels, *Karl der Grosse,* 1: 83–142, esp. 121–33.

20. The process of appropriation of offices was parallel to—indeed a subset of—that which turned the fief into an inheritance. Cf. Bloch, *Feudal Society,* pp. 190–208 passim.

21. On the importance of kin-structures among the Carolingian nobility, cf. G. Tellenbach, *Zur Bedeutung der Personenforschung für die Erkenntnis des früheren Mittelalters* (Freiburg, 1957); an important critique of some of Tellenbach's views is in K. Leyser, "The German Aristocracy from the Ninth to the Early Twelfth Century: A Historical and Cultural Sketch," *Past and Present,* no. 41 (1968), pp. 25–53, which, in turn, was critiqued by Bullough "Medieval Social Groupings" (supra Chapter 2, n. 26), p. 17. For a discussion of how family ties were overcome in at least the monastic world, cf. E. John, " 'Secularium Prioratus' and the Rule of St. Benedict," *Revue Bénédictine* 75 (1965): 212–39.

22. On the appropriation of Carolingian lands and monetary rights, cf. J. W. Thompson, *The Dissolution of the Carolingian Fisc in the Ninth Century* (Berkeley, 1935). On the contribution of the Viking invasions and dynastic wars, cf. Dhondt, *Etudes* (supra Chapter 2, n. 39), pp. 36–40; on the similar effect of the Saracens in Italy, cf. Toubert, *Structures du Latium* (supra, Chapter 2, n. 79), 2: 970–74.

23. On the contraction of royal power under the last Carolingians, cf. J.-F. Lemarignier, *Le gouvernement royal aux premiers temps capétiens (987–1108)* (Paris, 1965), maps 1 and 2. On Italy, cf. G. Falco, "La Crisi dell'autorità e lo sforzo della ricostruzione in Italia," *I problemi comuni dell'Europa post-carolingia,* Settimane di Studio del Centro italiano di studi sull'Alto Medioevo, no. 2, 6–13 aprile 1954 (Spoleto, 1955), pp. 39–51.

24. In Italy, there were the third and fourth factors of a Roman past and a papal administrative tradition.

25. See supra, Chapter 2, nn. 105–6.

26. This term is not applied to men who defy the norms. Their actions may be called deviation or innovation as defined by Merton, *SSA,* pp. 375–83, and L. Coser, "Some Functions of Deviant Behavior and Normative Flexibility," *American Journal of Sociology* 68 (1962): 172–81. Cf. also M. B. Clinard, "The Theoretical Implications of Anomie and Deviant Behavior," in Clinard, *Anomie,* pp. 18–20. The terms "deviation" and "innovation" are interchangeable, though, of course, there seems to be a value judgment inherent in the choice of one over the other. For the somewhat value-laden term "functional" as used by sociologists, cf. Clinard, *Anomie,* p. 20, n. 50.

27. H. Becker, "Normative Reactions to Normlessness," *American Sociological Review* 25 (1960): 803–10.

28. Cf. W. Bell, "Anomie, Social Isolation, and the Class Structure," *Soci-*

ometry 20 (1957): 105–16; R. Poblete and T. F. O'Dea, "Anomie and the 'Quest for Community'. The Formation of Sects Among the Puerto Ricans of New York," *American Catholic Sociological Review* 21 (1960): 18–36.

29. E. M. Lemert, "Social Structure, Social Control, and Deviation," in Clinard, *Anomie,* pp. 57–97, esp. 86–88.

30. R. Nett, "Conformity-Deviation and the Social Control Concept," *Ethics* 64 (1953): 38–45; Dubin, "Deviant Behavior," pp. 149–60. Cf. R. K. Merton, "Social Conformity, Deviation and Opportunity Structures: A Comment on the Contributions of Dubin and Cloward," *American Sociological Review* 24 (1959): 177–89.

31. The most recent discussion of these institutions is in Heath, *Crux imperatorum* (supra, Chapter 1, n. 111) pp. 73–86, and Wollasch, "Obituaires" (supra, Chapter 1, n. 74).

32. Cf. the anthropological approach of M. Douglas, *Natural Symbols. Explorations in Cosmology* (New York, 1970), where the key notion is a "replication hypothesis," i.e., that religious behavior reiterates the social structure.

33. For the Cluniac handling of violence in the eleventh century, from a psychological perspective, cf. B. H. Rosenwein, "Feudal War and Monastic Peace: Cluniac Liturgy as Ritual Aggression," *Viator* 2 (1971): 129–57.

34. For a recent discussion cf. Cowdrey, *The Cluniacs,* pp. 3–43.

35. Cf. supra, Chapter 3, pp. 36, 82–83.

36. For a slightly different approach to this same paradigm and its application to the mendicants as well, cf. B. H. Rosenwein and L. K. Little, "Social Meaning in the Monastic and Mendicant Spiritualities," *Past and Present,* no. 63 (1974), pp. 4–32. The paradigm should be applicable to the transformation of norms in any social context and may explain the "inventions" discussed by Dubin, "Deviant Behavior," pp. 150ff.

37. On medieval notions of reform, cf. G. Ladner, *The Idea of Reform: Its Impact on Christian Thought and Action in the Age of the Fathers,* 2d ed. (New York, 1967).

38. On the paradigmatic view, cf. E. Auerbach, "Figura," *Scenes from the Drama of European Literature. Six Essays* (New York, 1959), pp. 11–76.

39. Anarchy is not implied by the term disintegration. What is referred to here is the phenomenon of political fragmentation. For the view that disintegration was, in fact, anarchical, cf. Lemarignier, "Political and Monastic Structures," pp. 100–111. For the view that it was in fact the substitution of one order for another, cf. R. Aubenas, "Les châteaux-forts des Xe et XIe siècles: Contribution à l'étude des origines de la féodalité," *Revue historique de droit français et étranger* 17 (1938): 548–86.

40. Recent positive assessments of the tenth century include D. Parsons, ed., *Tenth-Century Studies* (London, 1975); G. Barraclough, *The Crucible of Europe. The Ninth and Tenth Centuries in European History* (Berkeley, 1976); T. Manteuffel and A. Gieysztor, eds., *L'Europe aux IXe–XIe siècles: Aux origines des états nationaux* (Warsaw, 1968).

Select Bibliography

PRIMARY SOURCES

Adalbero of Laon. *Carmen ad Rotbertum regem.* In G.-A. Hückel, ed, "Les poèmes satiriques d'Adalbéron," Bibliothèque de la Faculté des Lettres, Université de Paris. Vol. 13, pp. 49–184. Paris, 1901.

Adémar. *Historiarum libri tres.* In *Adémar de Chabannes. Chronique,* edited by J. Chavanon. Paris, 1897.

Aimo of Fleury. *Miracula Sancti Benedicti.* In *Les Miracles de Saint Benoît,* edited by E. de Certain. Paris, 1858.

Albers, B., ed. *Consuetudines monasticae.* Vol. 2. Monte Cassino, 1905.

Ambrose. *De Officiis ministrorum.* In *PL,* 16: cols. 23–184.

Augustine. *De civitate Dei.* Edited by B. Dombart and A. Kalb. In *CCSL,* vols. 47–48. Turnhout, 1955.

Balzani, J., ed. *Destructio Monasterii Farfensis.* In *Il Chronicon Farfense.* Rome, 1903.

Bautier, R.-H. and M. Gilles, eds. Translated by R-H. Bautier, M. Gilles, and A.-M. Bautier. *Chronique de Saint-Pierre-le-Vif de Sens, dite de Clarius (Chronicon Sancti Petri Vivi Senonensis).* Paris, 1979.

Bernard. *Ordo cluniacensis.* In *Vetus disciplina monastica,* edited by M. Herrgott, pp. 134–364. Paris, 1726.

Bernard, A. and A. Bruel, eds. *Recueil des chartes de l'Abbaye de Cluny.* 6 vols. Paris, 1876–1903.

Benedict. *Regula.* In *La Règle de Saint Benoît,* edited and translated by A. de Vogüé. *SC,* vols. 181–186a. Paris, 1972–77.

Bertrand de Broussillon, A., ed. *Cartulaire de Saint-Aubin d'Angers.* Vol. 1. Paris, 1903.

Bougaud, E. and J. Garnier, eds. *Chronique de l'abbaye de Saint-Bénigne de Dijon.* Dijon, 1875.

Bouquet, M. *Recueil des historiens des Gaules et de la France.* Paris, 1738–86.

Canat de Chizy, M. and P., eds. *Cartulaire du prieuré de Saint-Marcel-lès-Chalon.* Chalon, 1894.

Chevalier, U., ed. *Cartulaire du prieuré de Paray-le-Monial.* Paris, 1890.

Chevrier, G. and M. Chaume, eds. *Chartes et documents de Saint-Bénigne de Dijon, prieurés et dépendances des origines à 1300.* Vol. 2. Dijon, 1943.

D'Arbois de Jubainville, H. *Histoire des ducs et des comtes de Champagne.* 6 vols. Paris, 1859–1886.

Devic, C. and Vaissette, J. *Histoire générale de Languedoc.* 15 vols. Toulouse, 1872–92.

Duru, L.-M., ed. *Bibliothèque historique de l'Yonne.* 2 vols. Auxerre, 1861.

Einhard. *Vita Karoli Magni.* In *Vie de Charlemagne,* edited and translated by L. Halphen. 3d rev. ed. Paris, 1947.

Flodoard of Reims. *Annales.* In *Les Annales de Flodoard,* edited by P. Lauer. Paris, 1905.

———. *Historia Remensis ecclesiae.* In *MGH, SS,* 13: 409–599.

Gallia Christiana. 16 vols. Paris, 1715–1865.

Gesta pontificum Autissiodorensium. In L.-M. Duru, *Bibliothèque historique de l'Yonne.* 2 vols. 1:309–509. Auxerre, 1861.

Grandmaison, C. de. "Fragments de chartes du Xe siècle, provenant de Saint-Julien de Tours, recueillis sur les registres d'état civil d'Indre-et-Loire." In *Bibliothèque de l'École des Chartes* 46 (1885): 373–429.

Gregorio di Catino. *Il Regesto di Farfa.* Edited by I. Giorgi and U. Balzani. 5 vols. Rome, 1879–1914.

Gregory of Tours. *Historiae Francorum.* In *Grégoire de Tours, Histoire de France,* edited by H. Omont. Paris, 1886.

Gregory the Great. *Moralia in Job.* Books 1–22, edited by M. Adriaen in *CCSL,* vols. 143 and 143a. Turnhout, 1979. Books 23–35 in *PL,* vol. 76.

Guerard, M., ed. *Cartulaire de l'abbaye de Saint-Victor de Marseille.* 2 vols. Paris, 1857.

Hallinger, K., ed. *Corpus consuetudinum monasticarum.* Vol. 1: *Initia consuetudinis Benedictinae.* Siegburg, 1963.

Huygens, R. B. C., ed. *Monumenta Vizeliacensia. CCCM,* vol. 42. Turnhout, 1976.

John of Salerno. *Vita S. Odonis.* In *PL,* 133: cols. 43–86.

Jotsaldus. *De vita et virtutibus sancti Odilonis abbatis.* In *PL,* 142: cols. 897–962.

Juénin, P., ed. *Nouvelle histoire de l'abbaïe royale et collégiale de Saint Filibert, et de la ville de Tournus.* 2 vols. Dijon, 1733.

Liutprand. *Antapodosis.* In *Die Werke Liudprands von Cremona,* edited by J. Becker. 3d ed. Hanover, 1915.

Mabille, É., ed. *Cartulaire de Marmoutier pour le Dunois.* Châteaudun, 1874.

Marrier, M. and A. Duchesne, eds. *Bibliotheca cluniacensis.* Paris, 1614.

Odilo. *Epitaphium domine Adelheide auguste.* In *Die Lebensbeschreibung der Kaiserin Adelheid von Abt Odilo von Cluny,* edited by H. Paulhart, pt. 2 of *Festschrift zur Jahrtausendfeier der Kaiserkrönung Ottos des Grossen.* Graz, 1962.

Odo of Cluny. *Collationum libri tres.* In *PL,* 133: cols. 517–638.

———. *De vita Sancti Geraldi.* In *PL,* 133: cols. 639–704.

———. *Sermones Quinque.* In *PL,* 133: cols. 709–752.

Odo of St.-Maur-des-Fossés. *Vita Domni Burcardi.* In *Eudes de Saint-Maur, Vie de Bouchard le Vénérable,* edited by C. Bourel de la Roncière. Paris, 1892.

Prou, M. and A. Vidier, eds. *Recueil des chartes de l'abbaye de Saint-Benoît-sur-Loire.* 2 vols. Paris, 1900–1912.

Prudentius. *Psychomachia.* Edited by M. P. Cunningham. In *CCSL,* vol. 126. Turnhout, 1966.

Quantin, M., ed. *Cartulaire général de l'Yonne.* 2 vols. Auxerre, 1854–1860.

Richer. *Historiarum libri quatuor.* In *Histoire de France (838–995),* edited and translated by R. Latouche. 2 vols. Paris, 1937.

Ragut, M.-C., ed. *Cartulaire de Saint-Vincent de Mâcon.* Mâcon, 1864.

Series abbatum Flaviniacensium. In *MGH, SS,* 8.

Simon, P., ed. *Bullarium sacri ordinis cluniacensis.* Lyons, 1880.

Sitwell, G., ed. and trans. *St. Odo of Cluny. Being the Life of St. Odo of Cluny by John of Salerno and the Life of St. Gerald of Aurillac by St. Odo.* London, 1958.

Sulpicius Severus. *Dialogus.* In *CSEL,* vol. 1.

––––––. *Vita S. Martini.* Edited by J. Fontaine. In *SC,* vols. 133–34. Paris, 1967–68.

Syrus. *Vita Sancti Maioli.* In *PL,* 137: cols. 745–778.

Tyrannus Rufinus. *Orationum Gregorii Nazianzeni novem interpretatio.* In *CSEL,* vol. 46, pt. 1.

Ulrich. *Antiquiores consuetudines cluniacensis monasterii.* In *Spicilegium; sive collectio veterum aliquot scriptorum,* edited by L. D'Achery. 3 vols. Paris, 1723. Reprinted in *PL,* 149: cols. 635–778.

Vogel, C., ed. *Le Pontifical romano-germanique du dixième siècle.* 2 vols. Vatican, 1963.

SECONDARY SOURCES

A Cluny, Congrès scientifique. Fêtes et cérémonies liturgiques en l'honneur des Saints Abbés Odon et Odilon, 9–11 July 1949. Dijon, 1950.

Anselme, A. D. *Histoire généalogique et chronologique de la maison royale de France.* 9 vols. 3d ed. Paris, 1726–33.

Anton, H. H. *Fürstenspiegel und Herrscherethos in der Karolingerzeit.* Bonn, 1968.

Antonelli, G. "L'opera di Odone di Cluny in Italia." *Benedictina* 4 (1950): 19–40.

Arnaldi, G. "Alberico di Roma." *Dizionario biografico degle Italiani,* 1: 647–56.

––––––. "Il biografo 'romano' di Oddone di Cluny." *Bullettino dell'Istituto storico italiano per il Medio Evo e Archivio Muratoriano,* no. 71 (1959), pp. 19–37.

––––––. "Profilo di Alberic di Roma." *Atti, Academia nazionale di Scienze morali e politiche* 68 (1957): 138–58.

––––––. "La *Vita Odonis* di Giovanni Romano e la spiritualità cluniacense." *Spiritualità Cluniacense,* pp. 245–249.

Aubenas, R. "Les châteaux-forts des Xe et XIe siècles: Contribution à l'étude des origines de la féodalité." *Revue historique de droit français et étranger* 17 (1938): 548–86.

Auerbach, E. *Literary Language and Its Public in Late Latin Antiquity and in the Middle Ages.* Translated by R. Manheim. New York, 1965.

———. *Scenes from the Drama of European Literature. Six Essays.* New York, 1959.

Auzias, L. *L'Aquitaine Carolingienne.* Toulouse, 1937.

Baethgen, F. "Das Königreich Burgund in der deutschen Kaiserzeit des Mittelalters." In *Mediaevalia. Aufsätze, Nachrufe, Besprechungen,* vol. 2. Schriften der *MGH,* vol. 17, pt. 2. Stuttgart, 1960.

Bauchond, M. "Un sermon de Saint Odilon (962–1049), cinquième abbé de Cluny." *Millénaire de Cluny,* 2: 103–13.

Becker, H. "Normative Reactions to Normlessness." *American Sociological Review* 25 (1960): 803–10.

Becquet, J. "Les évêques de Limoges aux Xe, XIe et XIIe siècles." *Bulletin de la société archéologique et historique du Limousin* 104 (1977): 63–90.

Bell, W. "Anomie, Social Isolation, and the Class Structure." *Sociometry* 20 (1957): 105–16.

Berlow, R. "Spiritual Immunity at Vézelay (Ninth to Twelfth Centuries)." *Catholic Historical Review* 62 (1976): 573–88.

Berthelier, S. "L'expansion de l'Ordre de Cluny et ses rapports avec l'histoire politique et économique de X^e au XIIe siècles." *Revue archéologique* 11 (1938): 319–26.

Bligny, B. *L'Eglise et les ordres religieux dans le royaume de Bourgogne aux XIe et XIIe siècles.* Grenoble, 1960.

Bloch, M. *Feudal Society.* Translated by L. A. Manyon. Chicago, 1961.

———. *Les rois thaumaturges. Etude sur le caractère surnaturel attribué à la puissance royale, particulièrement en France et en Angleterre.* Strasbourg, 1924.

Bloomfield, M. *The Seven Deadly Sins. An Introduction to the History of a Religious Concept, with Special Reference to Medieval English Literature.* East Lansing, Michigan, 1952.

Boissonnade, P. "Cluny, la papauté et la première grande croisade internationale contre les Sarrasins d'Espagne. Barbastro (1064–1065)." *Revue des questions historiques* 21 (1932) 257–301.

———. *Du nouveau sur la chanson de Roland.* Paris, 1923.

Borst, A. *Mönche am Bodensee, 610–1525.* Sigmaringen, 1978.

Bösl, L. "Potens und Pauper. Begriffsgeschichtliche Studien zur gesellschaftlichen Differenzierung im frühen Mittelalter und zum 'Pauperismus' des Hochmittelalters." In *Alteuropa und die moderne Gesellschaft: Festschrift für Otto Brunner,* edited by A. Bergengruen and L. Deike, pp. 60–87. Göttingen, 1963.

Bouchard, C. B. "Laymen and Church Reform Around the Year 1000: The Case of Otto-William, Count of Burgundy." *Journal of Medieval History* 5 (1979): 1–10.

———. "Nobility, Church, and Reform in Eleventh- and Twelfth-Century Burgundy." As yet unpublished.

———. "The Origins of the French Nobility: A Reassessment." *American Historical Review* 86 (1981): 501–32.

Boussard, J. "Les origines de la vicomté de Turenne." In *Mélanges offerts à René Crozet.* 2 vols., 1: 101–9. Poitiers, 1966.

Bouyer, L. et al. *Histoire de la spiritualité chrétienne.* 3 vols. Paris, 1960–66.

Brackmann, A. *Zur politischen Bedeutung der Kluniazensischen Bewegung.* Darmstadt, 1958.

Braga, G. "Problemi di autenticità per Oddone di Cluny: l'Epitome dei 'Moralia' di Gregorio Magno." *Studi Medievali* ser. 3, 18, pt.2 (1977): 45–145.

Braunfels, W., ed. *Karl der Grosse.* 4 vols. Düsseldorf, 1965.

Brown, E. A. R. "The Tyranny of a Construct: Feudalism and Historians of Medieval Europe." *American Historical Review* 79 (1974): 1063–88.

Brown, P. *Augustine of Hippo. A Biography.* Berkeley, 1969.

———. *The World of Late Antiquity,* A.D. *150–750.* London, 1971.

Bullough, D. A. "Early Medieval Social Groupings: The Terminology of Kinship." *Past and Present,* no. 45 (1969), pp. 3–18.

Bulst, N. *Untersuchungen zu den Klosterreformen Wilhelms von Dijon (962–1031).* Bonn, 1973.

Bur, M. *La formation du comté de Champagne (v. 950–v. 1150).* Nancy, 1977.

Büttner, H. "Der Weg Ottos des Grossen zum Kaisertum." In *Das Kaisertum Ottos des Grossen,* edited by H. Beumann and H. Büttner, pp. 55–80. Constance, n.d.

Calmette, J. "La famille de Saint Guilhem." *Annales du Midi* 18 (1906): 145–65.

Capitani, O. "Motivi di spiritualità cluniacense e realismo eucaristico in Odone di Cluny." *Spiritualità cluniacense,* pp. 250–57.

Chagny, A. *Cluny et son empire.* Rev. ed. Lyon, 1938.

Chaume, M. "En marge de l'histoire de Cluny." *Revue Mabillon* 29 (1939): 41–61; 30 (1940): 33–62.

———. *Les Origines du Duché de Bourgogne.* 2 vols. Dijon, 1925.

———. "Observations sur la chronologie des chartes de Cluny." *Revue Mabillon* 16 (1926): 44–48; 29 (1939): 81–89, 133–42; 31 (1941): 14–19, 42–45, 69–82; 32 (1942): 15–20, 133–36; 38 (1948): 1–6, 39 (1949): 41–43; 42 (1952): 1–4.

Chaumont, L. *Histoire de Cluny depuis les origines jusqu'à la ruine de l'Abbaye.* 2d ed. Paris, 1911.

Chauney, M. "Deux évêques bourguignons de l'an mil: Brunon de Langres et Hugues Ier d'Auxerre." *Cahiers de civilisation médiévale* 21 (1978): 385–94.

Chédeville, A. *Chartres et ses campagnes, XIe–XIIIe siècles.* Paris, 1973.

Clinard, M. B., ed. *Anomie and Deviant Behavior. A Discussion and Critique.* New York, 1964.

Conant, K. J. *Cluny. Les églises et la maison du chef d'Ordre.* Cambridge, Mass., 1968.

———. "Cluny in the Tenth Century." *Medievalia et Humanistica* 9 (1955): 23–25.

———. "Les églises de Cluny a l'époque de Saint Odon et de Saint Odilon." *A Cluny, Congrès scientifique,* pp. 37–43.

———. "Medieval Academy Excavations at Cluny: The Season of 1928." *Speculum* 1–4 (1929): 3–26, 168–76, 291–302, 443–50.

Constable, G. *Cluniac Studies.* London, 1980.

———. "Cluniac Tithes and the Controversy between Gigny and Le Miroir." *Revue Bénédictine* 70 (1960): 591–624 and reprinted in *Cluniac Studies.* London, 1980.

————. *Monastic Tithes from Their Origins to the Twelfth Century.* Cambridge, 1964.

Coolidge, R. T. "Adalbero, Bishop of Laon." *Studies in Medieval and Renaissance History* 2 (1965): 3–114.

Coser, L., ed. *The Idea of Social Structure: Papers in Honor of Robert K. Merton.* New York, 1975.

————. "Some Functions of Deviant Behavior and Normative Flexibility." *American Journal of Sociology* 68 (1962): 172–81.

Les courants philosophiques, littéraires et artistiques en occident au milieu du XII ^{e} siècle, Pierre Abélard-Pierre le Vénérable. Abbaye de Cluny. 2–9 July 1972. Colloques internationaux du centre national de la recherche scientifique, no. 546. Paris, 1975.

Cousin, P. "La dévotion mariale chez les grands abbés de Cluny." *A Cluny, Congrès scientifique,* pp. 210–18.

Cowdrey, H. E. J. *The Cluniacs and the Gregorian Reform.* Oxford, 1970.

————. "Unions and Confraternity with Cluny." *Journal of Ecclesiastical History* 16 (1965): 152–62.

Cucherat, M. F. *Cluny au onzième siècle, son influence religieuse, intellectuelle et politique.* 2d ed. Mâcon, 1873.

Curtius, E. R. *European Literature and the Latin Middle Ages.* Translated by W. Trask. New York, 1953.

Dauphin, H. "Monastic Reforms from the Tenth Century to the Twelfth." *Downside Review* 70 (1952): 62–74.

David, M. *La souveraineté et les limites juridiques du pouvoir monarchique du IX ^{e} au XV ^{e} siècle.* Paris, 1954.

Deane, H. A. *The Political and Social Ideas of St. Augustine.* New York, 1963.

Déléage, A. *Le vie rurale en Bourgogne jusqu'au début du onzième siècle.* 3 vols. Mâcon, 1941.

Delehaye, H. *The Legends of the Saints.* Translated by D. Attwater. New York, 1962.

Devailly, G. *Le Berry du X ^{e} siècle au milieu du XIII ^{e}. Etude politique, religieuse, sociale et économique.* Paris, 1973.

Dhondt, J. *Etudes sur la naissance des principautés territoriales en France (IX ^{e}–X ^{e} siècle).* Bruges, 1948.

————. "Le titre du marquis à l'époque carolingienne." *Archivum latinitatis medii aevi. Bulletin du Cange* 19 (1948): 407–17.

Doppelfeld, O. "Das Inventar des fränkischen Knabengrabes." *Kölner Domblatt* 21 (1963): 49–68.

Douglas, M. *Natural Symbols. Explorations in Cosmology.* New York, 1970.

Dubin, R. "Deviant Behavior and Social Structure: Continuities in Social Theory." *American Sociological Review* 24 (1959): 147–64.

Duby, G. *The Chivalrous Society.* Translated by C. Postan. Berkeley, 1977.

————. *The Early Growth of the European Economy. Warriors and Peasants from the Seventh to the Twelfth Century.* Translated by H. B. Clarke. Ithaca, N.Y., 1974.

————. "Economie domaniale et économie monétaire. Le budget de l'Abbaye de Cluny entre 1080 et 1155." *Annales. Economies, sociétés, civilisations* 7 (1952): 155–71.

————. "Les laïcs et la Paix de Dieu." In *I Laici,* pp. 448–61. English translation in *Chivalrous Society,* translated by C. Postan, pp. 123–33. Berkeley, 1977.

————. "Lignage, noblesse et chevalerie au XIIe siècle dans la région mâconnaise." *Annales. Économies, sociétés, civilisations* 27 (1972): 803–23. English translation in *Family and Society. Selections from the Annales,* edited by R. Forster and O. Ranum, pp. 16–40. Baltimore, 1976. Also in *Chivalrous Society,* translated by C. Postan, pp. 59–80. Berkeley, 1977.

————. *The Making of the Christian West, 980–1140.* Translated by S. Gilbert. Geneva, 1967.

————. "Recherches sur l'évolution des institutions judiciaires pendant le Xe et le XIe siècles dans le sud de la Bourgogne." *Le Moyen Age* 52 (1946): 149–94, 53 (1947): 15–38. English translation in *Chivalrous Society,* translated by C. Postan, pp. 15–58. Berkeley, 1977.

————. *La société aux XIe et XIIe siècles dans la région mâconnaise.* Paris, 1953.

————. *Les trois ordres: ou L'imaginaire du féodalisme.* Paris, 1979. English translation in *The Three Orders: Feudal Society Imagined,* translated by A. Goldhammer. Chicago, 1980.

————. "La ville de Cluny au temps de saint Odilon." *A Cluny, Congrès scientifique,* pp. 260–64.

Duby, G. and Mandrou, R. *A History of French Civilization.* Translated by J. Atkinson. New York, 1964.

Dürig, W. "Disciplina: Eine Studie zur Bedeutungsumfang des Wortes in der Sprache der Liturgie und der Väter." *Sacris Erudiri* 4 (1952): 245–79.

Durkheim, E. *Le Suicide.* Paris, 1897. English translation in *Suicide, A Study in Sociology,* translated by J. A. Spaulding and G. Simpson. New York, 1951.

Egger, P.-B. "Die Schweizerischen Cluniacenserkloester zur Zeit ihrer Bluete." *Millénaire de Cluny,* 1: 374–86.

Erdmann, C. *Die Entstehung des Kreuzzugsgedankens.* Stuttgart, 1935. English translation in *The Origin of the Idea of Crusade,* translated and annotated by M. W. Baldwin and W. Goffart. Princeton, 1977.

————. "Das ottonische Reich als Imperium Romanum." *Deutsches Archiv für Geschichte des Mittelalters* 6 (1943): 412–41.

Estey, F. N. "The *Fideles* in the County of Mâcon." *Speculum* 30 (1955): 82–89.

Evans, J. "L'iconographie clunisienne." *A Cluny, Congrès scientifique,* pp. 44–50.

————. *Monastic Life at Cluny 910–1157.* London, 1931.

Falco, G. "La Crisi dell'autorita e lo sforzo della ricostruzione in Italia." *I problemi comuni dell'Europa post-carolingia.* Settimane di Studio del Centro italiano di studi sull'Alto Medioevo, no. 2. 6–13 April 1954. Spoleto, 1955.

————. *La Santa Romana Repubblica.* 4th ed. Milan, 1963.

Febvre, L. *A New Kind of History and Other Essays.* Edited by P. Burke and translated by K. Folca. New York, 1973.

Fechter, J. *Cluny, Adel und Volk. Studien über das Verhältnis des Klosters zum den Ständen (910–1156).* Stuttgart, 1966.

Fumagalli, V. "Note sulla 'Vita Geraldi' di Odone di Cluny." *Bullettino dell'Istituto storico italiano per il Medio Evo* 76 (1964): 217–40.

Fustel de Coulanges, N. D. *Histoire des institutions politiques de l'ancienne France.* 6 vols. Paris, 1875–1892.

Ganshof, F. L. *The Carolingians and the Frankish Monarchy. Studies in Carolingian History.* Translated by J. Sondheimer. Ithaca, N.Y., 1971.

Geary, P. *Furta Sacra: Thefts of Relics in the Central Middle Ages.* Princeton, 1978.

Gooch, G. P. *History and Historians in the Nineteenth Century.* London, 1913.

Graham, R. and A. W. Clapham. "The Monastery of Cluny 910–1155." *Archaeologia* 80 (1930): 143–78.

Graus, F. *Volk, Herrscher und Heiliger im Reich der Merowinger.* Prague, 1965.

Grazia, S. de. *The Political Community. A Study of Anomie.* Chicago, 1948.

Guépin, A. "La grande époque de Cluny. Ses causes, sa fin au XIIe siècle." *Millénaire de Cluny,* 2: 211–30.

Guilhiermoz, P. *Essai sur l'origine de la noblesse en France au Moyen Age.* Paris, 1902.

Guilloreau, L. "Les prieurés anglais de l'Ordre de Cluny." *Millénaire de Cluny,* 1: 291–373.

Hallinger, K. *Gorze-Kluny. Studien zu den Monastischen Lebensformen und Gegensätzen im Hochmittelalter.* 2 vols. Rome, 1950.

————. "Klunys Bräuche zur Zeit Hugos des Grossen (1049–1109). Prolegomena zur Neuherausgabe des Bernhard und Udalrich von Kluny." *Zeitschrift der Savigny–Stiftung für Rechtsgeschichte, Kanonistische Abteilung* 45 (1959): 99–140.

————. "Progressi e problemi della ricerca sulla Riforma pre-gregoriana." *Il monachesimo.* German translation in *Archiv für mittelrheinische Kirchengeschichte* 9 (1957): 9–32.

————. "Zur geistigen Welt der Anfänge Klunys." *Deutsches Archiv für Erforschung des Mittelalters* 10 (1953–54): 417–45. English translation in N. Hunt, ed. *Cluniac Monasticism in the Central Middle Ages,* pp. 29–55. Hamden, Conn., 1971.

Hamilton, B. "The Monastery of S. Alessio and the Religious and Intellectual Renaissance in Tenth-Century Rome." *Studies in Medieval and Renaissance History* 2 (1965): 265–310.

————. "The Monastic Revival in Tenth-Century Rome." *Studia Monastica* 4 (1962): 35–68.

Harnack, A. *Das Mönchtum, seine Ideale und seine Geschichte.* Giessen, 1908.

Heath, R. G. *Crux imperatorum philosophia: Imperial Horizons of the Cluniac "Confraternitas," 964–1109.* Pittsburgh, 1976.

Hessel, A. "Odo von Cluni und das französische Kulturproblem im früheren Mittelalter." *Historische Zeitschrift* 128 (1923): 1–25.

Hlawitschka, E., ed. *Königswahl und Thronfolge in Fränkischer-Karolingischer Zeit.* Darmstadt, 1975.

Hoffmann, H. *Gottesfriede und Treuga Dei.* Schriften der *MGH,* vol. 20. Stuttgart, 1964.

————. "Von Cluny zum Investiturstreit." *Archiv für Kulturgeschichte* 45 (1963): 165–209.

Hofmeister, A. "Die Gründungsurkunde von Peterlingen." *Zeitschrift für die Geschichte des Oberrheins,* n.s. 25 (1910): 217–38.

Hourlier, J. "Cluny et la notion d'Ordre religieux." *A Cluny, Congrès scientifique,* pp. 219–26.

Howard, D. R. *The Three Temptations: Medieval Man in Search of the World.* Princeton, 1966.

L'Huillier, A. *Vie de St. Hugues, Abbé de Cluny, 1024–1109.* Solesmes, 1888.

Hunt, N., ed. *Cluniac Monasticism in the Central Middle Ages.* Hamden, Conn., 1971.

———. *Cluny under Saint High, 1049–1109.* London, 1967.

Jacobs, H. "Die Cluniazenser und das Papsttum im 10. und 11. Jahrhundert." *Francia* 2 (1974): 643–63.

Jones, C. W. *Saints' Lives and Chronicles in Early England.* Ithaca, N.Y., 1947.

Jorden, P.W. *Das cluniazensische Totengedächtniswesen vornehmlich unter den drei ersten Äbten Berno, Odo und Aymard (910–954). Zugleich ein Beitrag zu den cluniazensischen traditionsurkunden.* Münster, 1930.

Knowles, D. *Cistercians and Cluniacs: The Controversy between St. Bernard and Peter the Venerable.* London, 1955.

———. *Great Historical Enterprises: Problems in Monastic History.* New York, 1963.

Kraus, F. X. "Nekrologium von St. Maximin." *Jahrbücher des Vereins von Alterthumsfreunden im Rheinlands* 57 (1876): 108–119.

Ladner, G. *The Idea of Reform. Its Impact on Christian Thought and Action in the Age of the Fathers.* 2d ed. New York, 1967.

———. *Theologie und Politik vor dem Investiturstreit. Abendmahlstreit, Kirchenreform, Cluni und Heinrich III.* Baden bei Wien, 1936.

I Laici nella "Societas christiana" dei secoli XI e XII. Atti della terza Settimana internazionale di Studio Mendola. 21–7 August 1965. Miscellanea del Centro di Studi Medioevali, vol. 5. Milan, 1968.

Lamma, P. *Momenti di storiografia cluniacense.* Istituto storico Italiano per il Medio Evo. Studi storici, vols. 42–44. Rome, 1961.

Laporte, J. "Saint Odon, disciple de Saint Grégoire le Grand." *A Cluny, Congrès scientifique,* pp. 138–43.

Lasko, P. *The Kingdom of the Franks. North-West Europe before Charlemagne.* New York, 1971.

Lasteyrie, R. de. *Etude sur les comtes et vicomtes de Limoges antérieurs à l'an 1000.* Paris, 1874.

Leclercq, J. *L'Amour des lettres et le désir de Dieu. Initiation aux auteurs monastiques du Moyen Âge.* Paris, 1957. English translation in *The Love of Learning and the Desire for God, A Study of Monastic Culture,* translated by C. Misrahi. New York, 1961.

———. "Cluny fut-il ennemi de la culture?" *Revue Mabillon* 47 (1957): 172–82.

———. "L'ideal monastique de saint Odon, d'après ses oeuvres." *A Cluny, Congrès scientifique,* pp. 227–32.

———. *Monks and Love in Twelfth-Century France: Psycho-Historical Essays.* Oxford, 1979.

———. "Pour une histoire de la vie à Cluny." *Revue d'histoire ecclésiastique* 57 (1962): 385–408, 783–812.

———. "Spiritualité et culture à Cluny." *Spiritualità cluniacense,* pp. 101–51.

———. "Y-a-t-il une culture monastique?" *Il monachesimo,* pp. 339–56.

Lemarignier, J.-F. *Etude sur les privilèges d'exemption et de jurisdiction ecclésiastique des abbayes normandes depuis les origines jusqu'en 1140.* Ligugé, 1937.

———. "L'exemption monastique et les origines de la réforme grégorienne." *A Cluny, Congrès scientifique,* pp. 288–340.

———. *Le gouvernement royal aux premiers temps capétiens (987–1108).* Paris, 1965.

———. "Structures monastiques et structures politiques dans la France de la fin du Xe et des débuts du XIe siècle." *Il monachesimo,* pp. 357–400. English translation and revision in *Lordship and Community in Medieval Europe, Selected Readings,* edited by F. L. Cheyette, pp. 100–127. Huntington, N.Y., 1975.

Lemert, E. M. "Social Structure, Social Control, and Deviation." In M. B. Clinard, ed., *Anomie and Deviant Behavior. A Discussion and Critique,* pp. 57–97. New York, 1964.

Letonnelier, G., *L'Abbaye exempte de Cluny et le Saint-Siège. Etude sur le développement de l'exemption clunisienne des origines jusqu'à la fin du XIIIe siècle.* Ligugé, 1923.

Levillain, L. "De quelques personnages nommés Bernard dans les Annales de Saint-Bertin." *Mélanges dédiés à la mémoire de Félix Grat,* 2 vols., 1: 169–202. Paris, 1946.

Lewis, A. R. " Count Gerald of Aurillac, and Feudalism in South-Central France in the Early Tenth Century." *Traditio* 20 (1964): 41–58.

Lex, L. "Un office laïque de l'abbaye. La prévôté et crierie de Cluny." *Millénaire de Cluny,* 1: 404–15.

Leyser, K. J. "The German Aristocracy from the Ninth to the Early Twelfth Century: A Historical and Cultural Sketch." *Past and Present,* no. 41 (1968), pp. 25–53.

———. *Rule and Conflict in an Early Medieval Society: Ottonian Saxony.* Bloomington, 1979.

Little, L. K. *Religious Poverty and the Profit Economy in Medieval Europe.* New York, 1978.

Lorain, P. *Histoire de l'abbaye de Cluny depuis sa fondation jusqu'à sa destruction à l'époque de la Révolution française.* 2d ed. Paris, 1845.

Mager, H.-E. "Studien über das Verhältnis der Cluniacenser zum Eigenkirchenwesen." In G. O. Tellenbach, ed. *Neue Forschungen über Cluny und die Cluniacenser,* pp. 167–217. Freiburg, 1959.

Marcson, S. *Automation, Alienation, and Anomie.* New York, 1970.

Merton, R. K. "Anomie, Anomia, and Social Interaction: Contexts of Deviant Behavior." In M. B. Clinard, ed. *Anomie and Deviant Behavior. A Discussion and Critique,* pp. 213–42. New York, 1964.

———. "Continuities in the Theory of Social Structure and Anomie." In *Social Theory and Social Structure.* New York, 1968.

———. "Social Conformity, Deviation and Opportunity Structures: A Comment on the Contributions of Dubin and Cloward." *American Sociological Review* 24 (1959): 177–89.

———. "Social Structure and Anomie." In *Varieties of Modern Social Theory,* edited by H. M. Ruitenbeek. New York, 1963.

Millénaire de Cluny. Congrès d'histoire et d'archéologie tenu à Cluny, 10–12 September 1910. 2 vols. Mâcon, 1910.

Il monachesimo nell'Alto medioevo e la formazione della Civiltà occidentale. Settimane di studio del Centro Italiano di Studi sull'Alto medioevo, no. 4. 8–14 April 1956. Spoleto, 1957.

Morghen, R. "Riforma monastica e spiritualità cluniacense." *Spiritualità cluniacense,* pp. 31–56. English translation in N. Hunt, ed. *Cluniac Monasticism in the Central Middle Ages,* pp. 11–48. Hamden, Conn., 1971.

Morrison, K. F. *Rome and the City of God: An Essay on the Constitutional Relationships of Empire and Church in the Fourth Century.* Philadelphia, 1961.

———. *Tradition and Authority in the Western Church, 300–1140.* Princeton, 1969.

———. *The Two Kingdoms. Ecclesiology in Carolingian Political Thought.* Princeton, 1964.

Murray, A. *Reason and Society in the Middle Ages.* Oxford, 1978.

Nett, R. "Conformity-Deviation and the Social Control Concept." *Ethics* 64 (1953): 38–45.

North, H. "Canons and Hierarchies of the Cardinal Virtues in Greek and Latin Literature." In *The Classical Tradition. Literary and Historical Studies in Honor of Harry Caplan,* pp. 165–83. Ithaca, N.Y., 1966.

Parsons, T. *The Social System.* New York, 1951.

Pignot, J. H. *Histoire de l'Ordre de Cluny depuis la fondation de l'abbaye jusqu'à la mort de Pierre-le-Vénérable (909–1157).* 3 vols. Autun, 1868.

Pizzorno, A. "Lecture actuelle de Durkheim." *Archives européennes de sociologie* 4 (1963): 1–36.

Poncelet, A. "La plus ancienne Vie de S. Gerard d'Aurillac." *Analecta Bollandiana* 14 (1895): 89–107.

Poulin, J.-C. *L'Idéal de sainteté dans l'Aquitaine carolingienne d'après les sources hagiographiques (750–950).* Quebec, 1975.

Poupardin, R. *Le royaume de Bourgogne (888–1038): études sur les origines du royaume d'Arles.* Paris, 1907.

———. *Le royaume de Provence sous les Carolingiens (855–933?).* Paris, 1901.

Pourrat, P. *La spiritualité chrétienne.* 4 vols. Paris, 1918–28.

Prinz, F. *Frühes Mönchtum im Frankenreich. Kultur und Gesellschaft in Gallien, den Rheinlanden und Bayern am Beispiel der monastischen Entwicklung (4. bis 8. Jahrhundert).* Munich, 1965.

———. "Heiligenkult und Adelsherrschaft im Spiegel merowingischer Hagiographie." *Historische Zeitschrift* 204 (1967): 529–44.

———. *Klerus und Krieg im früheren Mittelalter.* Stuttgart, 1971.

Riché, P. *Education and Culture in the Barbarian West, Sixth through Eighth Centuries.* Translated by J. J. Contreni. South Carolina, 1976.

Richter, H. "Die Persönlichkeitsdarstellung in cluniazensischen Abtsviten." Ph.D. dissertation, Nürnberg, 1972.

Rosenwein, B. H. "Feudal War and Monastic Peace: Cluniac Liturgy as Ritual Aggression." *Viator* 2 (1971): 129–57.

———. "Rules and the *Rule* at Tenth-Century Cluny." *Studia Monastica* 19 (1977): 307–20.

———. "St. Odo's St. Martin: The Uses of a Model." *Journal of Medieval History* 4 (1978): 317–31.

———. and L. K. Little. "Social Meaning in the Monastic and Mendicant Spiritualities." *Past and Present,* no. 63 (1974), pp. 4–32.

Sackur, E. *Die Cluniacenser in ihrer kirchlichen und allgemeingeschichtlichen Wirksamkeit bis zur Mitte des elften Jahrhunderts.* 2 vols. Halle a.S., 1892–94.

Schieffer, T. "Cluniazensische oder gorzische Reformbewegung (Bericht über ein neues Buch)." *Archiv für mittelrheinische Kirchengeschichte* 4 (1952): 24–38.

———. "Cluny et la Querelle des Investitures." *Revue historique* 225 (1961): 47–72.

Schmid, K. and J. Wollasch. "Die Gemeinschaft der Lebenden und Verstorbenen in Zeugnissen des Mittelalters." *Frühmittelalterliche studien* 1 (1967): 365–405.

Schmitt, J.-C. " 'Religion populaire' et culture folklorique," *Annales. Economies, sociétés, civilisations* 31 (1976): 941–53.

Schmitz, P. "La liturgie de Cluny." *Spiritualità cluniacense,* pp. 83–99.

Schreiber, G. *Gemeinschaften des Mittelalters. Recht und Verfassung. Kult und Frömmigkeit.* Münster, 1948.

Schultze, W. *Forschungen zur Geschichte der Klosterreform im 10. Jahrhundert.* Vol. 1: *Cluniacensische und lothringische Klosterreform.* Halle a.S., 1883.

Semmler, J. "Die Beschlüsse des Aachener Konzils im Jahre 816." *Zeitschrift für Kirchengeschichte* 74 (1963): 15–82.

Setton, K. M. *Christian Attitude to the Emperor in the Fourth Century.* New York, 1941.

Smith, L. M. "Cluny and Gregory VII." *English Historical Review* 26 (1911): 20–33.

———. *Cluny in the Eleventh and Twelfth Centuries.* London, 1930.

———. *The Early History of the Monastery of Cluny.* London, 1920.

Southern, R. W. *Saint Anselm and His Biographer: A Study of Monastic Life and Thought, 1059–c. 1130.* Cambridge, England, 1963.

Southern, R. W. *Western Society and the Church in the Middle Ages.* Harmondsworth, 1970.

Spiritualità cluniacense. Convegni del Centro di Studi sulla Spiritualità medievale, 2. 12–15 October 1958. Todi, 1960.

Tabuteau, E. Z. "Transfers of Property in Eleventh-Century Norman Law." Ph.D. dissertation, Harvard University, 1975.

Talbot, H. "Cluniac Spirituality." *The Life of the Spirit* 2 (1945): 97–101.

Tellenbach, G. O. *Libertas, Kirche und Weltordnung im Zeitalter des Investiturstreits.* Stuttgart, 1936. English translation in *Church, State and Christian Society at the Time of the Investiture Contest,* translated by R. F. Bennett. New York, 1970.

———. "Der Sturz des Abtes Pontius von Cluny und seine geschichtliche Bedeutung." *Quellen und Forschungen aus italienischen Archiven und Bibliotheken* 42 (1963): 13–55.

———. "Zum Wesen der Cluniacenser. Skizzen und Versuche." *Saeculum* 9 (1958): 370–78.

———. *Zur Bedeutung der Personenforschung für die Erkenntnis des früheren Mittelalters.* Freiburg, 1957.

———, ed. *Neue Forschungen über Cluny und die Cluniacenser.* Freiburg, 1959.

Teske, W. "Laien, Laienmönche und Laienbrüder in der Abtei Cluny. Ein Beitrag zum 'Konversen-Problem.'" *Frühmittelalterliche Studien* 10 (1976): 248–322; 11 (1977): 288–339.

Thompson, J. W. *The Dissolution of the Carolingian Fisc in the Ninth Century.* Berkeley, 1935.

Thrupp, S., ed. *Early Medieval Society.* New York, 1967.

Tomek, E. *Studien zur Reform der deutschen Klöster im XI. Jahrhundert.* Vol. 1: *Die Frühreform.* Vienna, 1910.

Toubert, P. *Les structures du Latium médiéval. Le Latium méridional et la Sabine du IX ͤ siècle à la fin du XII ͤ siècle.* 2 vols. Rome, 1973.

Ullman, W. *Carolingian Renaissance and the Idea of Kingship.* London, 1969.

Valous, G. de. "Cluny." *Dictionnaire d'histoire et de géographie ecclésiastiques,* 13: 35–174.

———. "Le domaine de l'abbaye de Cluny aux X ͤ et XI ͤ siècles." *Annales de l'Académie de Mâcon* 22 (3d ser., 1920): 299–481.

———. *Le monachisme clunisien des origines au XV ͤ siècle. Vie intérieure des monastères et organisation de l'ordre.* Ligugé, 1935. 2d ed., Paris, 1970.

Vauchez, A. *La spiritualité du Moyen Age occidental, VIII ͤ–XII ͤ siècles.* Vendôme, 1975.

Violante, C. "Il monachesimo cluniacense di fronte al mondo politico ed ecclesiastico (Secoli X e XI)." *Spiritualità cluniacense,* pp. 153–242.

Virey, J. "Note sur un manuscrit du XIV ͤ siècle sur parchemin, provenant de l'Abbaye de Cluny." *Millénaire de Cluny,* 1: 264–90.

Voorman, C. "Studien zu Odo von Cluny." Dissertation, Rheinischen Friedrich-Wilhelms Universität, Bonn, 1951.

Wallace-Hadrill, J.M. *The Barbarian West, 400–1000.* 2d ed. New York, 1962.

———. *Early Germanic Kingship in England and on the Continent.* Oxford, 1971.

———. *The Long-Haired Kings and Other Studies.* New York, 1962.

Wassèlynck, R. "Les compilations des 'Moralia in Job' du VII ͤ au XII ͤ siècle." *Recherches de théologie ancienne et médiévale* 29 (1962): 5–32.

Wathen, A. G. *Silence: The Meaning of Silence in the Rule of St. Benedict.* Washington, 1973.

Werner, E. *Die gesellschaftlichen Grundlagen der Klosterreform im 11. Jahrhundert.* Berlin, 1953.

Werner, K. F. "Untersuchungen zur Frühzeit des französischen Fürstentums (9.–10. Jahrhundert)." *Die Welt als Geschichte* 18 (1958): 256–89; 19 (1959): 146–93; 20 (1960): 87–119.

White, H. V. "Pontius of Cluny, the *Curia Romana* and the End of Gregorianism in Rome." *Church History* 27 (1958): 195–219.

Wollasch, J. "Königtum, Adel und Klöster im Berry während des 10. Jahrhunderts." In G. O. Tellenbach, ed. *Neue Forschungen über Cluny und die Cluniacenser,* pp. 18–165. Freiburg, 1959.

———. "Les obituaires, témoins de la vie clunisienne." *Cahiers de civilisation médiévale* 22 (1979): 139–171.

INDEX

and the empire, 9, 11, 15–16
and the laity, 10, 16, 19–20, 23. *See also* Cluny, and the poor; Cluny, and the rich; *names of sponsors of Cluniac reforms*
and the nobility. *See* Cluny, and the rich
and the papacy, 4, 8–9, 12, 15–17, 21, 23, 82. *See also* Cluny, and church reform
and the poor, 22, 32–38, 120n.94
and the rich, 22, 32, 38, 120n.94
and the society of the Mâconnais, 32–38. *See also* Mâconnais, the, society of
as model monastery, 44, 46, 100, 106–7
Benedictine *Rule* at, 90–96, 99
benefactors of, 30–56. *See also* Cluny, and anomie; Cluny, sponsors of reforms by; Gift-giving, patterns of; *names of individual benefactors*
charters of, 5, 22, 30, 71–72, 81–82
confraternities at, 107
customaries of, 96–97, 100
custom at, 94–95
donations to. *See* Gift-giving, patterns of
exemption of. *See* Cluny, liberty of
expansion of, 13, 21, 30–31. *See also* Cluny, and monastic reform
foundation charter of, xvii, 4, 43
immunity of. *See* Cluny, liberty of
in the twelfth century, 122n.111
liberty of, xvii, 4, 21, 23, 43, 82. *See also* Exemption, monastic
literalism at, 98–99, 101. *See also* Gerald, Saint, *Life,* liturgy and ritual in; Odo, Saint, *Life,* literalism in
liturgy and ritual at, xix, 43, 93–98, 100, 112
monasteries reformed by. *See* Cluny, and monastic reform
monastic life at, 13–14, 17, 32–33. *See also* Cluny, liturgy and ritual at
old-fashioned character of, 43
Order of, xvi, xviii, 17, 32

political and religious activity of contrasted, 11–13, 28
related, 14–16, 25
precarial gifts at, 35, 38, 109
social origins of monks at, 21–22, 120n.94
sponsors of reforms by, 42–56, 109–10. *See also names of individual sponsors of Cluniac reforms*
tenth-century gap in studies of, 26–28
"uniqueness" of, xx, 17–19, 26
Cluny Congress of 1910 *(Millénaire de Cluny),* 8
Cluny Congress of 1949 *(A Cluny, Congrès scientifique),* 14, 27
Collationes. See Odo, Saint, abbot of Cluny, writings
Conant, Kenneth John, 10–11
Concordia Regularum, 93
Confraternities, at Cluny, 107
Conrad the Pacific, king of Burgundy, 51–52
Constantine, 60
Coronation *ordines. See Ordines,* coronation
Council of Anse. *See* Anse, Council of
Courtois, C., 21
Cowdrey, H. E. J., 23, 25–26
Crescentius family, 53
Cucherat, M. F., 3–4
Cupidity. *See* Avarice
Custom, at Cluny, 94–95
Customaries of Cluny, 96–97, 100

Dauphin, H., 18
Delaruelle, E., 25
Déols. *See* Bourg-Dieu, Déols
Devil, 59
Disciplina. See Laws of God, binding effects of
Drunkenness, 58
Dubin, R., 106
Duby, Georges, 20, 33–35, 103–4
Durkheim, Emile, 102–3

Ebbo of Déols, 28, 43–44
Elisiardus, 48
Elisiernus, 48
Emma, queen of France, 45
Envy, 58

THE MIDDLE AGES
EDWARD PETERS, *General Editor*

Law, Church, and Society: Essays in Honor of Stephan Kuttner. Edited by Robert Somerville and Kenneth Pennington

The Fourth Crusade: The Conquest of Constantinople, 1201–1204. Donald E. Queller

The Magician, the Witch, and the Law. Edward Peters

Daily Life in the World of Charlemagne. Pierre Riché. Translated, with an Introduction, by Jo Ann McNamara

Repression of Heresy in Medieval Germany. Richard Kieckhefer

The Royal Forests of Medieval England. Charles R. Young

Popes, Lawyers, and Infidels: The Church and the Non-Christian World, 1250–1550. James Muldoon

Heresy and Authority in Medieval Europe. Edited, with an Introduction, by Edward Peters

Women in Frankish Society: Marriage and the Cloister, 500 to 900. Suzanne Fonay Wemple

The English Parliament. Edited by R. G. Davies and J. H. Denton

Rhinoceros Bound: Cluny in the Tenth Century. Barbara H. Rosenwein